WATER RESOURCES ENGINEERING (THEORY AND PRACTICE)

AUTHOR (S)

Prof. Prakash Chandra Swain
Professor (Retd.) and former Head, Department of Civil Engineering, Dean School of Infrastructure & Planning, and Dean Academic Affairs, VSS University of Technology Burla Sambalpur - 768018, Odisha India

Dr. Dillip Kumar Ghose
Associate Professor Department of Civil Engineering National Institute of Technology Silchar, Cachar - 788010, Assam, India.

REVIEWER

Dr. Manabendra Saharia
Assistant Professor, Department of Civil Engineering Associate Faculty, Yardi School of Artificial Intelligence Indian Institute of Technology Delhi New Delhi, 110016, INDIA.

KHANNA BOOK PUBLISHING CO. (P) Ltd.
4C/4344, Ansari Road, Darya Ganj, New Delhi, India

All India Council for Technical Education
Nelson Mandela Marg, Vasant Kunj, New Delhi, India

ISBN: 978-93-5538-428-7

Book Code: DIP478EN

Water Resources Engineering:
Theory and Practice

by Prof. Prakash Chandra Swain and
Dr. Dillip Kumar Ghose

First Edition: 2026

Originally Published by:
All India Council for Technical Education, Ministry of Education, GOI

Exclusively Published & Distributed by:
Khanna Book Publishing Co. (P) Ltd.
4C/4344, Ansari Road, Daryaganj,
New Delhi (INDIA)

Visit us at: **www.khannabooks.com**
Write us at: **contact@khannabooks.com**

To view complete list of books,
Please scan the QR Code:

KPH

Printed in Bharat.

प्रो. टी. जी. सीताराम
अध्यक्ष
Prof. T. G. Sitharam
Chairman

सत्यमेव जयते

आज़ादी का अमृत महोत्सव

अखिल भारतीय तकनीकी शिक्षा परिषद्
(भारत सरकार का एक सांविधिक निकाय)
(शिक्षा मंत्रालय, भारत सरकार)
नेल्सन मंडेला मार्ग, वसंत कुंज, नई दिल्ली–110070
दूरभाष : 011–26131498
ई–मेल : chairman@aicte-india.org

ALL INDIA COUNCIL FOR TECHNICAL EDUCATION
(A STATUTORY BODY OF THE GOVT. OF INDIA)
(Ministry of Education, Govt. of India)
Nelson Mandela Marg, Vasant Kunj, New Delhi-110070
Phone : 011-26131498
E-mail : chairman@aicte-india.org

FOREWORD

Engineers are the backbone of any modern society. They are the ones responsible for the marvels as well as the improved quality of life across the world. Engineers have driven humanity towards greater heights in a more evolved and unprecedented manner.

The All India Council for Technical Education (AICTE), have spared no efforts towards the strengthening of the technical education in the country. AICTE is always committed towards promoting quality Technical Education to make India a modern developed nation emphasizing on the overall welfare of mankind.

An array of initiatives has been taken by AICTE in last decade which have been accelerated now by the National Education Policy (NEP) 2020. The implementation of NEP under the visionary leadership of Hon'ble Prime Minister of India envisages the provision for education in regional languages to all, thereby ensuring that every graduate becomes competent enough and is in a position to contribute towards the national growth and development through innovation & entrepreneurship.

One of the spheres where AICTE had been relentlessly working since past couple of years is providing high quality original technical contents at Under Graduate & Diploma level prepared and translated by eminent educators in various Indian languages to its aspirants. For students pursuing 2nd year of their Engineering education, AICTE has identified 87 books, which shall be translated into 12 Indian languages - Hindi, Tamil, Gujarati, Odia, Bengali, Kannada, Urdu, Punjabi, Telugu, Marathi, Assamese & Malayalam. In addition to the English medium, books in different Indian Languages are going to support the students to understand the concepts in their respective mother tongue.

On behalf of AICTE, I express sincere gratitude to all distinguished authors, reviewers and translators from the renowned institutions of high repute for their admirable contribution in a record span of time.

AICTE is confident that these outcomes based original contents shall help aspirants to master the subject with comprehension and greater ease.

(Prof. T. G. Sitharam)

ACKNOWLEDGEMENTS

Writing this book has been a collaborative effort, and we are deeply grateful to the many individuals and organizations who have contributed to its completion.

We would first like to extend our heartfelt thanks to the authorities of AICTE, particularly Prof. T. G. Sitharam; Chairman, Dr. Abhay Jere; Vice-Chairman, Prof. Rajive Kumar; Member Secretary, and Dr. Sunil Luthra; Director of Training and Learning Bureau, for their vision and guidance in encouraging the publication of this book, **Water Resources Engineering (Theory and Practice)**.

We also express our sincere appreciation to Dr. Manabendra Saharia, Assistant Professor, Department of Civil Engineering, Associate Faculty, Yardi School of Artificial Intelligence, Indian Institute of Technology Delhi for his careful review and valuable feedback. His suggestions have greatly enhanced the clarity and quality of this work.

Our friends, colleagues, and students have been constant sources of inspiration and support throughout this project. We are especially grateful for their encouragement, which has sustained us during the many challenges of writing.

Finally, we wish to acknowledge the love and support of our families, who have shown incredible patience and understanding throughout this process. Without their unwavering support, this book would not have been possible.

We also express our deep appreciation to the numerous authors, researchers, and industry professionals whose books, papers, articles, and other resources provided us the invaluable knowledge and insights that shaped this book.

Prakash Chandra Swain
Dillip Kumar Ghose

PREFACE

This book: "**Water Resources Engineering (Theory and Practice)**" is an outcome of several years of intimate involvement in teaching, research, consultancy works, field projects and patents in the field of Water Resources Engineering. The purpose of writing this book is to create a basic foundation of Water Resources Engineering for students as well as enable them to use the knowledge so gained to solve real life problems of the society. Keeping in mind the purpose of wide coverage of water resources issues as well as to provide essential supplementary information, we have included the topics recommended by AICTE, in a very systematic and orderly manner throughout the book. Efforts have been made to explain the fundamental concepts of the subject in the simplest possible way.

During the process of preparation of the manuscript, we have considered the various standard textbooks, IS codes, Research Papers, internet resources freely. While preparing different sections, emphasis has also been laid on concepts, definitions, laws and on comprehensive synopsis of formulae for a quick revision of basic principles. The book covers all types of preliminary and medium level problems, and these have been presented in a very logical and systematic manner. Apart from illustrations and examples, we have enriched the book with solved problems in every unit for proper understanding of the related topics along with exercise for practice of students.

Under the title "**Water Resources Engineering (Theory and Practice)**" there is a set of five units covering different aspects and applications of Water Resources Engineering. Out of those, the first one covers "Introduction to Hydrology", the second one covers "Crop water requirements and Reservoir Planning", the third one is "Dams and Spillways for Engineers", the fourth one is on "Minor and Micro Irrigation" and the fifth one is related to "Diversion Headworks & Canals". It is important to note that in all units, we have included the relevant laboratory / practical experiments for better understanding of students. In addition, some essential information for the users under the heading "Know More" is presented in each unit.

We sincerely hope that the book will inspire the students to learn and discuss the ideas behind various concepts mentioned therein and will surely contribute to the development of a solid foundation on the subject. We would be thankful for all beneficial comments and suggestions which would contribute to the improvement of future editions of the book. It gives us immense pleasure to place this book in the hands of the teachers and students. Suggestions for improvement and correction of any mistake found in the book are welcome.

Prakash Chandra Swain
Dillip Kumar Ghose

OUTCOME BASED EDUCATION

For the implementation of outcome-based education, the first requirement is to develop an outcome-based curriculum and incorporate an outcome-based assessment in the education system. By going through outcome-based assessments evaluators will be able to evaluate whether the students have achieved the outlined standard, specific and measurable outcomes. With the proper incorporation of outcome-based education there will be a definite commitment to achieve a minimum standard for all learners without giving up at any level. At the end of the program running with the aid of outcome-based education, students will be able to arrive at the following outcomes:

PO-1: Engineering knowledge: Apply the knowledge of mathematics, science, engineering fundamentals, and an engineering specialization in the solution of complex water resources problems.

PO-2: Problem analysis: Identify, formulate, review and analyse complex engineering problems reaching substantiated conclusions using the principles of mathematics, natural sciences, and water resource engineering-based issues.

PO-3: Design/development of solutions: Design solutions for complex water resources engineering problems and design system components or processes that meet the specified needs with appropriate consideration for public and environmental considerations with applications.

PO-4: Conduct investigations of complex problems: Use research-based knowledge and research methods including the design of experiments, analysis, and interpretation of data, and synthesis of the information to provide valid design of Hydraulic structures.

PO-5: Modern tool usage: Create, select, and apply appropriate techniques, resources, and modern engineering and IT tools including prediction and modeling of complex water resources engineering activities with an understanding of the limitations.

PO-6: Environment and sustainability: Understand the impact of the professional engineering solutions in societal and environmental contexts, and demonstrate the knowledge of, and need for sustainable development in water resources engineering.

PO-7: Ethics: Apply ethical principles and commit to professional ethics and responsibilities and norms of engineering practices.

COURSE OUTCOMES

By the end of the course, the students are expected to learn:

CO-1: Estimate hydrological parameters.

CO-2: Estimate crop water requirements of a command area and capacity of canals.

CO-3: Execute Minor and Micro Irrigation Schemes.

CO-4: Select the relevant Cross Drainage works for the specific site conditions.

CO-5: Design, construct and maintain simple irrigation regulatory structures.

Mapping of Course Outcomes with Programme Outcomes :

Course Outcomes	Expected Mapping with Programme Outcomes (1- Weak Correlation; 2- Medium correlation; 3- Strong Correlation)						
	PO-1	**PO-2**	**PO-3**	**PO-4**	**PO-5**	**PO-6**	**PO-7**
CO-1	3	2	2	2	2	2	2
CO-2	3	3	3	3	1	3	3
CO-3	3	2	3	3	1	3	3
CO-4	3	2	2	3	2	2	2
CO-5	3	3	3	3	2	3	3

GUIDELINES FOR TEACHERS

To implement Outcome Based Education (OBE) knowledge level and skill set of the students should be enhanced. Teachers should take a major responsibility for the proper implementation of OBE. Some of the responsibilities (not limited to) for the teachers in OBE system may be as follows:

- Within reasonable constraint, they should manoeuvre time to the best advantage of all students.
- They should assess the students only upon certain defined criterion without considering any other potential ineligibility to discriminate them.
- They should try to grow the learning abilities of the students to a certain level before they leave the institute.
- They should try to ensure that all the students are equipped with the quality knowledge as well as competence after they finish their education.
- They should always encourage the students to develop their ultimate performance capabilities.
- They should facilitate and encourage group work and team work to consolidate newer approach.
- They should follow Blooms taxonomy in every part of the assessment.

Bloom's Taxonomy

Level	Teacher should Check	Student should be able to	Possible Mode of Assessment
Create	Students ability to create	Design or Create	Mini project
Evaluate	Students ability to justify	Argue or Defend	Assignment
Analyse	Students ability to distinguish	Differentiate or Distinguish	Project/Lab Methodology
Apply	Students ability to use information	Operate or Demonstrate	Technical Presentation/ Demonstration
Understand	Students ability to explain the ideas	Explain or Classify	Presentation/Seminar
Remember	Students ability to recall (or remember)	Define or Recall	Quiz

GUIDELINES FOR STUDENTS

Students should take equal responsibility for implementing the OBE. Some of the responsibilities (not limited to) for the students in OBE system are as follows:

- Students should be well aware of each PO before the start of the programme.
- Students should be well aware of each CO before the start of the course.
- Students should think critically and reasonably with proper reflection and action.
- Learning of the students should be connected and integrated with practical and real-life consequences.
- Students should be well aware of their competency at every level of OBE.

As the engineering education aims at translating the knowledge gained to solve real life problems of the society, the students are encouraged to correlate each and every portion of their study to the occurrences and engineering solutions. This will not only make their study interesting and charming; but also there will be a less need to memorize the concepts. The involvement in practical classes with an eye on solving the problems of society will shape their career as good engineers.

LIST OF FIGURES

CHAPTER 1

CHAPTER 2

CHAPTER 3

CHAPTER 4

CHAPTER 5

LIST OF TABLES

CONTENTS

1 INTRODUCTION TO HYDROLOGY

"जलमेव जीवनस्य आधारः। तस्य उपयुक्ता विनियोगः भवति पर्यावरणस्य संरक्षणं, मानवजीवनस्य उन्नतिः च।"

"Water is the foundation of life. Its proper utilization leads to the preservation of the environment and the advancement of human life."

परिचयः ॥
Introduction

Water is one of the most important natural resources on the globe. The importance of water is spelt out from the quote: "water is life". Although the earth is abundant with water, it is not always accessible in the ideal location, at the ideal time, or in the ideal quality. The growing evidence that chemical wastes inappropriately discharged or disposed of yesterday are finding their way into public water systems today exacerbates the issue. Hydrologists are essential in solving practical water-related issues, and individuals who pursue in-depth hydrology studies might pursue fascinating and demanding occupations.

UNIT SPECIFICS

This unit elaborately discusses the following aspects:

- The hydrological cycle.
- Precipitation - Its types and patterns.
- Rainfall intensity and its duration.
- Techniques for measuring rainfall.
- Calculating average rainfall over a watershed.
- Estimating runoff volume.

This chapter deals with the practical uses of the subjects covered to enhance curiosity, creativity, and problem-solving abilities. It features a vast array of multiple-choice and both short and long-answer questions, organized into two levels according to Bloom's taxonomy's lower and higher orders. Additionally, learners are provided with numerical assignments, along with a compilation of references and recommended readings for further practice.

To enrich the learning experience with more in-depth information on selected topics, QR codes are strategically placed throughout the text. These codes lead to additional supportive material upon scanning.

Following the practical exercises, the chapter introduces a "Know More" segment, carefully crafted to offer extra information that is of great value to readers. This segment focuses on the foundational activities, intriguing facts, analogies, and the historical progression of the subject, emphasizing key observations and discoveries. It outlines the timeline of the subject's evolution to present times and discusses its application in everyday life and various industries. Case studies addressing environmental, sustainability, social, and ethical considerations are also included, where relevant. The purpose is to stimulate curiosity and inquisitiveness about the topics discussed in the unit, enriching the reader's understanding and engagement with the material.

RATIONALE

This introductory course in hydrology is designed to build and improve students' knowledge and skills in the field. By the end of the course, students will have a solid foundation in hydrology, which they will be able to apply for solving field problems, specifically in civil and environmental engineering contexts. They will possess the capability to employ techniques for measuring runoff and precipitation in the hydrologic planning and construction of water resource facilities.

PRE-REQUISITES

Science: Fundamentals of mathematics and Science

Mechanics: Fundamentals of Fluid Mechanics

UNIT OUTCOMES

Specified results for this module include:

U1-O1: Differentiate various forms and types of precipitation
U1-O2: Measure rainfall using different types of rainguges
U1-O3: Compute the average rainfall over a catchment
U1-O4: Calculate runoff from a basin
U1-O5: Assess the dependable flow in a stream

ALIGNMENT WITH COURSE OBJECTIVES

UNIT OUTCOMES	EXPECTED ALIGNMENT WITH COURSE OUTCOMES (1: Low Correlation; 2: Moderate Correlation; 3: High Correlation)				
	CO:1	CO:2	CO:3	CO:4	CO:5
U1-O1	3	2	1	1	-
U1-O2	3	2	2	2	-
U1-O3	3	2	2	2	-
U1-O4	3	-	3	3	-
U1-O5	2	-	3	1	-

1.1 Definition of Hydrology

The terms "water" (hydōr) and "study" (logos) are the roots of the word hydrology. It is the branch of science that studies how water appears, moves, and is distributed across the Earth and its atmosphere. It's an important subject that affects both the environment and people. The following are a few real-world applications of hydrology, which make this area of engineering worthwhile to learn.

- The assessment of water resources for various purposes.
- Evolving solutions to fight droughts and floods
- Construction and management of hydraulic structures.
- Treatment and safe disposal of liquid waste.
- Hydropower production, irrigation and municipal water supply.
- Salinity control, navigation, erosion and sediment control
- Conservation of fish and wildlife

1.2 Hydrologic Cycle

In all three states water is present on Earth i.e. liquid, solid, and gas. It evaporates from water bodies like lakes and oceans; and it forms and moves as clouds. Water interacts with its environment, moves from the Earth's surface to the atmosphere, and then returns back to the Earth.

Figure 1.1 Diagrammatic illustration of the hydrologic cycle

1.2.1 Precipitation

It refers to all types of water that falls on to the ground from the atmosphere, e.g. rain, drizzle, dew, snow, sleet, glaze, frost and hail. Precipitation primarily refers to rainfall in India. Various forms of precipitation are as follows:

a) Rain

Rainfall is defined as precipitation that takes the shape of water droplets bigger than 0.5 mm. It is often represented as millimeters per hour (mm/h), or depth units per unit of time. Based on its intensity, rainfall is divided into the following categories.

Table 1.1 Classification of Rainfall based on intensity

Rainfall	Intensity
Light rain	Trace up to 2.5 mm/h
Moderate rain	2.5 mm/hr to 7.5 mm/h
Heavy rain	More than 7.5 mm/h

For simplicity of comprehension and for future record, the rainfall intensity is depicted visually. The graphical display of the distribution of rainfall intensity over a time period mapped as ordinate to the duration of rainfall as abscissa is known as the hyetograph. The area beneath the hyetograph is equal to the total precipitation which fell during the relevant time duration.

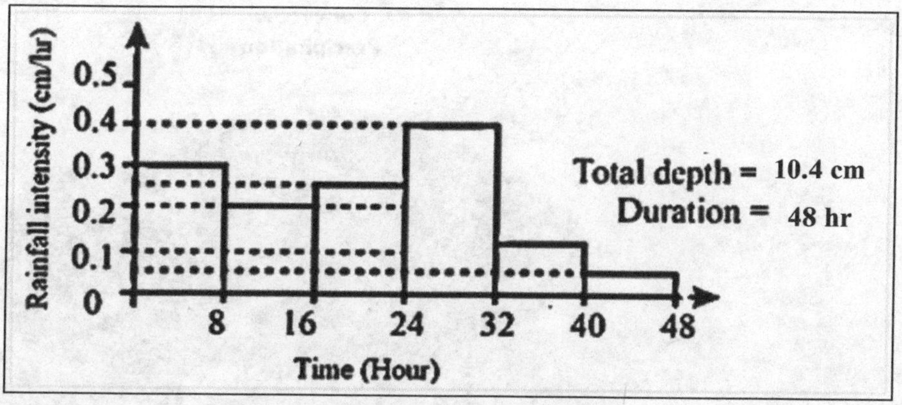

Figure 1.2 Typical hyetograph of rainfall

b) Snow

Snow, recognized as a distinct form of precipitation occurring in regions of high altitude and colder climates, is composed of ice crystals that aggregate to create flakes. Its density ranges from 0.06 to 0.15 grams per cubic centimeter, typically averaging around 0.1 grams per cubic centimeter.

c) Drizzle

Drizzle consists of a light mist comprised of numerous water droplets, each smaller than 0.5 mm on average, resulting in less than 1 mm of precipitation per hour. These tiny droplets appear like air bubbles suspended in the air.

d) Glaze

When drizzle or rain meets a cold surface at sub-freezing temperature, the water droplets freeze to create glaze.

e) Sleet

The clear, frozen droplets that develop when rain falls through subfreezing air are referred to as "sleet".

f) Hail

Precipitation that looks like ice chunks or irregular pellets larger than 8 mm. Hail forms during thunderstorms with strong vertical currents, generally occurring in areas with tropical climates.

1.2.1.1 Types of Precipitation

Precipitation may be of various types as follows:

a) Convective Precipitation

When the ground surface is heated up by sunrays, the adjoining air mass is lifted up and moves up. Upward movement of air with lesser density goes on rising to higher levels where the temperature is low or very low.

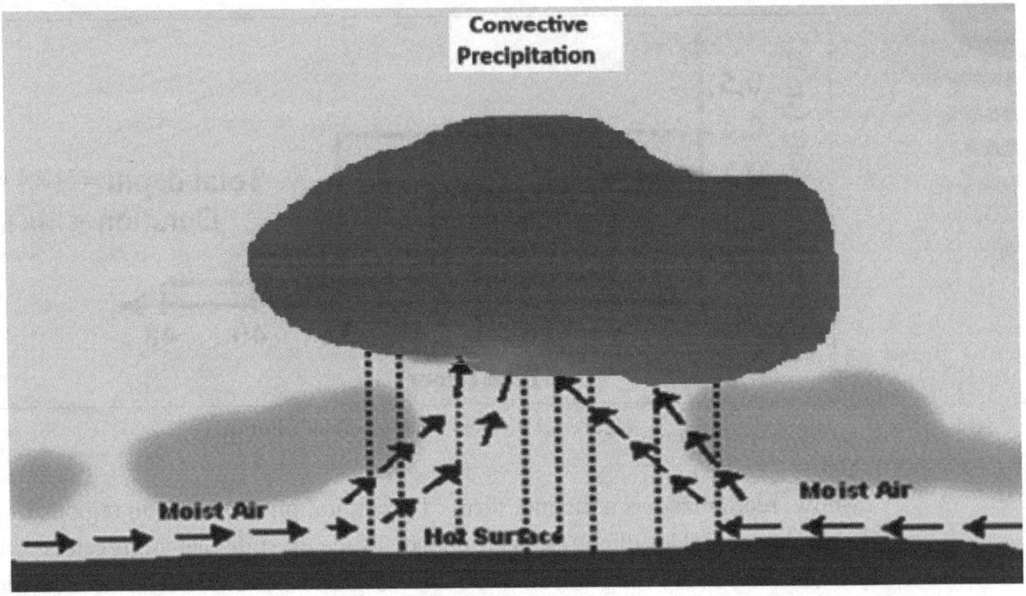

Figure 1.3 Schematic representation of the process of Convective Precipitation

This causes adiabatic cooling by reduction of pressure through lifting leading to showery precipitation. Its intensity may range from light rain to cloud bursts, depending on the temperature and moisture state.

b) Cyclonic Precipitation

This is a precipitation which occurs during the cyclones. Such a precipitation is classified as frontal or non-frontal. Frontal precipitation is caused due to lifting on warm air over cold air. Non- frontal precipitation occurs due to lowering of pressure caused due to horizontal inflow of air from adjoining areas.

i. Tropical Cyclone

Typhoons and hurricanes are other names for tropical cyclones that occur in tropical latitudes. Because of the strong circular storms that occur with wind speeds over 120 kmph and the rainfall that develops over warm tropical seas, these weather patterns are among the most hazardous. They go westward on the equatorial belt trade winds.

ii. Extratropical Cyclone

Extra-tropical cyclone is a low-pressure system with larger area and is less violent. They are typical low-pressure systems, and are responsible for much of the precipitation that falls on the continents at mid-latitudes.

iii. Anticyclone

A system of high air pressure when isobars are closer together is called an anticyclone. In the lower atmosphere, they are more worm-like than their surroundings. Here, condensation usually yields to evaporation, which prevents cloud droplets from forming. Rainfall does not occur as a result of this.

c) Orographic Precipitation

Orographic precipitation is the term for the precipitation that results from moist air rising when it crosses a mountain range. As the air rises and cools, orographic clouds develop, causing precipitation to mostly fall on the windward side of the mountains

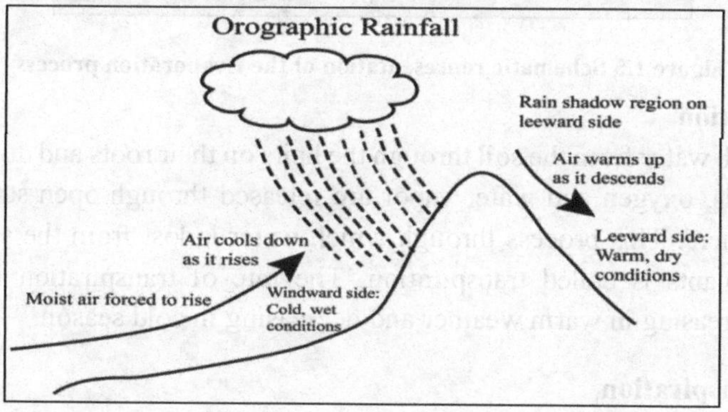

Figure 1.4 Schematic view of Orographic Rainfall

1.2.2 Interception

Some water received in the form of rain does not enter the ground or water bodies. Certain amount of water which is captured by vegetation or the top of roofs and then evaporates is called "Interception".

1.2.3 Evaporation

It's the process by which water from a lake, river, or ocean turns into vapour before being discharged into the sky. It is the hydrologic cycle's first stage. Energy is required to start the process, and the sun provides it. Figure 1.5 provides a schematic representation of evaporation and shows the evaporation process.

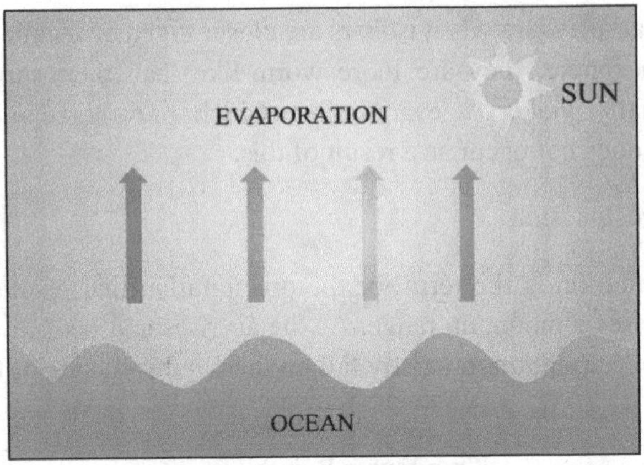

Figure 1.5 Schematic representation of the Evaporation process

1.2.4 Transpiration

The plants absorb water from the soil through the hairs on their roots and during the process of photosynthesis, oxygen and water vapor are released through open stomata of leaves into the atmosphere. This process through which water is lost from the surface of stems and leaves of plants is called transpiration. The rate of transpiration varies with the temperature, increasing in warm weather and decreasing in cold season.

1.2.5 Evapotranspiration

Evapotranspiration is the total amount of water lost through transpiration from plants and evaporation from the adjoining soil close to the plants. It is also known as consumptive use.

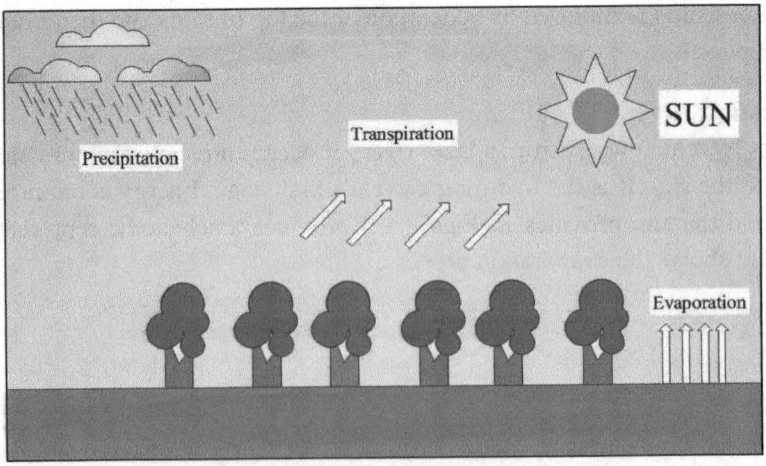

Figure 1.6 Evapotranspiration

1.2.6 Runoff

Following precipitation, a certain amount of water flows continuously across the surface and enters the catchment outlet. It is of two types, i.e. Surface runoff and Sub-surface runoff. Over-land flow is another name for surface runoff. Runoff that occurs below the surface is referred to as sub-surface runoff.

1.2.7 Infiltration

It is the major method of recharging the groundwater. In this process the surface runoff is converted to subsurface runoff. It has a lot of importance in the field of irrigation, pollutant transfer, groundwater recharge, etc.

1.2.8 Groundwater

Water infiltrates through the soil pores and joins the water present in the saturated zone below the ground surface with its top surface as water table is known as groundwater. Figure 1.7 below illustrates the groundwater, and different kinds of aquifers.

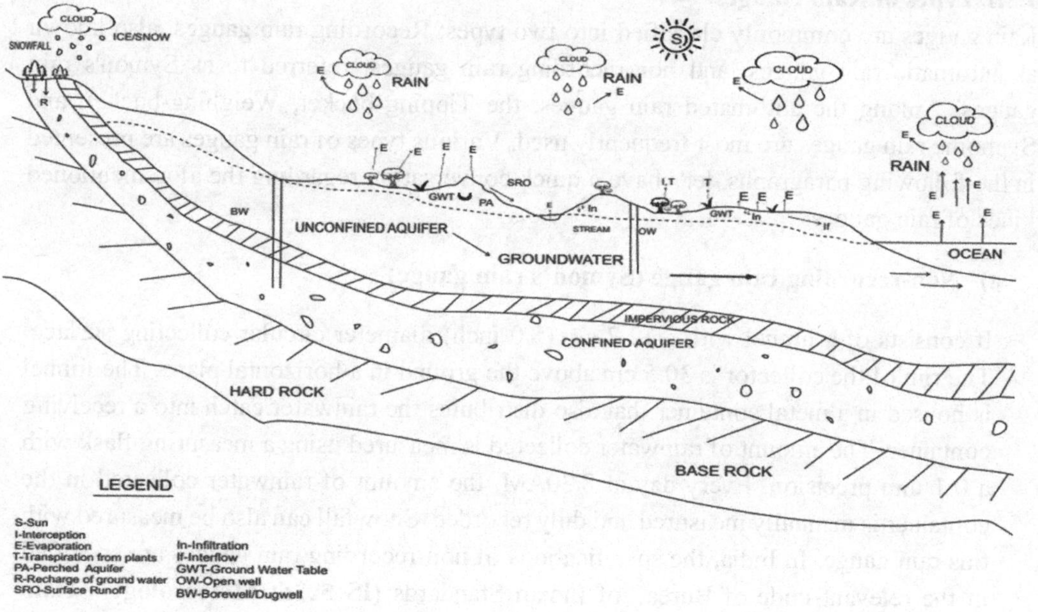

Figure 1.7 Schematic representation of groundwater in confined and unconfined aquifers

1.3 Rain Gauges

The measurement of rainfall is very important when we plan for designing hydraulic structures. The amount of precipitation that occurs in a region can be calculated with the aid of a rain gauge. Additionally, it aids in the computation, forecast, and management of floods and droughts. One of the most fundamental yet important equipment used to measure the weather is the rain gauge. It was first manufactured in the year 1441 for agricultural use. The rain gauge is still widely used to evaluate weather and climate trends. Hyetometer, pluviometer, and ombrometer are synonyms for rain gauge.

Setting up a rain gauge

- The instrument should be placed in a horizontal surface. A level surface is required for avoiding the tilting of the gauge. The gauge must be positioned as close to the ground as possible to minimize the effect of wind. Also, it should be kept 30cm higher than ground level to prevent splashing, flooding, etc.
- A minimum 5.5 m x 5.5 m open and secured area must be available surrounding the rain gauge.
- No object of higher elevation should be placed within 30 meters of the instrument and within a distance equal to two times the height of the obstruction

1.3.1 Types of Rain Gauges

Rain gauges are commonly classified into two types: Recording rain gauges, also known as automatic rain gauges, and non-recording rain gauges, referred to as Symon's rain gauges. Among the automated rain gauges, the Tipping-bucket, Weighing-bucket, and Syphonic rain gauges are most frequently used. Various types of rain gauges are presented in the following paragraphs, let's have a quick conversation regarding the aforementioned kinds of rain gauges.

a) Non-recording rain gauge (Symon's rain gauge)

It consists of a funnel with a 12.7 cm (5.0 inch) diameter circular collecting surface. The rim of the collector is 30.5 cm above the ground in a horizontal plane. The funnel is housed in a metal container that also distributes the rainwater catch into a receiving container. The amount of rainwater collected is measured using a measuring flask with a 0.1 mm precision. Every day at 8.30AM, the amount of rainwater collected in the container is manually measured and duly recorded. Snowfall can also be measured with this rain gauge. In India, the specifications of non-recording rain gauges are specified in the relevant code of Bureau of Indian Standards **(IS 5225: Meteorology - Rain gauge, non-recording – Specification)** and the details of procedure of installing a rain gauge and measuring rainfall are mentioned in **"IS 4986: Installation of Rain gauge (Non-Recording Type) and Measurement of Rain - Code of Practice".**

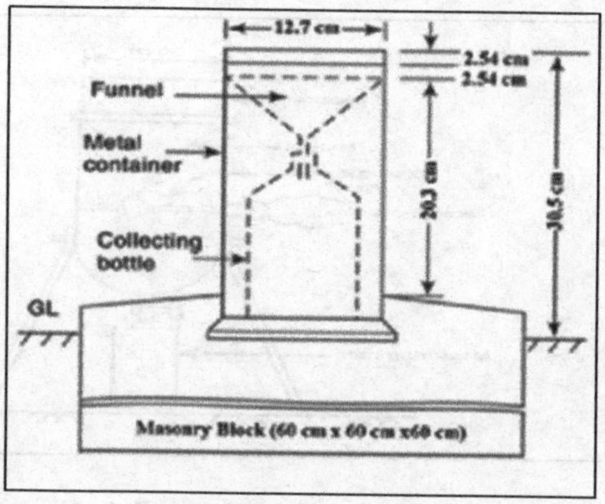

Figure 1.8 A typical Non-Recording Rain Gauge

b) Recording rain gauges

With the help of this rain gauge, one may get valuable data on the amount and duration of rainfall by creating a continuous plot of rainfall versus time. The automatic rain gage is generally used for measuring rainfall in remote places where it is very difficult to take the measurement manually. Few details of different types of automatic rain gauges are presented in following paragraphs.

i. Tipping-bucket type rain gauge

This is a rain gauge, where the receiver collects rainwater (please refer to the diagram below). One of the two little buckets, situated on each side of a lever, is where the funnel empties. The first bucket automatically tilts as it fills up, collecting water from tipped bucket in a container. Second bucket is raised and takes the place of the first bucket while this is happening. Filling and tipping keep happening as long as it is raining. An electronic record is made when the buckets turn and strike the stop/calibration screws, activating a switch. The apparatus keeps track of how many times the switch is activated. The capacity of each bucket is known; hence it is possible to record the total quantity of precipitation over time.

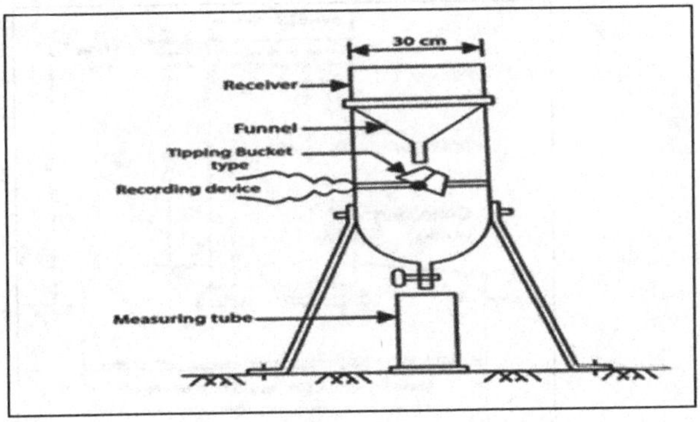

Figure 1.9 Tipping-Bucket type Rain Gauge
(Source: *http://ecoursesonline.iasri.res.in/mod/page/view.php?id=125261***)**

ii. Weighing-bucket type rain gauge

This particular kind of mechanical rain gauge collects rainfall using a funnel, which empties into a bucket/container that is secured to weighing machine. The amount of rainwater collected in the container is shown on a clock- or electrically-driven chart. A visual showing the total quantity of rainfall over time is shown in Figure 1.10.

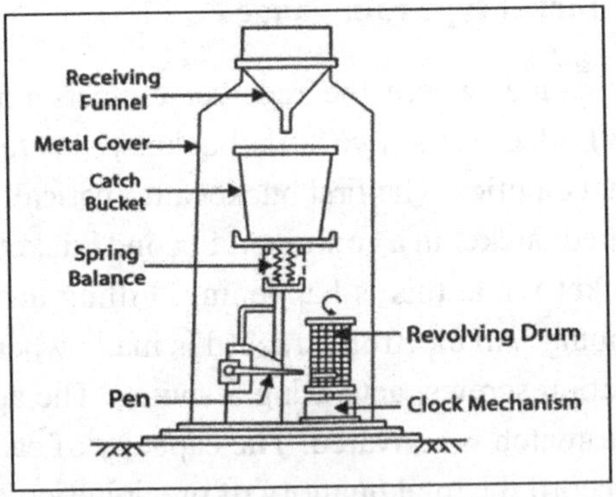

Figure 1.10 Weighing Bucket type Rain Gauge
(Source: *http://ecoursesonline.iasri.res.in/mod/page/view.php?id=125261***)**

iii. Syphonic Type Rain Gauge

The Siphonic type rain gauge is alternatively termed the float-type rain gauge. In this type of rain gauge, the rainwater is collected by a collector and is then directed into a float chamber through the funnel. As the rainwater enters the float chamber, the float goes on rising with rise of water level in the chamber. The elevation of the float is recorded by a pen coupled to the float, on a graph paper attached to a rotating disc, powered by an electricity or clockwork mechanism. When the float reaches a certain maximum level, a syphon evacuates the float chamber.

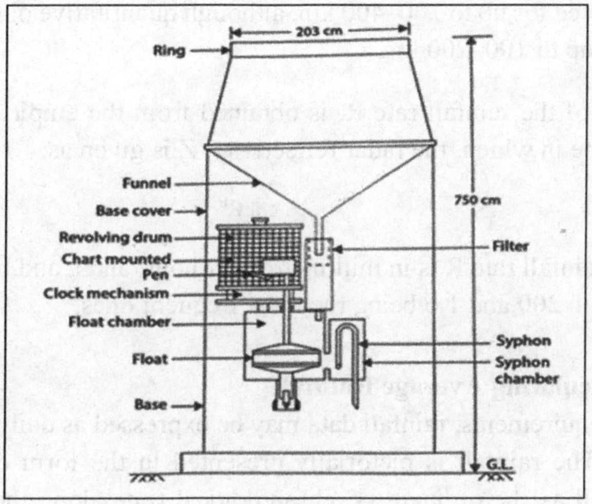

Figure 1.11 Syphonic type rain gauge

(**Source:** *http://ecoursesonline.iasri.res.in/mod/page/view.php?id=125261*)

Automatic Rain gauges are preferred for the places which are far off from the master control room. Each of the rain gauge mentioned above may be telemetered by providing a datalogger and sensors. The data logger receives the data through the rainfall sensors, stores and transmits the data to the remote computer` in the office room / master control room.

iv. RADAR measurement of Rainfall

Radar systems placed around a state or nation may also record rainfall. Numerous hydrological and meteorological uses, including short-term precipitation forecasting and monitoring and warning systems for severe weather, are made of it. Weather radar provides unique observations of precipitation systems at high geographical and temporal resolutions in contrast to conventional raingauge networks.

One of the main benefits of RADAR is that it offers an areal estimate of precipitation instead of a single-point measurement. Each station typically covers an area of more than 15,000 km^2. Additional advantages include the fact that it doesn't need installation in the region or even access to the area, and it gives data in real time.

A microwave pulse is sent out by the dish of a weather radar system, and it alternates between receiving the returned (or, more precisely, "scattered") pulse. The beam that is released is cone-shaped and diverges by one to two degrees. The return duration of the pulse may be used to calculate the target's range, and the reflected signal can be used to calculate the target's signal strength. Precipitation may be detected for up to 200–400 km, although quantitative observations can only be made for up to 100–200 km.

An estimate of the rainfall rate R, is obtained from the empirical equation of the following type in which, the radar reflectivity, Z is given as:

$$Z = a\,R^b$$

Where, the rainfall rate R is in millimetres per hour; and a and b have a wide range of values, with 200 and 1.6 being the most frequent ones.

1.4 Methods of Calculating Average Rainfall

Depending on the requirements, rainfall data may be expressed as daily, weekly, monthly, or annual rainfall. The rainfall is pictorially presented in the form of bar a chart with magnitude of rainfall as the ordinate vs. chronological time along the abscissa, the plot being called the "hyetograph".

Rain gauges only provide a point sample of a storm's overall dispersion. Rainfall is recorded at several gauges using the appropriate type of measuring equipment in order to calculate the average amount of precipitation over a catchment region or basin. An approximate count of the rain gauges that will need to be fitted in a basin depends on the hydrologist's experience in the practical domain and is also as set by the World Meteorological Organization (WMO)'s regulations. India Meteorological Organization (IMD) guidelines are followed in India.

The methods that follow may be used to determine the average rainfall in areas where there are several rain gauges installed:

1.4.1 Arithmetical-mean method

It is the simplest technique of calculating the average rainfall. It only works in areas with almost same amount of rainfall occurring at different rain gauge stations. This method is rarely adopted since the rainfall always varies substantially within a basin at different locations.

The average rainfall is equivalent to the mean rainfall when the precipitation amounts, denoted as P_1, P_2, and through P_n, are recorded at a specific time across n stations.

$$\overline{P} = \frac{P_1 + P_2 + \ldots + P_n}{n} = \frac{1}{n}\sum_{i=1}^{n} P_i \qquad (1.1)$$

Example 1. A catchment there are 5 rain gauge stations 1, 2, 3, 4 and 5. The rainfall collected by them in year 2018 are 58 cm, 59 cm, 60 cm, 63 cm, and 61 cm respectively. Compute the average rainfall by arithmetic mean method.

Solution: The average rainfall over the basin is the arithmetical mean of the data collected by the rain gauge stations.

$$\text{Mean value} = \frac{P_1 + P_2 + P_3 + P_4 + P_5}{5}$$

$$= \frac{(58 + 59 + 60 + 63 + 61)}{5}$$

$$= 60.2 \text{ cm}$$

1.4.2 Thiessen-polygon method

When the rainfall is unevenly distributed with respect to intensity of rainfall and duration, the arithmetic mean method cannot be applied to them. Hence, a better presentation of rainfall will be arrived at if each rain gauge station's rainfall data is weighted based on the area it represents. The following circumstances make this strategy more appropriate:

- If the catchment areas are of moderate size.
- When the number of rainfall stations is small with respect to the size of the catchment.
- If the terrain is reasonably rough.

This method was developed by Thiessen and hence known as Thiessen polygon method. In this method, the outline drawing of the catchment or basin is drawn to the scale. Then the points representing the rain gauge stations are connected with straight lines to form well-conditioned triangles. When determining the average rainfall for the region, rain gauge stations close to the catchment area are also taken into account. Every triangle has a perpendicular bisector drawn on each side. While drawing the triangle, sufficient care should be taken such that there is no overlap of triangles. Each station's rainfall data is given a weight equal to the area of the Thiessen polygon surrounding the station under consideration.

Following steps are followed for finding the mean rainfall as described above.

- Draw the outline map of the catchment area under consideration. In this case, he outline map of a catchment containing six rain gauge stations as shown in the Figure below. There are three stations which are located nearby but are outside the catchment. The position of the six stations is indicated on the outline map of the catchment drawn to the scale.

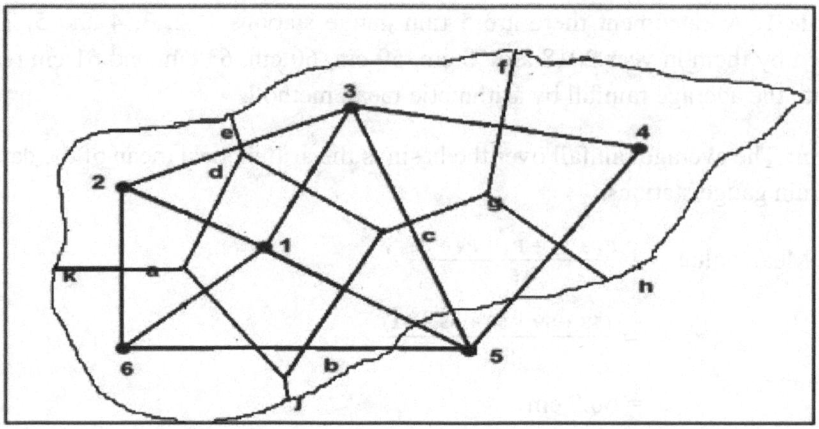

Figure 1.12 Thiessen-polygons drawn on outline map of a catchment

- The polygon's outer limit is defined as the point at which the boundary line intersects the perpendicular bisector of a triangle side, if the boundary line cuts a given bisector; if not, stations 1 through 6 are viewed as forming a network of triangles.

- Therefore, a-b-c-d is the enclosing polygon, the area of which is to be considered as the weight for station 1. The area of the polygon k-a-d-e with the portion of catchment boundary is used as the weight for station 2.

- The average rainfall calculation is based on the rainfall measurements recorded at locations 1 through 6, represented by P_1, P_2, ..., and P_6, respectively, in conjunction with A_1, A_2, ..., and A_6, which represent the areas of the Thiessen polygons associated with each location.:

$$\overline{P} = \frac{P_1A_1 + P_2A_2 + \ldots + P_6A_6}{(A_1 + A_2 + \ldots + A_6)} \tag{1.2}$$

Therefore for (*m*) number of locations,

$$\overline{P} = \frac{\sum_{i=1}^{m} P_iA_i}{A} = \sum_{i=1}^{m} P_i\frac{A_i}{A} \tag{1.3}$$

Example 2. Using the Thiessen polygon technique, calculate average depth of rainfall across a catchment. Rain gauge stations 1, 2, 3, 4, 5, 6, 7 and 8 recorded rainfall of 10, 20, 15, 12, 8, 14, 25 and 18 mm, respectively. The corresponding areas of Thiessen polygons are 7, 4, 10, 12, 5, 8, 4, and 10km 2 respectively. It is observed that the stations 4, 6, and 8 are outside the catchment boundary.

Solution:

The mean rainfall across the catchment area is determined by the formula:

$$\overline{P} = \frac{P_1A_1 + P_2A_2 + \ldots + P_6A_6}{(A_1 + A_2 + \ldots + A_6)}$$

$$\overline{P} = \frac{[(10 \times 7) + (20 \times 4) + (15 \times 10) + (12 \times 12) + (8 \times 5) + (14 \times 8) + (25 \times 4) + (18 \times 10)]}{[7 + 4 + 10 + 12 + 5 + 8 + 4 + 10]}$$

$$= 14.6\ mm$$

1.4.3 Isohyet method

Line that connects locations that get the same amount of rainfall—that is, points on a map. This method involves producing a to-scale map of the catchment area and labeling it with the locations of the rain gauge stations.

Let the rain gauge stations are with the assumed names as A, B, C, D, E and F as shown on the outline map of the catchment. In this method, the rainfall values are shown at the locations of the respective rain gauges and then the isohyets are drawn by choosing suitable intervals.

Let $P_1, P_2, \ldots\ P_n$ are isohyet values, and $a_1, a_2, \ldots\ldots a_{n-1}$ are inter-isohyet areas, lying between respective two isohyets

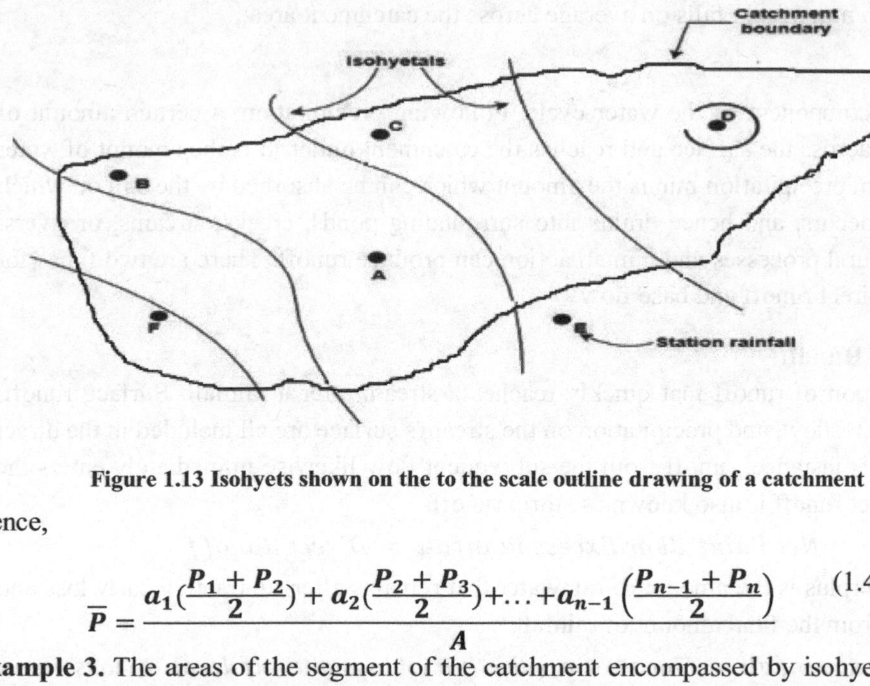

Figure 1.13 Isohyets shown on the to the scale outline drawing of a catchment

Hence,

$$\overline{P} = \frac{a_1\left(\frac{P_1 + P_2}{2}\right) + a_2\left(\frac{P_2 + P_3}{2}\right) + \ldots + a_{n-1}\left(\frac{P_{n-1} + P_n}{2}\right)}{A} \quad (1.4)$$

Example 3. The areas of the segment of the catchment encompassed by isohyets 12, 12-10, 10-8, 8-6, and 6-4 are computed as 30, 140, 80, 180, and 20 km2 correspondingly. The isohyets resulting from a storm in a catchment were taken (please refer to the figure as an illustration). Calculate the mean precipitation across the drainage basin.

Solution:

Isohyet(s)	Average Value of rainfall (mm)	Area to be considered or lying between the adjacent isohyets (sq Km)	$\frac{\text{Area lying between the adjacent isohyets}}{\text{Total Area}}$	Weighted value of rainfall (mm)
12	12	30	$\frac{30}{450} = 0.066$	$12 \times 0.066 = 0.792$
12-10	$\frac{(12+10)}{2} = 11$	140	$\frac{140}{450} = 0.311$	11×0.311 = 3.421
10-8	$\frac{(10+8)}{2} = 9$	80	$\frac{80}{450} = 0.177$	9×0.177 = 1.583
8-6	$\frac{(8+6)}{2} = 7$	180	$\frac{180}{450} = 0.4$	7×0.4 = 2.8
6-4	$\frac{(6+4)}{2} = 5$	20	$\frac{20}{450} = 0.044$	5 ×0.044 = 0.22
	TOTAL	450	TOTAL	8.816

Hence, 8.816 mm of rain falls on average across the catchment area.

1.5 Runoff

Runoff is a component of the water cycle. Following precipitation, a certain amount of water flows across the surface and reaches the catchment outlet. It is the amount of water received from precipitation minus the amount which can be absorbed by the soil on which the rainfall occurs, and hence drains into surrounding ponds, creeks, streams, or rivers. Both the natural processes and human action can produce runoff. There are two types for the runoff: direct runoff and base flow.

1.5.1 Direct Runoff

It is the portion of runoff that quickly reaches a stream after a rainfall. Surface runoff, immediate interflow, and precipitation on the stream's surface are all included in the direct runoff. In this instance, runoff from the subsequent flow likewise immediately enters the stream. Direct runoff is also known as storm runoff.

$$Net\ Rainfall\ or\ Excess\ Rainfall\ =\ Direct\ Runoff$$

Rainwater surplus is the amount of rainwater that remains after subtracting early loss and infiltration from the final amount of rainfall.

$$Excess\ rainfall\ =\ Total\ rainfall - \ Initial\ loss\ and\ infiltration\ loss.$$

Effective rainfall is the quantity of precipitation that causes direct drainage. The direct runoff includes surface runoff and interflow, therefore the effective rainfall is a little bit more than the previously stated rainfall surplus.

1.5.2 Factors Affecting Runoff

The subsequent points outline the key factors that impact the discharge originating from a watershed area.

a) Characteristics of Rainfall

The main element influencing runoff is precipitation. The length, intensity, and spatial distribution of precipitation are significant factors, which affect the runoff.

The amount of runoff depends on how long the precipitation continues. A longer-lasting rainfall event will produce greater runoff for a given rainfall intensity and other factors. Also, the runoff volume and runoff rate are influenced by rainfall intensity. An intense rainfall event will result in higher runoff volume and rate than a less intense storm. It is an established fact that areal distribution of rainfall affects volume and rate of runoff. Typically, the watershed as a whole contributes to the highest rate and amount of runoff.

b) Catchment characteristics

Catchment characteristics such as size, shape, topography, geology and storage characteristics affect the runoff. These are presented in following paragraphs.

i. Shape and Size of the Catchment

Size and shape of a catchment affect the runoff volume and its peak. More intense rainfall generally occurs over a smaller region; the larger the area, the less intense the rainfall will be. The peak often declines as the basin's size increases.

Fan-shaped catchments produce runoff with higher peak. On the other hand, runoff from fern leaf shaped basin has lower peak. The hydrograph, which is a graphical presentation of the variation of runoff volume shown on the ordinate versus time of arrival of the runoff or flow at the basin outlet, may have higher or lower peak; single or multiple peaks and early or late arrival of the peak runoff depending upon the shape and size of the basin.

ii. Topography

The topography significantly influences the runoff resulting from rainfall. Runoff is determined by factors such as soil composition, slope gradient, and land utilization. Contrary to what might be expected, a flat surface typically generates more runoff than terrain characterized by peaks and valleys. A steep surface slope will also speed up water flow and decrease evaporation and infiltration losses, enhancing runoff. However, there will be more runoff in hilly areas due to the increased intensity of rainfall in these areas.

iii. Geologic Characteristics

Types of soil, and their permeability, influence the rate of infiltration and percolation. For soils of low infiltration capacity such as clay, the discharge will be more than for the soils with high infiltration capacity such as sand.

iv. Storage Characteristics

Peak flow is typically decreased by the presence of both natural and manmade storage, such as lakes, ponds, and reservoirs. These structures lead to more loss from surface runoff due to increased infiltration and evaporation.

c) Meteorological Characteristics

The primary meteorological factors that impact runoff are humidity, wind speed, and temperature. The aforementioned factors have a significant impact on transpiration and evaporation rates. Runoff volume, infiltration rate, and soil moisture regime are all significantly impacted by these variables.

1.5.3 Computation of Runoff

Estimating the volume of water that leaves a basin or catchment area after precipitation is necessary for calculating runoff. The following techniques are generally used for this purpose:

a) Rational method

This common empirical technique is used to calculate peak runoff rates. It is suitable for small catchments and urban regions with distinct features. The method to get the peak runoff rate (Q) uses the formula Q = CIA, where C is the runoff coefficient (dependent on soil type and land use), I is the design rainfall intensity, and A is the catchment area. We shall talk about the specifics of this approach in the next chapter.

b) SCS Curve Number Method

The Soil Conservation Service (SCS) curve number approach was suggested by the United States Department of Agriculture's Natural Resources Conservation Service to estimate the amount of direct runoff based on hydrological conditions, land use, and soil type. The SCS curve number technique uses a hydrological soil group, a land use, and an antecedent moisture state to obtain a curve number that is then utilized to calculate runoff volume.

Direct runoff (Q) is forecasted using a simple, steady, and dependable conceptual process that is dependent on the depth of storm rainfall.

$$Q = \frac{(P - \lambda S)^2}{P + \lambda S} \; ; \; for\ P \geq \lambda S \tag{1.5}$$

$$Q = 0;\ for\ P < \lambda S$$

Where, P is daily precipitation, Q is direct runoff, value & S is retaining factor

Curve Number:

It is denoted by CN and it depends on the type of earth, vegetation, and land use of catchment with AMC

Where,

S expresses in term of dimension less parameter CN through equation.

$$S = 254\left(\frac{100}{CN} - 1\right) \quad (1.6)$$

When CN = 100 then S = 0 (impervious catchment); and

when CN = 0 then S = infinity (impervious large catchment)

CN Depends upon the following Parameters.

i. Soil type:

Group A – low runoff potential; Group B – moderate low; Group C – moderate high runoff potential; and Group D – high runoff potential

ii. Antecedent Moisture Condition (AMC):

AMC-1 indicates that the land is dried, not where enough agriculture has been done.

AMC-2 denotes average circumstances

AMC-3 denotes that sufficient rainfall has fallen over the last five days, resulting in saturated soil conditions.

iii. Land-Use and Land-Cover

Value of λ for small size catchment = 0.2

Hence, for P > 0.2 S

$$Q = \frac{(P - 0.2S)^2}{P + 0.8S} \quad (1.7)$$

SCS-CN for Indian Conditions –

Here, λ varies in the range 0.1< λ > 0.4

For Indian condition λ = 0.1 or 0.3

It is valid for black soil under AMC 2 and AMC 3

When λ = 0.3

$$Q = \frac{(P - 0.3S)^2}{P + 0.7S} \text{ for } P > 0.3S \tag{1.8}$$

It is valid for black soil of AMC 1, AMC 2 and AMC3

Example 4. In a 350-hectare watershed the curve no. value is 70 for AMC 3.

i. Calculate the direct runoff value based on the four days of rainfall data provided.

ii. What could be the runoff value for CN 80.

Date of rainfall	Rainfall (m)
1st July	50
2nd July	20
3rd July	30
4th July	18

Solution:

$$S = 254\left(\frac{100}{CN} - 1\right)$$

For CN = 70;

$$S = 254\left(\frac{100}{70} - 1\right) = 108.85$$

Here, λ = 0.2

$$Q = \frac{(P - (0.2 \times 108.85))^2}{P + 0.8 \times 108.85}$$

P = (0.2S) = 0.2 × 108.85 = 21.77

So, 2nd July and 4th July P will be not considerable.

For 1st July –

$$Q = \frac{(50 - (21.77))^2}{50 + 87.08} = 5.81 \text{ cm}$$

For 3rd July –

$$Q = \frac{(30 - 21.77)^2}{30 + 87.08} = 0.57 \text{ cm}$$

Total Runoff depth = 5.81 + 0.57 = 6.38 cm

$$\text{Runoff volume} = \frac{6.38}{100} \times 350 \times 10^4 = 223300 \text{ m}^3$$

For CN = 80;

$S = 254(\frac{100}{80}-1) = 63.5$

$Q = \frac{(P - 0.2 \times 63.5)^2}{P + 0.8\,S}$

P = (0.2S) = 0.2 × 63.5= 12.7

So, it will consider P for all case –

For 1st July –

$Q = \frac{(50 - 12.5)^2}{50 + 50.8} = 13.80$ cm

For 2nd July –

$Q = \frac{(20 - 12.7)^2}{20 + 50.8} = 0.75$ cm

For 3rd July –

$Q = \frac{(30 - 12.7)^2}{30 + 50.8} = 3.70$ cm

For 4th July –

$Q = \frac{(18 - 12.7)^2}{18 + 50.8} = 0.40$ cm

Total Runoff depth = 13.80 + 0.75 + 3.70 + 0.40 = 18.65 cm

Runoff volume $= \frac{18.65}{100} \times 350 \times 10^4 = 652750\ m^3$

c) Empirical Formulae

Numerous empirical equations have been produced in the past; however they are only applicable to the area from whence they were formed. Furthermore, if the region's characteristics have undergone artificial disturbance (settlement, change in land use pattern), caution must be exercised in their implementation. These are just connections between runoff and precipitation that take into consideration catchment or climatic characteristics by adding a third or fourth component. The following list contains several significant empirical runoff estimation formulae that are often used in India:

i. Binnie's Percentages

Alexander Binnie created curves that showed the relationship between cumulative rainfall and runoff and determined the proportion of runoff that came from rainfall. The Vidarbha area of Maharashtra and Madhya Pradesh have estimated yield using these percentages

ii. Barlow's Tables

In 1915, Barlow, who served as the first Chief Engineer of the Hydro-Electric Survey of India, delineated Runoff R based on his research conducted in small catchments (less than 130 square kilometers) located in Uttar Pradesh. (Subramanya, 2008), as

$$R = K_b P \tag{1.9}$$

Where Kb, the runoff coefficient, and P, the rainfall, are influenced by the kind of catchment and monsoon.

Table 1.2 Barlow's Tables

Class	Description of catchment	K_b (%)		
		Season I	Season II	Season III
A	Flat, cultivated, and absorbent soil	7	10	15
B	Flat, partly cultivated, and stiff soil	12	15	18
C	Average catchment	16	20	32
D	Hills and plains with little cultivation	28	35	60
E	Very hilly, steep and no cultivation	36	45	81

iii. Strange's Tables

Strange (1892) examined harvest ratios as purposes of variables describing watershed features, rainfall, and runoff potential in the boundary zones of Maharashtra and Karnataka,. Three categories were applied to the catchments: excellent, average, and terrible. There are two methodologies that make use of tables to approximate the runoff volume for a given season.

- Runoff Volume from all of the Monsoon Season's Rainfall
- Calculating Runoff Volume Based on Daily Rainfall

iv. Inglis and Desouza Formula

Following meticulous stream flow measurements at 53 locations, two equations were developed as follows:

For the Western Ghats regions of India

$$R = 0.85P - 30.5 \tag{1.10}$$

For the deccan plateau

$$R = \frac{1}{254} P\,(P - 17.8) \tag{1.11}$$

v. Khosla's Formula

In an attempt to establish an experimental relationship between runoff and rainfall, Khosla (1960) examined temperature, runoff, and rainfall data for several catchments in the USA and India. The duration regarded as single month. In terms of monthly runoff, his connection is $R_m = P_m - L_m$ and $L_m + 0.48\, T_m$ for $T_m > 4.5°c$, where T_m is the catchment's average monthly temperature in °C; R_m is the monthly runoff in cm; and P_m is the monthly rainfall in cm. L_m is the monthly losses in cm. If T_m is less than 4.5°C, the losses concluded as

Table 1.3 Monthly losses and Catchment's average monthly temperature

T°C	4.5	-1	-6.5
L_m (cm)	2.17	1.78	1.52

$$\textbf{Runoff (Annual)} = \sum R_m$$

Khosla's equation, accounting for evapotranspiration losses through the integration of average monthly catchment temperatures, is indirectly derived from the theory of water balance. This formula has been tested across various catchments in India, and the results indicate it yields a reasonably good annual output, making it suitable for application in pilot projects.

1.6 Maximum Flood Discharge Measurement

A flood is a river's highest point. The most frequent kind of natural catastrophe is flooding, which occurs when an excessive amount of water submerges usually dry terrain. Long-duration severe rainstorms, rapid snowmelt, storm surges from tropical cyclones, or tsunamis in coastal areas are often the causes of flooding.

According to annual calculations, floods and cyclones are responsible for 60% of all destructions. The GDP growth of a nation has also been impacted by the flood.

1.6.1 Maximum Flood Discharge Measurement Techniques

For the purpose of designing spillways, culverts, bridges, and hydraulic structures as well as estimating scour at such locations, the peak flood measurement is necessary. Only the first two approaches—the rational method, the empirical method, the unit-hydrograph method, and flood-frequency studies—will be discussed in this book among the many ways available for determining the maximum flood flow. Nevertheless, the following limitations must be addressed before using a certain approach. While the rational technique is only appropriate for tiny watersheds with areas less than 50 sq. km. While empirical equations may be used to other basins with appropriate changes and care, they are only useful for the catchments for which they were designed.

a) Rational Method

The rational approach dates from the middle of the nineteenth century. In many nations, applying the Rational approach in urban settings has had some success. The application of the Rational Method in rural catchments has come under heavy criticism. When specific storms and resulting peak discharges are taken into account, international experts have discovered that the method gives low accuracy. They used observed data to test the strategy and assessed it as a deterministic model. Nonetheless, research by French et al. (1974), who examined the validity of the system, has shown that, statistically speaking, the approach supports the goal of engineering practice, which links peak discharges at a certain frequency to comparable rainfall intensities.

The incapacity of this method to replicate specific flood situations when real rainfall is utilized as the input has drawn criticism. Such critique suggests that the approach is deterministic and does not accurately capture the physical processes involved in the rainfall–runoff process. This is not how the approach is supposed to be used. Using the Rational Method as a statistical correlation between the frequency distribution of rainfall and runoff is the most practical use. Because of this, it offers a way to calculate the design flood for a certain return period, where the length of the rainfall corresponds to the concentration time.

- Assume that a basin is completely covered by a long-lasting, consistently heavy downpour. The graphic shows the progressive rise in runoff rate from 0 to a constant level.
- As more and more water from far-off catchment regions reaches the outlet, the runoff rises.

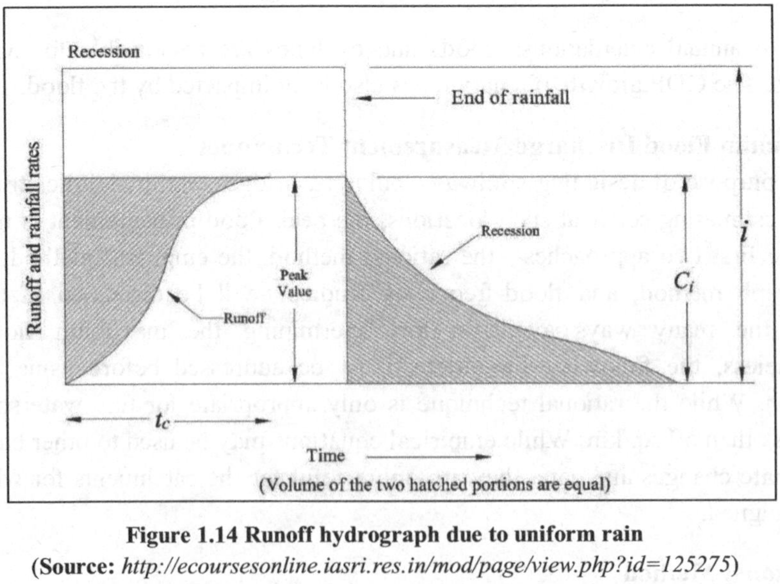

Figure 1.14 Runoff hydrograph due to uniform rain
(**Source:** *http://ecoursesonline.iasri.res.in/mod/page/view.php?id=125275*)

$$Q_p = C\,A\,i\,, t > t_c \quad (1.12)$$

This is the rational method's fundamental equation. It is created for field application using the widely used units such as:

$$Q_p = 1/3.6\, C\, (it_{c,p}) A \quad (1.13)$$

Here,

Q_P = Highest discharge (m^3/Sec)

C = Runoff coefficient

($i\, t_{c,p}$) = the average rainfall intensity (mm/h)

A = area of drainage (km^2)

Kirpich equation

This widely used formula, which state as

$$t_c = 0.01947\, L^{0.77}\, S^{-0.38} \quad (1.14)$$

The time of concentration can also be expressed in terms of K_1

$$t_c = 0.01947\, K_1^{0.77} \quad (1.15)$$

Where,

$$K_1 = \sqrt{\frac{L^3}{\Delta H}}$$

Rainfall intensity

$$i\, t_{c,p} = KT^x / (t_c + a)^n \quad (1.16)$$

Where, K, a, x and n = specific to a given area

Runoff coefficient (C)

$$C = \sum_{i=1}^{n} \frac{(C_i * A_i)}{A_i} \quad (1.17)$$

Where, Ai = the areal extent of the sub area i having a runoff coefficient Ci .and

n = no. of sub area in catchment.

Suggested intervals for different kinds of infrastructure utilized in Indian watershed restoration efforts are as follows:

Table 1.4 Frequencies for various types of structures in India

SL. No	Infrastructure Types	Return Period (RP) (Years)
1	Dams for storage and diversion with permanent spillways	50-100

2	Earthen dams with natural spillways	25-50
3	Dams for livestock water	25
4	Small, permanent stone and green water channels	Oct 15
5	Terrace outlets and green water channels	10
6	Agricultural water diversions	15

Coefficient of runoff (C)

The kind of surface, surface slope, and intensity of rainfall all affect coefficient C, which is the integrated impact of catchment losses. Table 1.3 shows some typical values for C (a and b).

Table 1.5 Values of C in Rational Formula for Watersheds with Agricultural and Forest Land Covers

Types of area	Value of C
A. Urban area (P = 0.05 to 0.10)	
Lawns: Sandy-soil, flat, 2%	0.05-0.10
Sandy soil, steep, 7%	0.15-0.20
Heavy soil, average, 2.7%	0.18-0.22
Residential areas:	
Single family areas	0.30-0.50
Multi units, attached	0.60-0.75
Industrial:	
Light	0.50-0.80
Heavy	0.60-0.90
Streets	0.70-0.95
B. Agricultural Area	
Flat: Tight clay; cultivated	0.5
woodland	0.4

Sandy loam: cultivated	0.2
woodland	0.1
Hilly: Tight clay;	0.7
cultivated	
woodland	0.6
Sandy loam: cultivated	0.4
woodland	0.3

The assumption of equation (1.14) is a homogenous catchment surface. In the event that the catchment is non-homogeneous and may be segmented into discrete subareas, each with a unique coefficient of runoff, the runoff from each subarea is computed independently and combined according to the correct temporal order.

It is discovered that the rational formula works well for estimating peak flow in minor catchments with an area of up to 50 km2. It is widely used in the design of minor culverts, bridges, and urban drainage systems.

b) Empirical Formulae

An empirical formula for calculating the flood peak is created for a particular catchment after the flood peaks that have historically occurred across the watershed for various rainfalls of varying lengths and intensities are measured or gathered. The empirical methods used to estimate flood peaks are based on the statistical relationship between the recorded peak and important watershed factors. The empirical formulas are limited to usage within the watershed region for which they were created, although they may be applied to other watersheds to at least approximate a value.

i. Dicken's formula

$$Q_p = C_D A^{3/4} \tag{1.18}$$

Where C_D is the Dicken's Constant, whose value varies depending on the characteristics of the watershed between 2.8 and 5.6 for catchments in plains and 14 to 28 for catchments in hills. Q_P is the peak flood discharge (m^3/sec); A is the catchment area (km^2).

Dickens' formula, despite being straightforward and useful, cannot produce flood volume at various required frequencies. It is important to utilize this formula very carefully. Selecting the incorrect value for the constant C_D will result in very deceptive numbers when assessing the catchment's flow. Many cross drainage structures designed using inappropriate value of C_D have failed to serve the purpose for which they were constructed.

ii. Ryve's Formula

$$Q_p = C_R A^{\frac{2}{3}} \tag{1.19}$$

Where,

Q_P = Highest overflow discharge (m^3/sec)

C_R = Ryve's coefficient

C_R = 6.8 (ranges inside 80 km from east)

= 8.5 (ranges inside 80-160 km from east)

= 10.2 (limited ranges nearby hills)

iii. Inglis formula

Data on catchment floods from the Western Ghats of Maharashtra is the basis for this equation. The Q_P for the flood peak is expressed in m^3/sec.

$$Q_P = \left(\frac{124A}{A+10.4}\right) \tag{1.20}$$

Where, A is the catchment area.

iv. Nawab Jung Bahadur formula:

Calculated for Deccan catchments of Hyderabad.

States that,

$$Q_P = C.A'^{[0.92-\left(\frac{1}{14}\right)logA]} \tag{1.21}$$

Where, Q_p is the peak flow in m^3/s;

C = 48 to 60, maximum value 86

A′ = Area in square miles = 0.39 A

Where A = Area in sq. km.

This formula is widely used in India.

v. Creager's formula:

It states,

$$Q_p = C.A'(0.894A'^{-0.048}) \quad (1.23)$$

where Q_p, or peak flow, is measured in m^3/s, and C ranges from 40 to 130. Higher values are considered for strong floods, while lower values correspond to typical floods. When A is the catchment area in square kilometers,

Then A′ is catchment area in square miles i.e. 0.39 A.

vi. Jarvis formula:

States that,

$$Q_p = C\sqrt{A} \quad (1.24)$$

where the constant C ranges from 1.77 to 177 and Q_p is the peak flow expressed in m^3/s. Floods with a 100 percent or limiting likelihood are indicated by a C rating of 177.

(g) **Modified Mayer's formula**: It states that

$$Q_p = 177p(A)^{1/2} \quad (1.25)$$

Where Q_p is the peak flow in m^3/s and p is the percentage of the stream's flood flow that is greater than the maximum shown above for any other river. P is assumed to have a value of unity for the river with the highest local flood flow. P values for various streams range from 0.002 to 1.0, with 1 being the typical interpretation.

1.7 Yield and dependable yield from a catchment

The yield is the total amount of water from the catchment area that is available at the outflow over the course of a calendar year. The units of this amount are Mm3 or ha-m. To calculate yield, one may utilize rainfall analysis or river gauging (mass curve analysis). Because it impacts a proposed reservoir's storage capacity, yield calculation is important. Dependable yield is the sustainable yield of water from a surface or ground water source or sources that is continuously available under anticipated future circumstances, even in the event of a recurrence of the worst drought on record, with no adverse effects. It is the yield value that each rainy cycle will have for a certain amount of years. There are two methods to find the predictable yield: one is to adopt the yearly rainfall during an average dry year, and the other is to assume a certain level of predictability.

1.7.1 Dependability percentage

Assume that while planning a dam and reservoir, the minimal yield value is used. This will result in a modest height and low cost for the dam, but it won't use the yield entirely every year. However, if the design is based on the maximum yield, the dam will have a huge height, the reservoir will fill up to 5% of the time, and more investment will be unnecessarily obstructed.

For instance, if minimum and maximum yields from a catchment are 100 and 500 Mm3 in 50 years, respectively, then the design should be based on dependability percentage (p) between 100% and 2% for economy and optimal resource use. Larger reservoirs are intended for p=75%, while smaller and medium reservoirs are designed for p=60%.

When precise data is not available for small projects, the design may be based on the average dry year's rainfall. A dry year is one in which the yearly rainfall falls below 80% of the average. The yield that can be obtained from this rainfall will be dependable yield, and rainfall for an average bad year will be equal to 80% of the average annual production. This approach is closer to the reality.

To get an acceptable agreement, the design yield or the dependable yield may be determined using an intermediate dependability percentage figure, such 50 to 75 percent. It is considered the stable yield or the secure yield even if it coincides with the worst or most memorable year in history. The term "secondary yield" refers to the quantity of water that is accessible in years when inflows surpass the firm yield. Hydropower may be produced by using this secondary water.

1.7.2 Computation of Design or Dependable Yield from a catchment

The reliable yield, which corresponds to a certain dependability percentage p, is calculated using the approximately 35 years' worth of historical data that is now accessible. For this reason, the reservoir catchment's yearly rainfall statistics are often used. As a consequence, the reliable rainfall value corresponding to the specified dependability percentage p is found using the rainfall data from previous years. The established empirical formulae that connect the yearly rainfall and the annual runoff are then used to translate this consistent rainfall value into the consistent runoff value.

1.7.3 Flow Duration Curves for Computing Dependable Flow

Plotting flow duration curves for the specified streams allows one to study the large fluctuation in stream flow that occurs over the course of a water year. A curve drawn between stream flows (Q) and the percentage of time the flow is equal to or greater than (P) is known as a flow duration curve, also known as a discharge frequency curve.

If the amount of discrete values is quite big, then the stream flow values may be first arranged using class intervals in decreasing order in oKirder to depict such a curve. If N data items are used the data may be of daily, weekly, or monthly values.

$$\mathbf{Pp} = \frac{\mathbf{m}}{\mathbf{N+1}} \times \mathbf{100} \qquad (1.26)$$

Here PP = the percentage chance that the flow magnitude will be equal to or greater than the discharge, and m = the discharge's order number (or class value). The following example shows the flow duration curve and its general characteristics.

Example 5. Flow measurement of Mahanadi river at Hirakud Dam yielded the following annual flow volumes. Draw the flow duration curve and estimate the 75% dependable yield from the catchment of Mahanadi River upstream of Hirakud (83400 km2).

Year	Monsoon runoff (Macft)
1979	8.87
1980	34.77
1981	19.06
1982	17.45
1983	24.37
1984	26.90
1985	28.53
1986	29.86
1987	15.77
1988	15.87
1989	1.007
1990	33.188
1991	24.77
1992	20.183
1993	21.173
1994	59.9
1995	19.304
1996	18.278

Solution:

The flow values are entered in the tabular form and the unit of Million Acre-ft (Macft) is converted to Million cubic meter (Mm3). In the next step, the flow values are arranged in descending order of their magnitudes. The percentage probability of each is calculated using the formula, Pp = m/(N+1)×100

Years	Monsoon runoff (Macft)	Runoff volume (Mm^3)	Rank (m)	Percentage probability (Pp)	Descending order of magnitude of runoff Volume (Mm^3)
1979	8.871	10949.24	1	5.26	73933.01
1980	34.773	42919.41	2	10.53	42919.41
1981	19.057	23521.56	3	15.79	40963.09
1982	17.449	21536.85	4	21.05	36852.95
1983	24.37	30079.26	5	26.32	34995.37
1984	26.896	33197.03	6	31.58	33197.03
1985	28.353	34995.37	7	36.84	30572.97
1986	29.858	36852.95	8	42.11	30079.26
1987	15.767	19460.80	9	47.37	26133.28
1988	15.871	19589.16	10	52.63	24911.35
1989	1.007	1242.91	11	57.89	23826.43
1990	33.188	40963.09	12	63.16	23521.56
1991	24.77	30572.97	13	68.42	22560.06
1992	20.183	24911.35	14	73.68	21536.85
1993	21.173	26133.28	15	78.95	19589.16
1994	59.9	73933.01	16	84.21	19460.80
1995	19.304	23826.43	17	89.47	10949.24

1996	18.278	22560.06	18	94.74	1242.91
Total		517244.74			517244.74

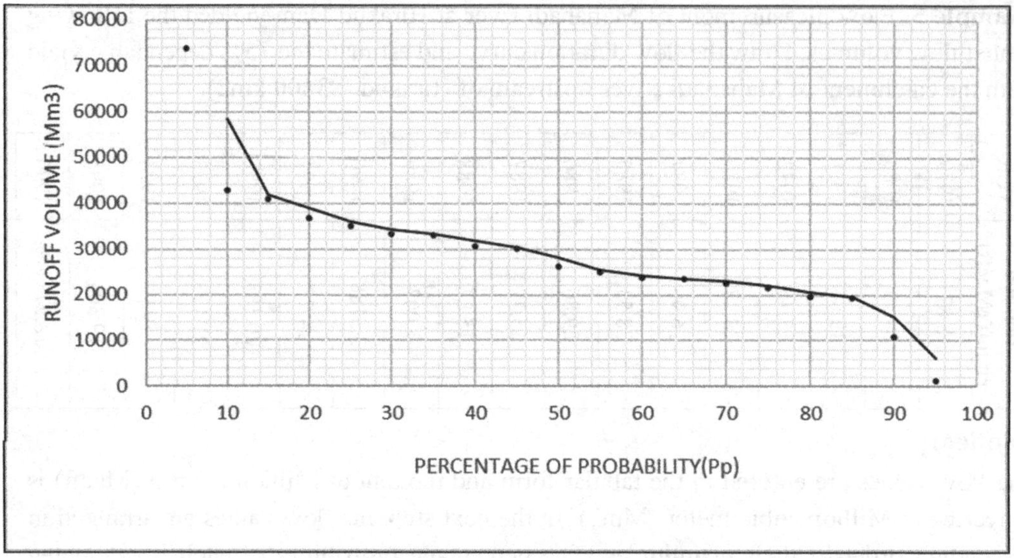

Figure 1.15 Flow duration curve

Percentage of Probability (P_p) = $\frac{m}{N+1} \times 100$

The 75% dependable flow can be calculated from the table by the method of interpolation. It is cross checked with the value obtained from the graph of flow duration curve by finding the runoff volume corresponding to the percentage probability of 75%.

$$75\ \%\ \text{Dependable yield} = 21536.85 - \frac{(21536.85 - 19589.16)}{(0.78 - 0.73)}(0.75 - 0.73) = 20757.77\ \text{Mm}^3$$

It is observed that the values obtained by interpolation and from flow duration curve are very close to each other.

Planning and development operations involving water resources make extensive use of flow duration curves. The following list includes some significant applications for flow duration curves:

a) Assessing consistent flows at different percentages (e.g., 75%, 60%, etc.) in order to design projects using water resources.
b) Assessing a river's hydropower potential features.
c) Drainage system design
d) Research on flood control.

UNIT SUMMARY

- Hydrology is the study that focuses on the ways in which water appears, moves, circulates, and is distributed on and beneath the Earth's surface, including in rivers, lakes, oceans, soil moisture, groundwater, and in the atmosphere as vapor or clouds.
- Precipitation, encompassing rain, snow, hail, frost, and dew, is the atmospheric contribution to the Earth's surface, with rain and snow playing the most crucial roles. Rainfall, in particular, is the primary source of stream flow and is responsible for flooding in many of India's rivers.
- The hydrologic cycle, also known as the water cycle, is an ongoing, cyclical process that has no start or end point. It illustrates how water continuously moves through and between the atmosphere and the Earth's surface.
- Hydrological challenges, such as floods and droughts, arise from significant variations in rainfall both spatially and over time. Understanding the relationship between rainfall intensity and duration is critical for the planning and design of water resources projects.

EXERCISE

MULTIPLE CHOICE QUESTIONS

1. Which is the most convenient method of calculating average rainfall?

   a. Arithmetic mean method c. Isohyetal method

   b. Thiessen-polygon method d. All of above

2. What is the term for a line that connects points having the same amount of rainfall?

   a. Isohyet c. Contour line

   b. Isotherm d. Isobar

3. The total time during which catchment contributes flow at the section is known as-

   a. Lag time c. Rising Limb

   b. Hyetograph d. Crest segment

4. Which is a graphical representation of the discharge flowing in the river at the given location with the passage of time?
   a. Hydrograph
   b. Hyetograph
   c. Rising Limb
   d. None of the above

5. The lower part of the falling limb and expresses the relation between base flow and time is known as-
   a. Time
   b. Base flow separation
   c. Base flow recession
   d. Lag time

6. Identify the year when the Soil Conservation Service (SCS) of the USA developed the Curve Number (CN) method.
   a. 1969
   b. 1959
   c. 1979
   d. 1999

7. The formula derived from the examination of flood data for basins situated in the Western Ghats of Maharashtra is:
   a. Empirical method
   b. Kirpich equation
   c. Dickens formula
   d. Inglis formula

8. The equations that are tailored for application in the regions where they were formulated, noting that their use beyond these specified areas may yield only estimated values is:
   a. Empirical method
   b. Dickens formula
   c. Kirpich equation
   d. Inglis formula

9. What method is employed to compute rainfall with uniform intensity and prolonged duration over a catchment area?
   a. Rational method
   c. Kirpich equation

b. Empirical method d. Dickens formula

10. In Odisha how many percentages of people depend upon cultivation and fishery?

a. 80 c. 50

b. 60 d. 20

Answers

1	2	3	4	5	6	7	8	9	10
d	b	b	b	a	a	a	b	c	c

SHORT ANSWER TYPE QUESTIONS

1. Write a short note on average rainfall over a watershed.
2. What is the arithmetic mean method? Explain.
3. What do you mean by Thiessen- polygon method?
4. When and how should we use Isohyetal method to find average rainfall over a basin?
5. What is the basic different between isohyetal and Thiessen polygon methods?
6. What are the factors affecting runoff?
7. What is effective rainfall?
8. Justify the importance of flood discharge measurement.
9. What is flood and why does it occur?
10. What is rational method? In which condition is it applicable?
11. What is an empirical method? Why should we go for applying it?
12. What is dependable yield? Explain.

LONG ANSWER TYPE QUESTIONS

1. Briefly discuss about the methods of calculation of average rainfall.
2. Briefly discuss the factor affecting runoff?
3. Briefly describe two techniques of maximum flood discharge measurement.
4. What is the rationale of rational method? How do you find the coefficient used in this method for more realistic estimation of peak of the flood?

5. What are the empirical methods commonly used for finding flood peak? Describe any two equations in detail.
6. Why flood discharge measurement is important? Briefly describe its each term.

NUMERICAL PROBLEMS

1. In a catchment there are 5 rain gauge stations a, b, c, d, and e. The rainfall data collected by them in the year 2022 are 5cm, 9cm, 6cm, 3cm, 1cm respectively. Find the average rainfall of that catchment.
2. The Isohyets due to a storm in a catchment were taken and the areas of the catchment bounded by Isohyet were found to be 301, 140, 180, 480, 200 sqKm for or between the isohyets 5, 5-10, 10-15, 15-20, 20-25 respectively. Find the average rainfall of the storm.
3. Calculate the average depth of rainfall using Thiessen polygon method. The station 3, 5, 8 are outside the catchment area.

   Station – 1, 2, 3, 4, 5, 6, 7, 8

   Rainfall (mm) – 12, 30, 25, 16, 28, 44, 65, 48 respectively.

   Bounding Area $(km)^2$ for each station - 3, 5, 10, 13, 15, 28, 34, 20
4. Calculate the average depth of rainfall. The station 4, 6, 8 are outside in catchment area. (Figure is given below).

   Station – 1, 2, 3, 4, 5, 6, 7, 8

   Rainfall (mm) collected in each rain gauge – 100, 206, 153, 122, 80, 141, 205, 180 respectively.

   Bounding Area $(km)^2$ for each station- 42, 70, 45, 8, 51, 15, 47, 19

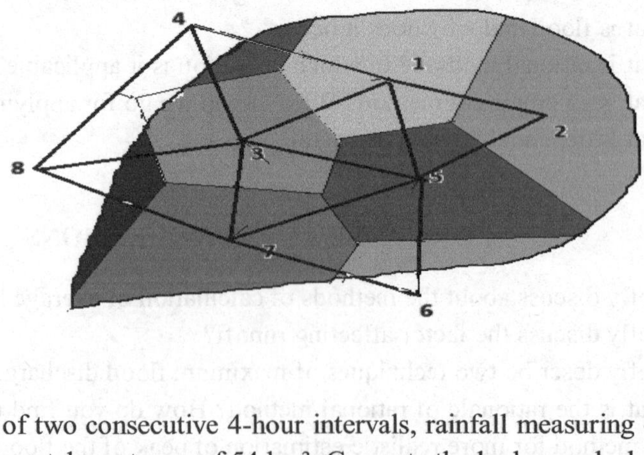

5. Over a period of two consecutive 4-hour intervals, rainfall measuring 4.1 cm and 5.7 cm fell on a catchment area of 54 km². Generate the hydrograph showing flow

at the catchment's outlet, assuming a base flow of 5.5 m³/s, and calculate the excess rainfall using a bar chart.

Time from start of storm(h)	0	2	4	6	8	10	12
Accumulated rainfall (cm)	0	1.6	6.8	3.2	5.5	7.8	9.4
Discharge (in m^3/sec)	6	13	22	31	18	11	29

6. An 8.0 km² catchment experienced a storm lasting 16 hours. The accumulated rainfall from the storm is described by its mass curve. Given a ϕ index (representing the infiltration rate) of 0.25 cm/hr for this catchment, calculate the hyetograph of effective rainfall and estimate the total direct runoff volume resulting from the storm, including a figure for illustration.
7. In a 550-hector watershed the curve no. value is 50 for AMC 2.

   i. Calculate the direct runoff value based on the provided rainfall data for the four specified days.

   ii. What could be the runoff value for CN 70?

DATE	P (cm)
1st June	55
2nd June	25
3rd June	38
4th June	12

PRACTICAL

RAINFALL MEASUREMENT

EXPERIMENT 1

Aim of the experiment

This practical exercise equips students with the ability to accurately measure rainfall using both manual (non-recording) and automated (recording) rain gauges, essential for understanding and monitoring hydrological processes.

Theory

Rainfall, a crucial natural resource, supports various needs including public health, industrial operations, and agricultural activities. Precise rainfall measurements are essential for the effective conservation and management of water resources. The practice of rainwater harvesting, conservation, and utilization is fundamental for the agricultural development and economic progress of regions. Rainfall measurement is conducted using either non-recording or automatic (recording) rain gauges. Non-recording gauges capture cumulative rainfall data (typically over 24 hours), and are often used in remote areas where readings are taken infrequently. Conversely, recording gauges continuously monitor rainfall, providing detailed insights into its intensity, frequency, duration, and total amount, which are critical for assessing the potential impact on runoff rates and volumes.

Equipment Needed

- Manual rain gauge
- Automatic rain gauge

Method

i. Manual rain gauge:

Rain is collected into a plastic container fitted with a funnel. The quantity of rain collected over a 24-hour period is measured using a glass measuring cylinder provided by the maker of the gauge, with readings taken at 8:30 A.M. The measuring cylinder, which is an essential part of the gauge, should be made of clear glass or plastic, with its diameter not exceeding one-third of the gauge's rim diameter. It must have precise markings in 0.2 mm increments for accurate reading. To measure the rainfall, the collected water is poured from the storage container into the cylinder, and the volume is read off the marked graduations. If the rainfall is significant, multiple measurements might be needed. The water's meniscus bottom marks the reading level, and it's important to keep the cylinder vertical during this process. After measurement, the storage container is emptied and placed back under the collector for future collection.

Precautions

- Confirm that the rain gauge is completely leak-proof to prevent loss of collected rainwater.
- The measuring cylinder must be maintained in a clean condition, and any plant leaves or foreign debris should be diligently removed from the collection area.

ii. Automatic rain gauge:

The device is composed of a cylindrical shape with a funnel at the top, leading into an inner brass tube. It features a recording system powered by a clock mechanism that drives a drum. This drum carries a chart where a pen plots a hydrograph, mapping rainfall against time. The clock's mechanism is designed to complete a full rotation every 24 hours. A pen, connected to a lever linked to a float inside the inner tube, ascends as the float lifts with accumulating rainwater, recording the amount of rainfall. When the tube is full, a mechanism connecting to the inner tube activates a siphon, which empties all the water, returning the pen to its initial position. To monitor rainfall intensity variations, especially during heavy rainfall, the depth recorded on the chart is checked every half hour.

Precautions

- Replace the recording chart daily, ideally between 8:30 and 9:00 AM, to ensure continuous and accurate data collection.
- Regularly check the pen to ensure it has enough ink for clear and consistent recording of rainfall data.
- Keeps the instrument clean, making sure it is clear of leaves and any other foreign materials that could obstruct the collection or recording process.

Observations

At 8:30 AM, document the rainfall measurements gathered from both the manual and automatic rain gauges. This standardized practice guarantees uniform and comparable data acquisition, enabling precise evaluation of daily precipitation trends.

Results

i. Non-recording rain gauge Depth of rainfall = _______mm

ii. Recording rain gauge Depth of rainfall = _______mm

EXPERIMENT 2

COMPUTATION OF AVERAGE RAINFALL

Aim of the experiment

After this practical exercise, students will be skilled in determining the catchment's average rainfall using the Thiessen polygon method, which calculates weighted averages from multiple gauge readings.

Theory

The Thiessen polygon method assigns a weight to the rainfall data from each station based on the area closest to that station. This method considers all stations inside and surrounding the catchment area, presuming a linear change in rainfall intensity between any two locations.

Following steps are involved to estimate the mean rainfall:

- Plot all rain gauges within and surrounding the catchment area on a scaled map.
- Connect adjacent stations to form a network of triangles.
- Draw perpendicular bisectors for each triangle's side, forming polygons. This is based on the principle that the most accurate rainfall estimate at any point is from the nearest gauge, achieved by constructing perpendicular bisectors between each pair of rain gauges, thus defining closed areas within the watershed boundary.
- Calculate the area of each Thiessen polygon.
- Let R_1, R_2, R_3, ..., R_n denote the amounts of rainfall recorded at stations 1, 2, 3, ..., n, respectively, and A_1, A_2, A_3, ..., A_n represent the areas of the respective Thiessen polygons associated with each station.
- Compute the average rainfall R across the catchment using the specified formula, which typically involves weighting each station's recorded rainfall by the area of its corresponding polygon and summing these products.

$$\bar{R} = \frac{(A_1R_1 - A_2R_2 - A_3R_3 - \cdots - A_nR_n)}{A_1 + A_2 + A_3 + \cdots + A_n}$$

Where,

$\bar{R}$ = mean precipitation over the catchment;

R_1, R_2.........R_n = point rainfall values for 'n' number of stations; and

A_1+ A_2 +A_3 +. . . + A_n = area of each polygon.

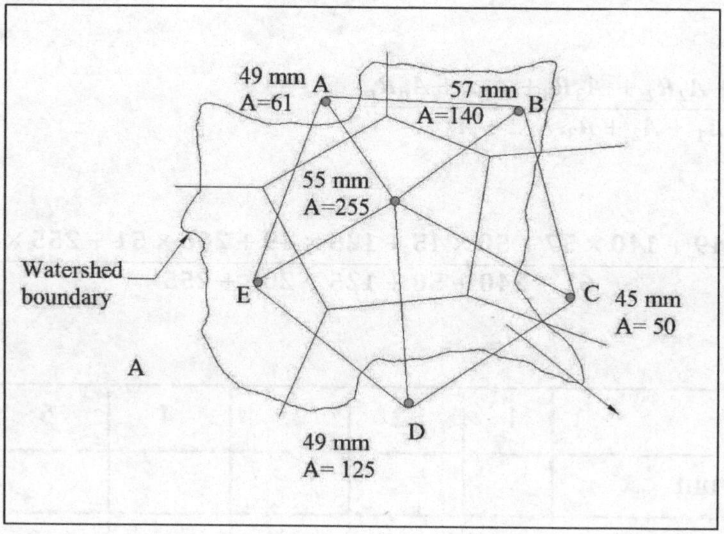

Figure 1.16 Thiessen polygon

Observations and calculations

The rainfall at different stations is given in the following Table.

Station	1	2	3	4	5	6
Rainfall, mm	49	57	45	49	51	55

Following the described approach, rain gauges located both within and around the catchment area, as illustrated in the figure, are accurately placed on a scaled map, and links between these stations form a series of triangles. Polygons are created by drawing perpendicular bisectors to each side of the triangles. The areas of these polygons are then precisely determined as outlined.

Station	1	2	3	4	5	6
Rainfall, mm	49	57	45	49	51	55
Area of polygon, h	61	140	50	125	206	255

$$\bar{R} = \frac{A_1R_1 + A_2R_2 + A_3R_3 + \ldots\ldots + A_nR_n}{A_1 + A_2 + A_3\ldots\ldots + A_n}$$

$$\bar{R} = \frac{(61 \times 49 + 140 \times 57 + 50 \times 45 + 125 \times 49 + 206 \times 51 + 255 \times 55)}{61 + 140 + 50 + 125 + 206 + 255} = 52.4mm$$

Station	1	2	3	4	5	6
Rainfall, mm						
Area of polygon, ha						

Results

Average rainfall for the catchment = mm

Limitations

- Whenever a rain gauge is added or removed, new polygons must be constructed.
- The method does not take into account orographic (elevation-related) influences on precipitation.
- It assumes a linear variation in rainfall, which may not accurately reflect real meteorological conditions and catchment features.
- Topographical and other physical barriers that could affect rainfall distribution are not accounted for.

EXPERIMENT 3

DELINEATION OF WATERSHEDS

Aim of the Experiment

Delineation of contributory area for the given outlet from the topo-sheet. Also, delineate the sub-watersheds within the watershed by using the topo-sheet of the catchment.

The Concept

A watershed is a fundamental hydrologic unit that is derived from a natural border. Any site enclosed inside a watershed from which rainfall will contribute water to the outlet (watershed outlet) are considered to be part of the watershed. In order to identify the sub-

or micro-watersheds within a watershed, it is important to keep in mind the following two fundamental ideas:

a. Determine the micro-watershed outlet point. When creating a structure, monitoring site, water body, or tributary merging into a larger stream, this is typically our point of interest.
b. Upstream-pointing contours, also known as contour lines, indicate valleys and serve as a watershed's drainage line. Ridges are shown by contours pointing downstream, and these boundaries are referred to as a micro- or sub-watershed.

Requirements

Survey of India Topo-sheet of study area, Pencil, Eraser, Planimeter and Calculator.

Procedure

Following steps are used for watershed delineation:

Step 1: Take a topo-sheet and mark the location of the water body or tributary joining the main stream.

Step 2: Study the contour lines (lines connecting points of equal elevation above mean sea level or GTS Benchmark) on the topo-sheet for the area. Contours (contour lines) that point upstream denote valleys and form the drainage line in a watershed. The contours that point downstream denote ridges. Contours spaced far apart indicate that the landscape is more or less flat and have gentle sloping land. Contour lines spaced very close together indicate sudden changes (rise or fall) in elevation over a short distance; i.e. the area with steep slopes.

Step 3: Trace the drainage line or waterway from its catchment source to its outlet, including the tributaries. This step helps in determining the beginning and end boundaries of the drainage area.

Step 4: A valley line or drainage line is represented by a series of contour lines "pointing" towards the highest elevation. Determine the direction of drainage in the area by drawing arrows perpendicular to a series of contour lines that decrease in elevation. Runoff water travels the path of least resistance while going down slope. The runoff travel path is the perpendicular route between contours.

Step 5: A higher area or ridge line is represented by a series of contour lines "pointing" towards the lowest elevation.

Step 6: Identify and mark the divide points /highest elevations where part of the runoff would drain towards one body of water, and the rest part would drain towards another body of water.

Step 7: Connect the divide points to form the line of highest elevations in the area which is called as watershed boundary.

Step 8: Thus the process of watershed delineation through topo-sheet is complete.

Step 9: Now this delineated watershed or sub-watershed map can be taken to the field for ground truth verification.

Step 10: Take different measurements, e.g. total number and length of channels, watershed boundary etc. and convert to the actual length in line with the scale mentioned in the map.

Step 11: Calculate the area of the watersheds and sub watersheds using a transparent graph sheet placed over the toposheet or with the use of a planimeter.

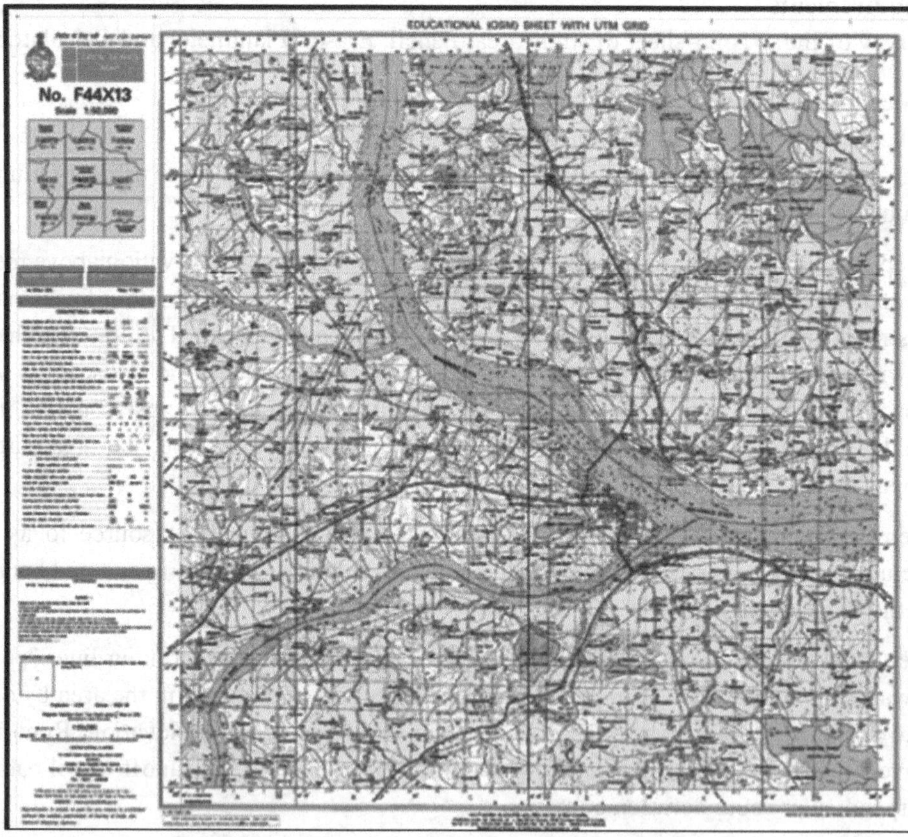

Figure 1.17 Survey of India Educational Toposheet showing parts of Mahanadi River and its major Tributaries "Tel" and "Ong" downstream of Hirakud Dam, with all other details.

(Source: *https://www.surveyofindia.gov.in/files/64P13.jpg*)

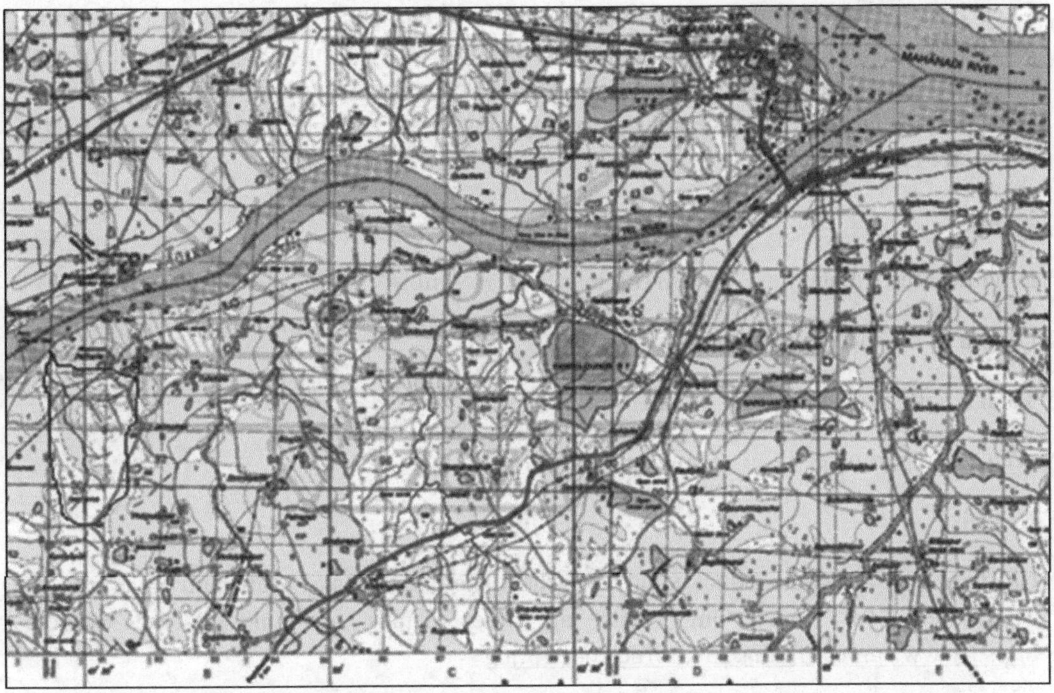

Figure 1.18 Survey of India Educational Toposheet showing parts of Mahanadi river and its Tributary "Tel" with all other details.

(**Source:** *https://www.surveyofindia.gov.in/files/64P13.jpg*)

OBSERVATION

Example 6. A watershed delineated from a sub-basin has one tributary (length 5.4 cm as measured on map) and one main drain/river (length 24.6 cm on map). The perimeter or length of watershed boundary is 72 cm measured on map. Assuming the map scale as 1: 50,000, calculate the total length of main river, total channel length and watershed perimeter in km.

Solution

Length conversion 1 cm (map): 500 m = 0.5 km on ground (1: 50,000 Scale Topo-sheet)

Length of the tributary = 5.4 cm (on map) = 5.4 x 0.5 = 2.7 km

Length of the main river= 24.6 cm (on map) = 24.6 x 0.5 = 12.3 km

Total length of channel = 2.7 + 12.3 = 15.0 km

Watershed perimeter = 72.0 cm (on map) = 72 x 0.5 = 36 km

Exercise. A watershed delineated from a sub-basin has one tributary (length 6.5 cm as measured on map) and one main drain/river (length 35.3 cm on map). The perimeter or length of watershed boundary is 85 cm measured on map. Assuming the map scale as 1 : 50,000, calculate the total length of main river, total channel length and watershed perimeter in km.

Results

Length of the tributary = cm (on map) = km

Length of the main river = cm (on map) = km

Total length of channel = km

Watershed perimeter = cm (on map) = km

Exercise

Use the Survey of India Educational Toposheet showing parts of Mahanadi River and its Tributaries "Tel" and "Ong" with all other details available in the Source: https://www.surveyofindia.gov.in/files/64P13.jpg

By use of the toposheet, delineate two watersheds with one sub watershed of each watershed of streams joining the river Ong close to its confluence with river "Mahanadi".

Classify the streams with respect to the stream order and shape. Calculate the area of the watersheds and sub watersheds using a transparent graph sheet placed over the toposheet or with the use of a planimeter.

Take the snapshots and paste as the figure mentioned above.

EXPERIMENT 4

WATERSHED DELINEATION BY THE USE OF GIS PACKAGE

Aim of the Experiment

Watershed Delineation by the use of GIS package and findout the area of the catchment considering the strategic location on the stream.

Requirements

Survey of India Topo-sheet of study area, Computer system with GIS software.

The Concept

- Using a DEM within a Geographical Information System (GIS), we can perform digital terrain analysis (DTA) such as calculating slopes, flow lengths, and delineate watershed boundaries and stream networks.
- Any GIS package can be used – eg. ArcGIS, GRAM++
- The major tools used are ArcMap and ArcCatalog
- ArcMap is used for performing the operations on the data
- ArcCatalog is used for maintaining the data and files
- The input required are topo sheets which can be obtained from Bhuvan or USGS sites
- Then the topo sheets are geo-registered.
- ArcMap contains the ArcTool box, which has all the tools required for modifying, reading, determining and viewing maps
- Shape files (.shp) are the files that can be created in ArcCatalog and edited in ArcMap
- The map we provide acts as a background for creating the shape files
- For watershed delineation, the contours are to be digitized from the scanned toposheet

Procedure

Major steps involved in delineating a watershed using ARC GIS are:

Geo-registering the topo sheets – Creating shapefiles – Contour digitization – Preparation of DEM – Filling of DEM – Flow Direction Raster generation – Flow Accumulation Raster – Determining Pour Points – Watershed Delineation.

- Creation of Shapefile: Initially a shape file is to be created in ArcCatalog. For contours, the polyline shape files are used.
  The coordinate system of the shape file be determined. An existing coordinate system can be used or a coordinate system being used in another file can be imported. Open the attribute table of this shape file and add a new attribute elevation (any name can be given).
- Contour Digitization:
  This shape file must now be added to the ArcMap as a layer. Open the editor tool bar and click on start editing. If there are multiple shape files in the ArcMap at the same time, specify the target file in the box provided.
  Now, select the Create new feature tool (pencil tool) and start sketching along the contours. After a contour is completed, specify its elevation in the attribute table.
- Preparation of DEM:
  In the Arc Tool box, open the spatial analyst extension. Open interpolation tools and then open the topo to raster option. In the topo to raster window, specify the

input file as the shapefile created. Change the type as contour and field to elevation. Run the topo to raster to get the DEM.

- Filling the DEM:
  After getting the DEM, there is need to fill the depressions if any in the DEM to get avoid false routings.
  Open the Hydrology tool box in the spatial analyst extension and then open the fill tool. Give the DEM as the input file. Now It fills the sinks in the surface raster and removes small imperfections in the data.
- Preparing Flow Direction map:
  Choose the Flow direction tool available in the hydrology tool box in spatial analyst extension. It creates the raster with flow direction to the steepest neighbouring cell down the slope. It is used to determine the direction of flow of water in the given topography.
  Direction of flow should be known for each cell, because it is the direction of flow that determines the direction of flow of water over the surface.
- Watershed Delineation:
  Use the watershed tool in hydrology tool box, to delineate a watershed.
  The flow direction raster and the pour point shape file are the inputs.
  If there are multiple watersheds in the topo-sheet, the watersheds corresponding to the drainage paths also can be determined.

Watershed Coding

To provide uniformity and fixing identity to each watershed use combination of letters and digits or by using name of stream.

- Find the name of river/stream, draining the watershed. e.g. Mahanadi
- Take first letter of main river Mahanadi e.g "M"
- Find name of sub-catchment. e.g. Ong of Mahanadi
- Use first letter of sub-catchment "O" Now Combine MO
- Use digits for watershed delineated within sub-catchment e.g. MO1, MO2 etc.
- Finally, code sub-watershed by adding another digit after MO1 after a hyphen e.g. MO1-1; MO1-2 and so on.
- Coding should be from downstream, i.e. confluence point with main river to upstream. Also, 'L' be adopted for the Left of stream "R" for right of the stream.

Example 7. Following the above-mentioned procedure, the watershed of Lawa river is delineated. Data on Bhuvan site are used for this purpose. The output Fern leaf shaped catchment is visible with green colored boundary line and the basin area being shown with whitish background. The strategic location on Lowa river is the location where the road crosses the stream. There is a need of all-weather road to cross the stream. It is proposed to construct a High-Level Bridge over the river Lowa to make the road fit for all weather traffic to cross the stream.

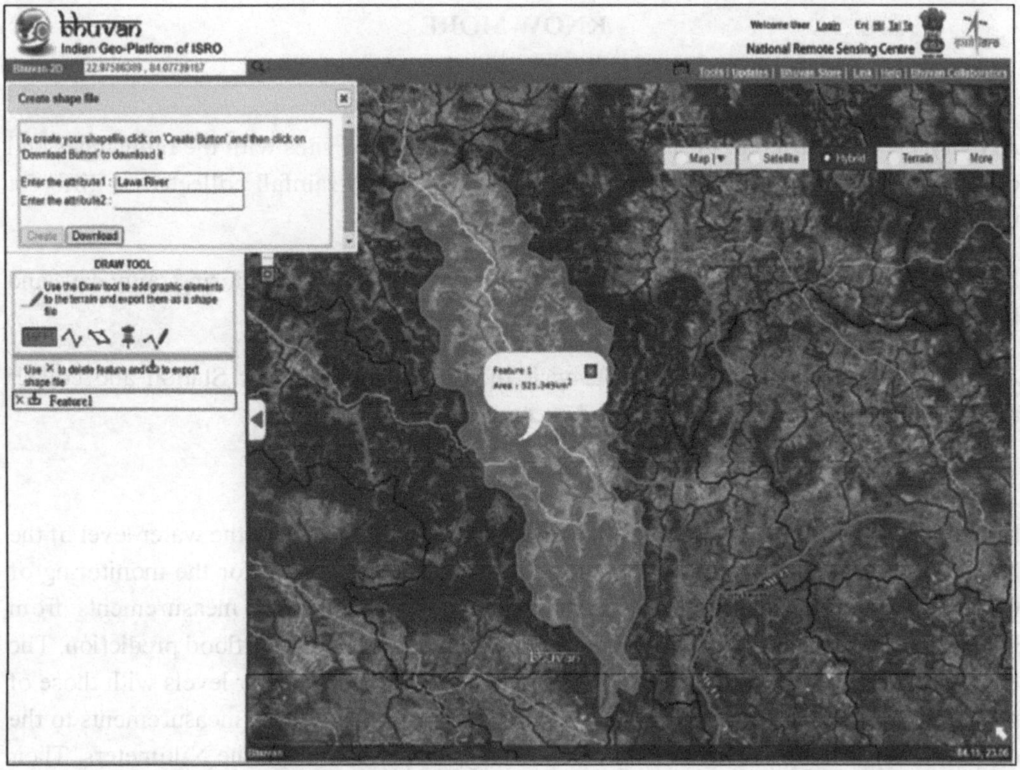

Exercise Use the toposheet. By use of data available in Bhuvan site or USGS site, delineate two watersheds with one sub watershed of each watershed of streams joining the river Ong close to its confluence with river "Mahanadi".

Classify the streams as per the stream order and calculate the area of the watersheds and sub watersheds.

Take the snapshots and paste as the figure mentioned above.

For further reading, please scan the QR Code or visit the web site: https://www.wvca.us/envirothon/pdf/Watershed_Delineation_2.pdf	

EXPERIMENT No. 5. Compute the yield of the Catchment area referring to the Watershed / Sub-watershed delineated by the use of Survey of India Toposheet or GIS package. Use the methods applicable for this purpose. Draw the observation table, present the detailed calculations and results. Mention the peak runoff and volume of runoff separately by using different methods / formulae. Give your comments after comparing the results obtained.

KNOW MORE

Activity

Activity 1: Make different groups of students to visit nearby sites with the raingauges and collet rain and report. Ask them to compare the amount of rainfall collected in different types of raingauges and at different places.

Activity 2: Let the groups collect the rainfall amount from the media during rainy days and find out the average rainfall over a catchment.

Activity 3: Let the group of students visit the Automatic Weather Station and collect rainfall data and other weather data and prepare a report.

Interesting facts

In ancient Egypt, the Nilometer was the device employed to measure the water level of the Nile River. This instrument was crucial before 600 B.C., allowing for the monitoring of the Nile's water levels, especially during the flood season. The measurements from Nilometers, particularly in locations like Memphis, were essential for flood prediction. The historical practice involved observing and comparing the Nile's water levels with those of previous years to anticipate flooding. To rapidly communicate these measurements to the capital, exceptionally skilled rowers would navigate upstream from the Nilometers. Their speed was critical, as they needed to move faster than the floodwaters to provide downstream populations with enough warning to evacuate in advance of floods.

In a significant advancement in meteorological instrumentation, Sir Christopher Wren and Robert Hooke were responsible for developing the tipping-bucket rain gauge. This invention marked a pivotal moment in the quantification of rainfall. Furthermore, in the 17th century, the Italian physician Santorio, together with Robert Hooke, introduced the modern current meter. This device was instrumental in measuring the speed of water flow, reflecting the period's burgeoning interest in accurately understanding and measuring various hydrological and meteorological phenomena.

Sir Christopher Wren (1632-1723)

Robert Hooke (1635–1703)

Timeline

The beginnings of civilization are deeply linked to the control and comprehension of water, highlighted by early advancements near the Tigris and Euphrates rivers in Mesopotamia, the Indus River in India, and the Yellow River in China. These early societies developed the initial water management infrastructures, such as water supply networks, dams, levees, enhancements to river beds, and irrigation and drainage systems, as far back as 3000 B.C. Notably, ancient Egyptian artefacts indicate meticulous records of Nile water levels dating back to 3000-3500 B.C.

The rational study of nature, devoid of mythological explanations, began in Ionia, along the Aegean Sea, after 600 B.C. Thales of Miletus, recognized as the first philosopher in the history of science, posited water as the fundamental substance of everything on Earth. The regular flooding of the Nile River captured the fascination of early Ionian thinkers such as Thales, Anaxagoras, Herodotus, Diogenes, and Democritus. Anaxagoras was the first to propose a rational explanation, attributing the floods to the melting snow from the mountains where the river originates.

Plato and Aristotle, philosophers of ancient Greece, contributed significantly to the understanding of the hydrologic cycle. Plato explained that rivers and springs stem from rainfall, while Aristotle, in his work "Meteorologica," delved into precipitation mechanics and discussed winds and seas. During this period, India saw the beginnings of systematic rainfall measurement, with non-recording rain gauges used for agricultural taxation based on rainfall amounts.

Roman engineering feats included the construction of sophisticated aqueducts, sewer systems, and harbors, along with significant water management structures in Istanbul, exemplifying their practical engineering prowess.

However, the scientific progress in hydrology stalled during the scholastic era (200-1500), with the notable exception of rain gauge development in China by the 13th century, and later in Korea by the 15th century. Renaissance polymath Leonardo da Vinci furthered the understanding of water flow, and Italian architect Giovan Fontana analyzed and provided solutions for the flooding of the Tiber in Rome.

The 17th century was a pivotal period for hydrology, characterized by the embracement of the principle of continuity and experimental contributions from Pierre Perrault, Edmé Mariotte, and Edmond Halley. These developments laid the groundwork for the field of experimental hydrology. The 18th century introduced the Pitot Tube by Henry de Pitot and the development of the Chézy equation by Antoine Chézy. The 19th century saw further advancements with the formulation of the Kutter equation by Ganguillet and Kutter, the Manning equation by Robert Manning, and substantial progress in groundwater hydrology, including the formulation of Darcy's Law and Dupuit's equations for well discharge.

These milestones highlight the evolution of hydrology from ancient civilizations' practical applications to a deeply analytical and scientific discipline, shaping our understanding and management of water resources through centuries of innovation and discovery.

Empirical Era (1900-1930): This era saw the proposal of numerous empirical formulas, the application of which heavily relied on the engineer's judgment and prior experience, as noted by Chow in 1964. The era was characterized by a reliance on empirical methods that eventually led to the pursuit of more scientific approaches in hydrology, driven by the realization that these methods often fell short in addressing real-world hydrological challenges effectively.

Rational Era (1930-1950): This period marked significant advancements in hydrology with the development of foundational theories and equations. In 1933, Sherman introduced the Unit Hydrograph Theory, revolutionizing the way rainfall excess was translated into runoff hydrographs. The same year, Horton formulated an infiltration equation critical for determining rainfall excess. This contributed new equations to well hydraulics in 1935, and Gumbel introduced the extreme value distribution method for analysing flood frequency data, laying the groundwork for modern hydrological analysis.

Theoretical Era (1950-Present): Hydrology entered a phase where theoretical and mathematical analyses became pivotal in understanding hydrologic processes. The advent of advanced computational tools and sophisticated measuring instruments has enabled the detailed study and application of hydrologic theories. This era is distinguished by the extensive use of linear and nonlinear system analysis, transient and statistical methods in groundwater dynamics, and theories of heat and mass transfer in evaporation studies. Moreover, it includes the systematic collection of hydrologic data and the use of operational research methods in the planning and design of water resources systems, showcasing the extensive scope and depth of contemporary hydrological science.

After World War II, significant strides were made in the field of hydrology, marking the beginning of focused research and educational efforts in this discipline. In 1959, the establishment of the Water Resources Development Center (WRDC) by the United Nations marked a significant shift towards a worldwide focus on hydrological research. This movement was further reinforced by the support of international entities like the United Nations Educational, Scientific and Cultural Organization (UNESCO), the World Meteorological Organization (WMO), the Food and Agricultural Organization (FAO), and the World Health Organization (WHO), each contributing crucially to the advancement of hydrologic studies and their practical applications.

The declaration of an International Hydrologic Decade (IHD) in 1961 was a landmark event, aiming to foster international collaboration in hydrologic research and training programs. Since then, the field of hydrology has witnessed continuous development, characterized by a myriad of investigations, seminars, conferences, and the publication of numerous papers in various scientific journals. These activities have been instrumental in advancing the understanding of hydrology and disseminating knowledge across the globe, contributing to the on-going evolution of this vital scientific discipline.

REFERENCES & SUGGESTED READING

- Garg, S.K. (1977). Water Resources and Hydrology. Delhi: Khanna Publishers, New Delhi.
- Michael, A.M. (2008). Irrigation Theory and Practices. Vikash Publishing House Pvt. Ltd., New Delhi.
- Raghunath, H.M. (1985). Hydrology : Principle, Analysis and Design. Wiley Eastern Limited, New Delhi.
- Raghunath, H.M. (2003). Groundwater. New Age International Pvt. Ltd. Publishers, New Delhi.
- Reddy, P J R (2016). A Textbook of Hydrology, Laxmi Publications, New Delhi
- Sharma, R.K. (1993). A Text Book of Hydrology and Water Resources. Dhanpat Rai & Sons Publisher, New Delhi.
- https://archive.nptel.ac.in/content/storage2/courses/105101010/downloads/Lecture13.pdf
- https://www.researchgate.net/figure/Watershed-delineation-methodology-flow-chart_fig3_257718233
- https://dolr.gov.in/sites/default/files/JR%20Sharma%20IWMP%20-JAN%208%202014%20-%20ONE.pdf

Dynamic QR Code for Further Reading

Dynamic QR Codes for Further Reading		

2 CROP WATER REQUIREMENTS & RESERVOIR PLANNING

परिचयः ॥
Introduction

Crops require water in order to grow. The primary and most important source of water supply is rainfall. Due to insufficient supply of water from rain, artificial water supply technologies must be used in addition to rainwater. Water must be carried or directed to the field by individuals, even in the case of other natural water sources such rivers, streams, lakes, and ponds. Irrigation can therefore be classified as either natural or artificial.

सुवर्णरौप्यमाणिक्यवसनैरपि पुरिताः ।
तथापि प्रार्थयन्त्येव कृषकान् भक्ततृष्णया ॥

Even after having all the riches of the world, you are dependent on the farmer for food.

सोना, चांदी, मानिक्य एवं वस्त्रों से पूर्ण होने पर भी मनुष्यों को भोजन के आवश्यकतावश किसान पर निर्भर रहना पडता है ।

वृष्टिमूला कृषिः सर्वा वृष्टिमूलं च जीवनम् । तस्मादादौ प्रयत्नेन वृष्टिज्ञानं समाचरेत् ॥

All agriculture depends on rainfall, and rainfall is the foundation of life. Therefore, one should strive to understand rainfall first and foremost.

UNIT SPECIFICS

This unit elaborately discusses the following aspects:

- Irrigation and its classification.
- Crop Water requirements
- Methods of application of irrigation water and its assessment.
- Surveys for irrigation project
- Area capacity curve.
- Silting of reservoirs
- Control levels in a reservoir

The practical applications of the subjects are covered to enhance curiosity, creativity, and problem-solving abilities. It features a vast array of multiple-choice and both short and long-answer questions, organized into two levels according to Bloom's taxonomy's lower and higher orders. Additionally, learners are provided with numerical assignments, along with a compilation of references and recommended readings for further practice.

To enrich the learning experience with more in-depth information on selected topics, QR codes are strategically placed throughout the text. These codes lead to additional supportive material upon scanning.

Following the practical exercises, the chapter introduces a "Know More" segment, carefully crafted to offer extra information that is of great value to readers. This segment focuses on the foundational activities, intriguing facts, analogies, and the historical progression of the subject, emphasizing key observations and discoveries. It outlines the timeline of the subject's evolution to present times and discusses its application in everyday life and various industries. Case studies addressing environmental, sustainability, social, and ethical considerations are also included, where relevant. The purpose is to stimulate curiosity and inquisitiveness about the topics discussed in the unit, enriching the reader's understanding and engagement with the material.

RATIONALE

India's terrain is a tapestry of contrasting landscapes, encompassing the towering peaks and deep gorges, fertile deltas, and the majestic high-altitude forests of the Himalayas. This extends to the vast grasslands of the Indo-Gangetic Plain and the undulating plateaus of the southeastern and southwestern regions, among other unique geographical features. The Indian climate is characterized by its dramatic range, with temperatures spanning from the frigid conditions akin to the Arctic to the sweltering heat found at the equator. Precipitation also varies wildly, from the arid regions receiving less than 100 mm of rainfall in the Thar Desert to the super-humid conditions in Mowsinram, Meghalaya, which sees the world's highest rainfall at 11,200 mm. Such diversity in geology and climate contributes to India's multifaceted agricultural sector that includes both well-watered and arid zones, yielding a broad spectrum of global food and horticultural produce.

For strategic planning and enhanced management of natural resources to mitigate environmental impact and boost agricultural yields for the burgeoning population's food and nutrition needs, India has been categorized into 20 agro-climatic zones and 60 sub-regions based on soil type, ecological parameters, and topography. The country boasts a cultivated expanse of approximately 142 million hectares, with 57 million hectares irrigated and the remaining 85 million dependent on rainfall. While the current cropping intensity lingers at 1.35, there is potential for growth through expanded irrigation and mechanization, particularly in India's eastern regions. The principal cereal crops include rice, wheat, maize, sorghum, and millet, complemented by a variety of pulses, oilseeds, and commercial crops like cotton, jute, sugarcane, and potatoes. Pulses predominantly encompass gram (chickpea) and pigeon pea, while the oilseed category mainly consists of groundnut, mustard, rapeseed, soybean, and sunflower.

Each crop's water needs vary according to its growth stage, and factors such as crop variety, seasonality, existing soil moisture play a role. For instance, water-intensive crops like sugarcane thrive in heavy soils, whereas cereals like wheat demand less water and are suited to sandy loam soils. Crops like cotton and maize fall somewhere in between. Accurate knowledge of the specific water requirements for diverse crops under the regional climatic conditions is crucial for developing irrigation strategies, designing efficient irrigation systems, and making mid-term adjustments during seasonal droughts. Such information guides the planning of reservoirs to meet the water needs across different crop growth stages, thereby ensuring optimal harvests.

PRE-REQUISITES

Mathematics: Basic Fundamentals of mathematics

Science: Basic Fundamentals of Science

UNIT OUTCOMES

After undergoing this module, the students will be able to perform the followings:

U2-O1: Differentiate various types and methods of irrigation

U2-O2: Estimate the capacity of a canal to irrigate a command area with various crops

U2-O3: Design a Water Reservoir to supply water into the irrigation canals

U2-O4: Suggest various silt control measures for a reservoir in a given situation with justifications

U2-O5: Calculate various control levels of a reservoir.

ALIGNMENT WITH COURSE OBJECTIVE

UNIT OUTCOMES	EXPECTED ALIGNMENT WITH COURSE OUTCOMES (1: Low Correlation; 2: Moderate Correlation; 3: High Correlation)				
	CO:1	CO:2	CO:3	CO:4	CO:5
U2-O1	-	3	2	-	3
U2-O2	-	3	2	-	2
U2-O3	-	3	2	-	2
U2-O4	-	-	3	3	2
U2-O5	1	3	3	3	3

2.1 Irrigation

2.1.1 Introduction

Watering crops on a regular basis is known as irrigation. It involves applying a controlled amount of water to land artificially, which helps in the production of crops. It can also be used for watering landscaping plants and lawns. Irrigation plays a crucial role in promoting agricultural growth, maintaining landscapes, and restoring damaged soils in dry regions and periods of low rainfall. Over the course of the twentieth century, irrigation has significantly expanded worldwide. In 1800, irrigation covered 8 million hectares globally, which increased to 94 million hectares in 1950 and 235 million hectares in 1990. By 1990, irrigated land accounted for 30% of global food production. Various irrigation techniques are employed worldwide, including canal systems, groundwater pumping, and diverting water from dams and other sources. While many irrigation projects are led by national governments, some are funded and organized by private investors and other countries like the United States, China, and European nations such as the United Kingdom. Irrigation has facilitated the cultivation of more crops, especially commodity crops, in regions where they would not naturally thrive. Many countries, often in collaboration with the World Bank, have invested in irrigation to boost wheat, rice, and cotton production. The Indian government has initiated a water management program targeting 8,350 water-stressed villages across seven states over a five-year period. The program aims to harvest rainwater, improve the water table, and increase irrigation rates.

2.1.2 Requirement in India

Irrigation is essential due to the cyclical nature of rainfall, which only occurs for four months each year in India. Some crops require irrigation to satisfy their water requirements due to the restricted quantity of rainfall. Archaeological studies have uncovered evidence of irrigation in regions where natural rainfall alone cannot sustain rainfed agriculture. Given the seasonal nature of rainfall in India, irrigation plays a crucial role. The predominant irrigation systems in India are based on groundwater. In the year 2013-2014, only approximately 36.7% of India's agricultural land received reliable irrigation, leaving the remaining two-thirds dependent on the monsoon season. Groundwater supplies about 65% of India's irrigation needs.

2.1.3 Advantages of Irrigation

Irrigation serves as the most effective solution to prevent drought and famine in regions experiencing insufficient rainfall, which can intermittently lead to these challenges. By providing a reliable water supply, irrigation offers several benefits, including:

a. Irrigation is essential in regions with limited rainfall, combating water scarcity.
b. It promotes soil fertility, enhancing agricultural productivity.
c. Irrigation projects have the potential to generate hydroelectric power.

d. It uplifts farmers' quality of life by enabling continuous cultivation and increased crop yields.
e. Effective irrigation methods aid in weed management, benefiting crop health.
f. By preventing famine and reducing reliance on deforestation, irrigation plays a critical role.

2.1.4 Disadvantages of Irrigation:

a. Overflowing seepage and leaking from ponds and marshes beside canals can encourage mosquito populations that spread diseases like malaria.
b. Irrigation can lower the temperature and create a damp environment due to the presence of water, impacting the local climate.
c. Irrigation canal systems can result in the loss of valuable residential and industrial land.
d. The high initial cost of irrigation projects leads to increased taxes and levies for cultivators.
e. During the rainy season, irrigation infrastructure can prevent water from draining freely, submerging crops and even villages.

2.1.5 Classification:

There are many irrigation techniques, the goal is to effectively and efficiently provide water to the plant. Since the rain is a seasonal phenomenon, as it is in the temperate zone, irrigation techniques are necessary for agriculture. Farmers carry out various types of irrigation depending on the soil, climatic conditions, area, and so on. The artificial method of applying water to the earth using a variety of tools, including sprayers, tubes, and pumps, is known as irrigation.

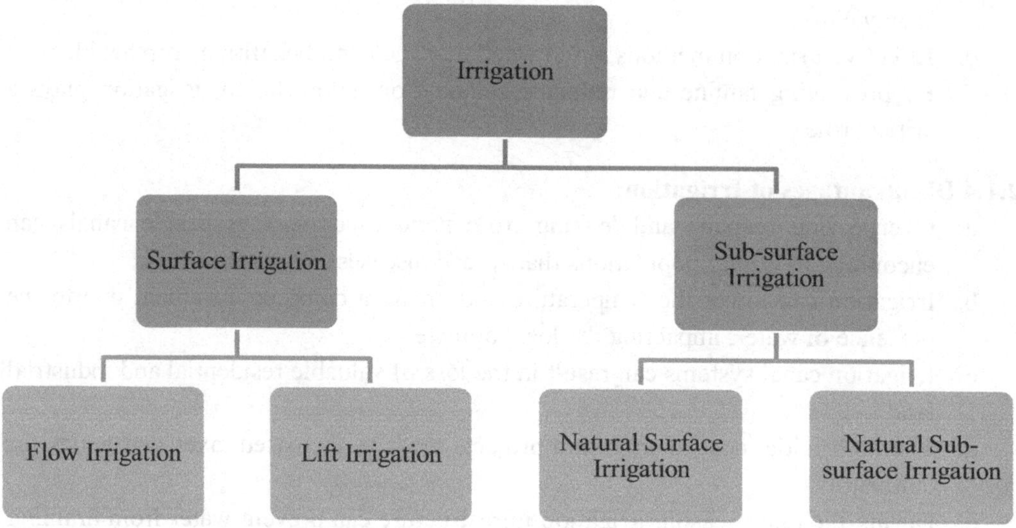

2.1.5.1 Surface Irrigation

Surface irrigation is a farming method where fields are flooded with water, which then spreads and seeps into the soil. It distributes water using gravity and functions best on level or gently sloping terrain. To guarantee uniform distribution over the field, water is redirected via channels from a water supply. Due to water losses from evaporation, runoff, and deep percolation, surface irrigation can be inefficient even though it is straightforward, affordable, and appropriate for a variety of crops.

2.1.5.2 Flow Irrigation

Flow irrigation uses the force of gravity to move water through canals from higher to lower levels. It doesn't need much upkeep, doesn't need an external power source, and in certain designs, it can even produce electricity. But since certain crops don't require a steady supply of water, it could not be appropriate for all crops, and some might not be ideal for summer crops.

2.1.5.3 Lift Irrigation:

The process of using pumps to raise water levels mechanically and then distributing it to agricultural regions for irrigation. A consistent and year-round supply of water is required for this technique. There are several ways to access the water source, including river canals, weirs, dams, and more.

Lifting Medium: Pumps are needed to raise the water so that it may be transported to a certain location. The necessary head and discharge are among the criteria that influence the choice of pumps. Concrete, steel, and other appropriate materials can be used for medium-rising and transporting.

2.1.5.4 Subsurface Irrigation

Subsurface irrigation, often known as subsurface drip irrigation (SDI), is a technique that involves injecting water directly into the ground beneath plant roots. Instead of putting water on the top, drip lines or emitters are buried beneath the soil's surface.

This technique has benefits including lessened weed growth and foliar diseases, as well as less water loss from evaporation and runoff. It makes it possible to precisely regulate the flow of nutrients and water, which maximises plant development and increases water usage efficiency. For consistent water distribution and to avoid emitter clogging, proper design, installation, and maintenance are essential.

2.1.6 Methods of Irrigation

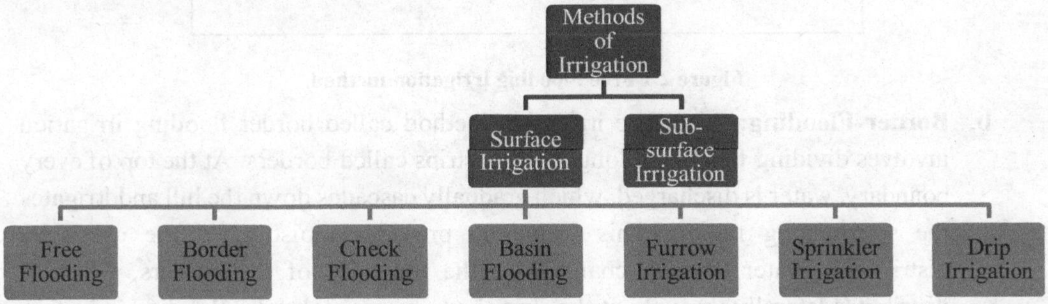

a. **Free Flooding:** Fields are inundated with water using the free flooding irrigation surface irrigation technique, which operates without any set rules or guidelines. Water is poured over the field, where it distributes organically and seeps into the ground to hydrate crops. This method is easy to use and reasonably priced; it works well in regions with lots of water resources and level terrain. On the other hand, it can lead to more water loss by evaporation and runoff as well as unequal water distribution throughout the field, which might cause fluctuations in soil moisture and perhaps waterlogging.

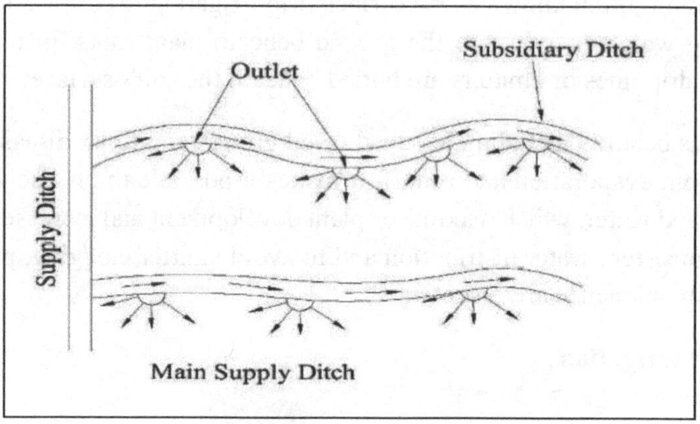

Figure 2.1 Free Flooding irrigation method

b. **Border Flooding:** A surface irrigation method called border flooding irrigation involves dividing fields into long, narrow strips called borders. At the top of every boundary, water is discharged, which gradually cascades down the hill and irrigates the surrounding region. This technique provides moisture to the crops by distributing water through channels to the top ends of the borders, where it distributes laterally throughout the strip. For row crops, border flooding irrigation works well in areas that are level or gradually sloping. It provides effective water distribution and simplicity. On the other hand, cautious management is required to avoid runoff or excessive irrigation, and frequent upkeep of borders and channels is crucial for the best possible water flow.

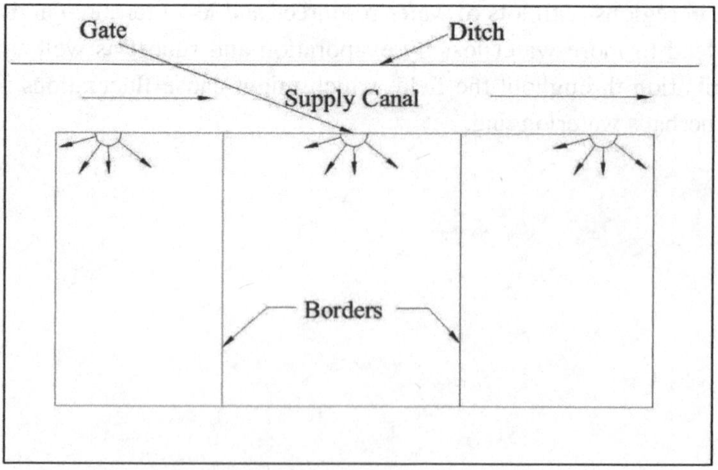

Figure 2.2 Border Flooding Irrigation method

c) **Check Flooding**: Check flooding is a type of flooding in which levees create a specified check area within which water is managed. Built following the contour, these levees can have different lengths, including sections that are usually between 0.2 and 0.8 hectares in size. Water enters the check area by a supply ditch and remains there until the proper degree of penetration is achieved. Verify whether flooding is appropriate for different permeability soils. Water is quickly dispersed and absorbed in permeable soils, while it is held in less permeable soils for a longer period of time to guarantee sufficient penetration.

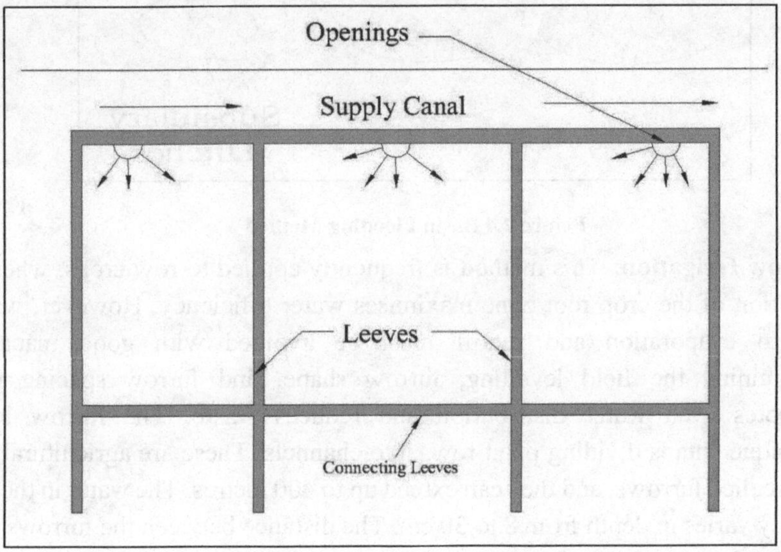

Figure 2.3 Check Flooding Method

d) **Basin Flooding:** By using the basin flooding approach, fields are divided into discrete basins with elevated edges. Before infiltration, water is let out of each basin and allowed to fill and saturate the soil. This method, which offers effective water utilisation and better water distribution within each basin, is frequently applied in flat terrain and clayey soils. But effective water management, which necessitates cautious border maintenance and field levelling, is essential to preventing over-irrigation or waterlogging.

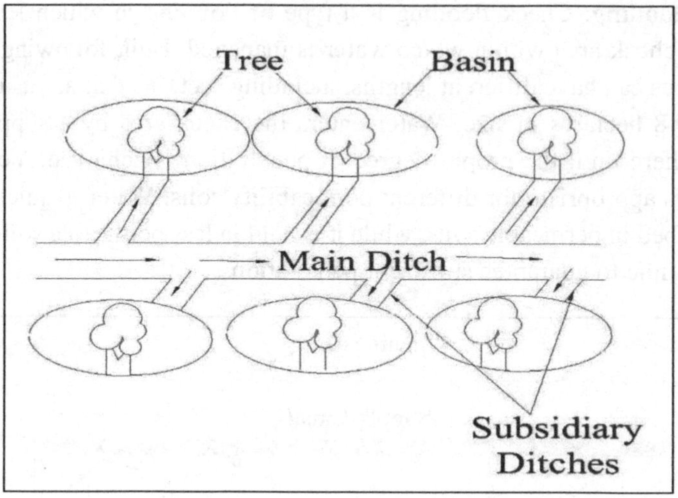

Figure 2.4 Basin Flooding Method

e) **Furrow Irrigation:** This method is frequently applied to row crops, where direct irrigation of the crop root zone maximises water efficiency. However, water loss due to evaporation and runoff must be avoided with good management. Maintaining the field levelling, furrow shape, and furrow spacing properly promotes even water distribution and reduces waste. The furrow irrigation technique entails dividing plant rows into channels. These are agricultural ditches, often called furrows, and they can extend up to 400 metres. The water in the furrows usually varies in depth from 8 to 30 cm. The distance between the furrows depends on how the crops are arranged.

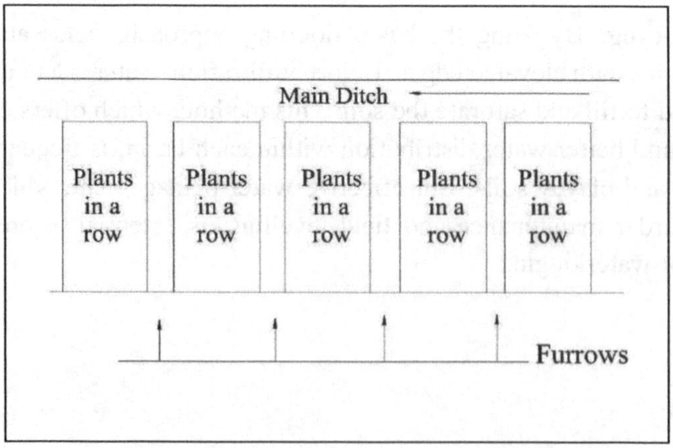

Figure 2.5 Furrow Irrigation Method

f) **Sprinkler Irrigation:** The practise of cultivating agricultural fields and other areas with a sprinkler system is known as sprinkler irrigation. This method works by evenly distributing pressurised water across crops or plants from above, replacing the need for hand watering. The sprinkler heads' shape makes it easier to distribute water evenly, giving off a fine mist or tiny droplets that mimic a light rainstorm. This technique has a number of advantages, such as careful control over water dispersal, automation possibilities, and landscape adaptation.

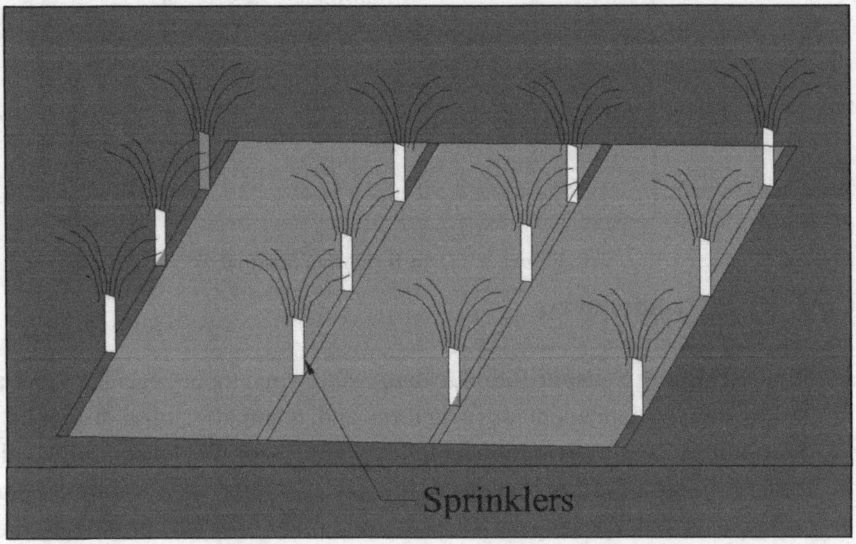

Figure 2.6 Sprinkler Irrigation

g) **Drip Irrigation:** A particular way of watering plants that is very careful and controlled is drip irrigation. By directly supplying water to each plant's root zone, this technology minimises water loss due to evaporation or runoff. This system uses a series of emitters, tubes, and pipelines to distribute consistent, modest amounts of water to the plants. This creative irrigation technique is especially useful in areas that struggle with salty water sources and water shortages. A head, laterals, drop nozzles, mains, and sub-mains are some of the parts of a standard drip irrigation system that work together to make sure plants get water precisely and effectively.

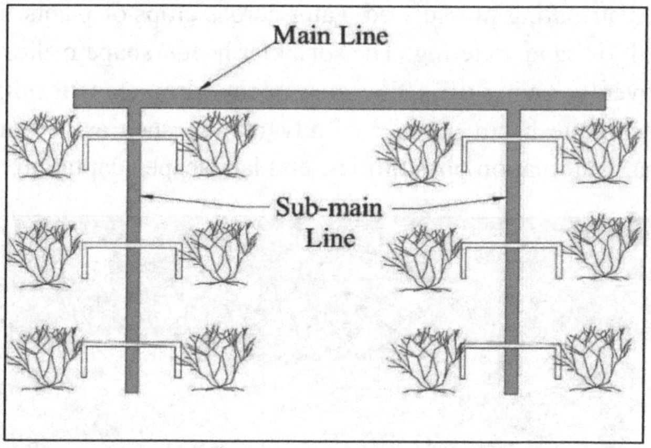

Figure 2.7 Drip Irrigation Method

2.2 Crop Water Requirements

2.2.1 Cropping seasons:

a. **Rabi Cropping Season:** Rabi farming usually occurs between October and March and is mostly dependent on irrigation and residual rainfall from the preceding monsoon. Access to irrigation water is essential for the successful development of Rabi crops. Rabi crops that thrive in milder winter temperatures include wheat, barley, oats, chickpeas, peas, mustard, and other oilseeds. Following the monsoon season, farmers cultivate Rabi crops after preparing their fields throughout the previous wet season.

b. **Kharif Cropping Season:** Harvesting usually occurs in September and October. Kharif crops are cultivated in various parts of the nation once the monsoon season starts. This cropping season is when important crops including paddy (rice), maize, jawar, bajra, tur (arhar), moong, urad, cotton, jute, peanuts, and soy beans are cultivated. Among the states that cultivate the most rice are Bihar and Uttar Pradesh. Furthermore, Punjab and Haryana have seen an increase in the importance of rice agriculture. In regions like as West Bengal, Orissa, and Assam, rice is grown three times a year.

c. **Zaid Cropping Season:** Zaid crops are those that are planted during the brief period of time between the Rabi and Kharif agricultural seasons, often from March to June. There is a brief period of time in the summer called the Zaid season. During "Zaid," crops such as cucumbers, muskmelon, watermelon, vegetables, and fodder crops are cultivated. It takes sugarcane over a year to mature. Tamil Nadu, Gujarat, Haryana, and Uttar Pradesh are the states where Zaid crops are mostly cultivated. In order to maximise the little water available, heat-tolerant, short-duration crops must be grown. Zaid cropping increases the amount of fresh product available, boosts farmer revenue, and lengthens the agricultural calendar. Zaid cropping plays a crucial role in diversifying agricultural production and extending the cropping calendar beyond the monsoon and winter seasons.

Kharif-Rabi ratio: The Kharif-Rabi ratio is the proportion of suggested irrigation fields to Rabi regions during the Kharif season. In India, the Kharif-Rabi ratio signifies the equilibrium between crops cultivated during the monsoon season (Kharif) and the winter season (Rabi). It demonstrates how farmers distribute their resources, such as land, labor, and inputs, between these two periods.

Kor-watering: Kor-watering refers to the initial irrigation given to a crop when it reaches a few centimetres in height. It is the first watering provided to the crop during its early growth stage. The Kor-period is the time frame during which this irrigation is done. The length of the Kor-period varies according to the particular crop being grown. For example, the Kor-period for paddy usually lasts between two and four weeks.

2.2.2 Crop Period

The crop period refers to the time taken by a crop to grow from planting to harvest. It varies depending on the crop and can range from a few weeks to several months or more. Farmers do consider the crop period when planning their farming activities.

Table 2.1 Crop Periods of few selected crops

Crops	Crop period (Days)
Wheat	40
Sugarcane	120
Rice	120
Cotton	50

2.2.3 Base Period

In irrigation, the "base period" is the time between a crop's initial irrigation during sowing and its last irrigation immediately prior to harvesting. Often, the crop period extends beyond the base period. Base period and crop period are similar phrases that are sometimes used interchangeably and are expressed in days. Water requirements for crops are determined by taking into account the crop, base, and growth periods which all represented by the letter 'B' and stated in days.

2.2.4 Duty (D)

Duty is a metric that connects the amount of water given to the area of land that is consistently watered during a particular crop's growth stages.

Duty of water, a key term in irrigation management, measures how much land can be irrigated with a constant flow of water. It's calculated as the number of hectares that can be fully irrigated for the complete growing season of a crop by a steady water flow of one cubic meter per second, commonly referred to as one Cumec. This ratio illustrates the efficiency of water use in agricultural practices and is typically expressed in hectares per cumec (ha/cumec), symbolized by the letter 'D'.

$D = A / Q$ is used to calculate irrigation duty, where:

D represents the Duty in hectares per cumec

A denotes the Area in square meters

Q refers to the Discharge in cubic meters per second, also known as Cumec

Irrigation duty can be categorized into:

Flow Duty: This type of duty applies to direct irrigation methods where water from the source is directly delivered to the fields without any form of storage. This immediate transfer of water to the irrigating area is referred to as flow duty.

Quantity Duty: In contrast, storage irrigation involves collecting water from the source into a reservoir or storage facility before it is distributed to the fields. This method's duty is thus known as Quantity Duty or Storage Duty.

Quantity duty is measured in hectares per million cubic meters of water stored in a reservoir, indicating the amount of land that can be irrigated with every million cubic meters of water from the reservoir for a specific crop.

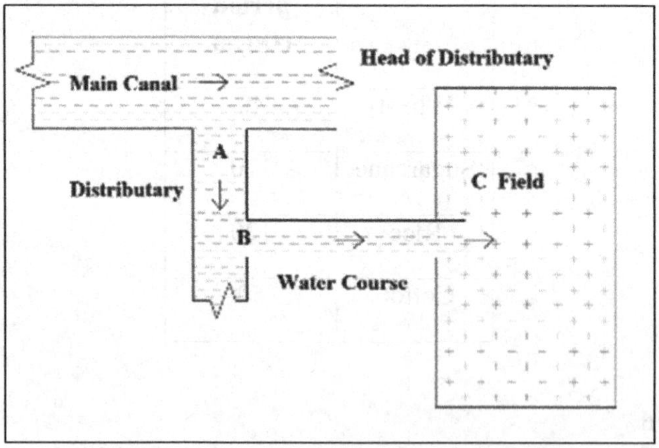

Figure 2.8 Duty at various locations of a canal

As water progresses along its course, its duty—indicating the area that can be irrigated per unit volume of water—tends to increase. To illustrate, consider a scenario where "C" represents the entry point of water into the field, "B" signifies the beginning of the water course or field channel, and "A" marks the start of the distributary. In this context, the water duty at point B, the head of the water course, is lower than that at point C, the head of the field, yet it is higher than the duty at point A, the start of the distributary.

2.2.5 Delta of a crop (Δ)

The "delta" for a crop, which is usually expressed in centimetres, represents the entire amount of water required for its growth. Crops require varied amounts of water at different stages of growth, which may be controlled by the frequency of irrigation. Depending on the particular requirement of the crop, water depths vary from 5 to 10 centimetres, and the frequency of irrigation last anywhere from 6 to 15 days. The total amount of water needed for crop nutrient uptake is represented by the cumulative water depth during the growing season, expressed in million cubic feet, million cubic metres, or hectare-meters.

Relationship between Duty and Delta of a crop

$\Delta=8.64\ B/D$

Where, Δ is the Delta of the crop; B is the Base period of the crop expressed in number of days; and D is the Duty of water epressed in hectare per cubic meter per second.

Water requirement of various crops

A crop requires water for their growth and consumptive use. The crop water requirement depends on:

Type of Crop: Different types of crops require different amount of water. Crops e.g. paddy and sugarcane require much more water then crops e.g. maize and Wheat.

Climate of the place where it is grown: Crops grawn in hot climate like Rajasthan, Iran, etc need much more water than cool climates like Himachal Pradesh or Kashmir

Type of soil: Crops grown in sandy or sandy – loamy soil needs more water than Clayey soil due to more water being lost in the process of infiltration and percolation.

Growth stage of the crop: Growth stage of crop has a bearing on the amount of water required by the crop for that time period as the full-grown crop needs more water than a crop of few days. To have a feel of the growth stages, various stages of growth of Lentil crop if presented below as an illustration.

Table 2.2 Approximate values of crop water requirement of few selected crops

Name of the Crop	Crop water requirement (mm) during the growing period)	Name of the Crop	Crop water requirement (mm) during the growing period)
Rice (paddy)	450-700	Sugarcane	1500-2500
Melon	400-600	Sunflower	600-1000
Onion	350-550	Tomato	400-800

Alfalfa	800-1600	Cabbage	350-500
Banana	1200-2200	Cotton	700-1300
Barley/Oats/Wheat	450-650	Maize	500-800
Bean	300-500	Peanut	500-700
Sorghum/Millet	450-650	Pepper	600-900
Soybean	450-700	Potato	500-700

Source: Brouwer and Heibloem (1986).

Frequency of Irrigation

Design Frequency

$$\frac{(\text{"Net irrigation requirement in the effective crop root zone"} - \text{"Moisture content of the same zone at the time of starting of irrigation"})}{\text{"Peak period moistures rate of crop"}}$$

Amount of Water to Apply per Irrigation

For 'full irrigation,' the calculation of the water volume needed for each irrigation event is determined as follows:

$$1 = \frac{D_r(f_c - f_m)}{\text{Irrigation efficiency}}$$

in which,

1= Amount of water to be applied,cm,

D_r= Depth of root zone, cm,

f_c= Soil moisture content at field capacity, and
f_m = Soil moisture content prior to irrigation.

Example 1. Calculate the delta for the crop given a Duty of 1500 hectares per cubic meter per second (cumec) over a base period of 120 days

Solution: Given,

$$D = 1500\ hectares/cumec\ and\ B = 120\ days$$

$$\Delta = 8.64\frac{B}{D} = \frac{8.64 \times 120}{1500} m = 0.69 = 9\ cm$$

2.2.6 Gross command Area

The Gross Command Area (GCA) refers to the complete land area that can be effectively irrigated by an irrigation system, without considering any water restrictions or limitations. It includes both cultivable land and non-cultivable areas like roads, wastelands, forests, and barren lands. The GCA is calculated by summing up the cultivable command area (CCA) with the uncultivable area.

GCA = [CCA + Uncultivable area.]

2.2.7 Culturable Command Area

The Culturable Command Area (CCA) represents the segment of the gross command area that is suitable for agricultural cultivation. It specifically excludes non-cultivable land from the gross command area. The CCA refers to the actual area where crops are grown during a particular time or season. While uncultivable lands are not included in the CCA, it does encompass canal networks and supply ditches as they serve the purpose of transporting water to the irrigation fields.

2.2.8 Net Command Area:

It represents the Culturable Command Area derived after subtracting canal networks, supply ditches, and additional field structures. NCA serves as an abbreviation for Net Command Area.

NCA = [CCA – The area occupied by canals, canals network, and ditches.]

2.2.9 Intensity of Irrigation

It is the proportion of cultivated agricultural area that can be submerged with irrigation water for a given season.

2.2.10 Factors affecting duty

The following factors have a bearing on the duty of water.

a. The characteristics of the soil through which the canal runs: Water obligation will be decreased if the canal is not lined and the coarse soil it runs through causes high seepage and percolation losses. In contrast, the canal is either lined or passes through finely ground earth. The water tariff will increase, but the losses will be negligible.
b. Field soil characteristics: Greater percolation losses occur when the soil in the field is both deep and composed of coarse grains. Nevertheless, the presence of a hard pan at a depth of 1 or 2 meters can alter this outcome. Percolation losses will be lower, but duty will be higher.
c. Undulating terrain: If the fields to be irrigated are undulating, the water duty will be reduced. Lower portions receive more water, whereas higher portions receive less water depth.

d. Weather conditions: Temperature, wind, rainfall, and humidity are the climatic conditions that affect water duty. High winds, high temperatures, little rain, and low humidity. More irrigation water is required, so the duty is reduced. If rainfall is taken into account when calculating duty figures. It is referred to as Duty inclusive of rainfall. Duty exclusive of rainfall is used when rainfall is not considered.
e. The crop's base period: Crops with a longer base period necessitate more frequent waterings, so duty will be increased.
f. Crop pattern: Because various crops need varying amounts of water to grow and mature, their duties will also vary.
g. Method of cultivation: If the cultivation method is faulty and inefficient, resulting in water waste, the water duty will naturally be reduced.

2.2.11 Problems with water requirements

Every crop needs a certain amount of water at certain times during its development cycle. If these requirements are sufficiently met by rainfall, irrigation might not be required for the crop to reach maturity. In Europe, for example, year-round steady rainfall suffices to fulfil agricultural demands, negating the need for irrigation. On the other hand, erratic or inadequate rainfall in tropical places such as India need irrigation for agricultural development. Because of differences in soil properties, climate, and rainfall, various crops may require different amounts of water in the same location or in different regions. A major worry is that around 60% of all farmed area still significantly depends on rainfall, even after enormous investments in irrigation infrastructure.

A variety of irrigation-related issues must be addressed.

a. Project completion delays: The primary issue facing our major and medium irrigation sectors has been the propensity to launch an increasing number of new initiatives, which has prevented project proliferation from occurring since the First Five Year Plan. Utilising the potential that already exists is also delayed. The majority of projects have encountered setbacks when it comes to building field canals and water courses, as well as flattening and contouring the ground.

b. Interstate Water Disputes: Irrigation is a state topic in India. States therefore plan the development of their water resources according to their own demands and specifications. On the other hand, every big river has an interstate character. States differ from one another as a result in terms of priority, usage, and storage of water. A restricted regional perspective exacerbates interstate rivalry over the allocation of water supplies.

c. Disparities in irrigation development across regions: The Ninth Five Year Plan Document states that whereas water resource development in the Northern area is around 95.3%, it is only 28.6% in the North Eastern region through large, medium, and small schemes. This illustrates the significant geographical diversity in the construction of irrigation facilities.

d. Water-logging and salinity: In certain states, the use of irrigation has led to salinity and water-logging. A working committee established by the Ministry of Water Resources in 1991 estimated that water logging damaged 2.46 million hectares in irrigated districts. The working committee also calculated that 3.30 million hectares of irrigated commands were impacted by salinity/alkalinity.

e. Rising irrigation costs: Irrigation has been more expensive over time, from the first five-year plan to the tenth.

f. Operating irrigation project losses: While public irrigation schemes showed a surplus before independence (1945-46) after meeting operating expenses and other charges, the situation deteriorated significantly after independence.

g. Water table decline: The over-exploitation of groundwater and inadequate recharging from rainfall have resulted in a steady decline in the water table in numerous regions of the nation, especially in the western arid zone.

2.2.12 Capacity of canal

The capacity factor of a canal is the relationship between its maximum intended capacity and its average supply discharge over time. At any given moment during all seasons, canal capacity is to be adequate enough to fulfil the highest peak demand of crops that require irrigation. Design capacity of the canal is Q

$$\textbf{Design Capacity} = \frac{\textbf{Duty of water at the canal outlet} \times \textbf{CCA (considering all losses)}}{\textbf{Time}}$$

Example 2. A water course has a 2800-hectare cultivable controlled area, of which 20% and 40%, respectively, are irrigated with perennial sugarcane and rice crops. The required acreage for these crops near the head of the water flow is 800 and 1850 hectares, respectively. The peak demand is 120% of the average need. At the head of the water stream calculate its discharge.

Solution:

Area for sugar cane =2800 x 0.2 = 560 hectares.

Area for rice = 2800 x 0.4 = 1120 hectares.

Water required for sugar-cane =560/800 = 0.7 cumec

Water required for rice =1120/1850= 0.605 cumecs.

Sugar cane needs water all year round since it is a perennial crop.

Therefore, total discharge of [0.7 + 0.605] = 1.305 cumecs which must be carried by the stream.

To fulfil the demand,

Design discharge =1.305 x 1.2 = 1.56 cumecs.

Example 3. A 1000-acre irrigation system is controlled by a water stream. In this region, 70% of the rice is irrigated. The planting of a rice crop requires 15 days, and during that time, the crop needs 500 mm of water in total on the field. The field receives 120 mm of beneficial rain during the transplanting season. Calculate the obligation of irrigation water for crops on field during transplanting at the head of the field and also at the head of the water course. Calculate the water course's needed discharge as well. [Assume 20% water loss in water channel]

Solution:

Area for irrigation = 1000 × 0.7 = 700 hectares

During the transplantation period,

Effective depth of water required =500 – 120 = 380 mm = 0.38 m

Duty of water at the field = $(8.64\ b)/\delta$ = (8.64 × 15) ÷ 0.38=341hec/cumec

Duty at the head of water course = (341×80) ÷ 100 = 272.8 hec/cumec

Discharge required in water, course =700 ÷ 272.8≅2.57cumec

2.3 Methods of application of irrigation water and its assessment.

a. Assessment on an area basis or crop basis
    - Crop areas are assessed by patrolling during sowing, maturity, and demand statement' for every irrigator using this irrigation water evaluation technique at the conclusion of the crop period.
    - Monetary value of the crops.
    - Specific water needs of various crops.
    - Timing and water required for irrigation.
    - Drawback of the system lies in its wasteful water use as charges are determined based on crop area rather than the actual water quality.

b. Volumetric Assessment
    - The amount of money charged is determined by the actual volume of water supplied at the output source.
    - The irrigated area grows as water efficiency in the field is maximised.
    - Every canal system exit needs to have water metres installed.

c. Composite rate assessment
    - The combined land revenue and water taxes apply to cultivators.
    - This technique of assessment is not commonly utilised.

d. Permanent Assessment or Betterment Levy
    - Farmers in areas who have drought insurance pay a yearly set fee, regardless of how much water they use.
    - In years when there is a drought, farmers may receive canal water at no additional cost over the standard improvement levy.

2.3.1 Types of Irrigation Efficiency

Various types of irrigation efficiencies are

a. Water Conveyance Efficiency (ηc):

This is a reference to how well water is transported from its source to the field. It evaluates losses from seepage, evaporation, and leaks in canals, pipelines, and other conveyance systems that happen in the water delivery system. Represented by the symbol ηc

$$\eta c = \frac{W_l}{W_r} \text{x } 100$$

Where,

$$W_l = \textbf{water applied to land}$$
$$W_r = \textbf{water supplied from reservoir}$$

b. Water Application Efficiency (ηa):

This indicates the proportion of water applied that the crops really use. It takes into account variables including runoff, deep percolation, and evaporation. The objective is to minimise losses while optimising the quantity of water that supports plant development and expressed as $\eta a = \frac{W_z}{W_l} \times 100$

Where,

$$W_z = \textbf{water stored in root zone}$$
$$W_l = \textbf{water applied to land}$$

c. Water Use Efficiency (ηu):

Water use efficiency gauges how well plants utilise the available water. It is the proportion of biomass or yield generated to water used. It's a vital indicator of how well crops use water to produce agricultural goods.

$$\eta u = \frac{W_u}{W_l} \times 100$$

Where,

$$W_u = \textbf{water used}$$
$$W_l = \textbf{water applied to land}$$

d. Consumptive use Efficiency (ηcu):

It is used to describe the proportion of applied irrigation water to real crop water usage, or evapotranspiration. It calculates the efficiency with which irrigation water promotes plant development and yield. Determined as ηcu,

Derived from the formula

$$\eta_{cu} = \frac{C_u}{W_p} \times 100$$

Where,

$$C_u = \textbf{Consumptive use of water}$$

$$W_p = \textbf{water depleted from root zone}$$

Example 4. A 35-hectare field receives 14 cumecs of water each hour for 4 hours. During irrigation, soil probing shows that 0.4 meters of water have been retained in the root zone. Calculate the efficiency of water application.

Solution:

Volume of water supplied by 14 cumecs of water applied for 4 hours

$$= (14 \times 4 \times 60 \times 60)\, m^3 = 2,01,600\, m^3$$

$$= 20.1 \text{ x } 104m^3 = 20.1 \text{ m x } 104\text{m}^2 = 20.1 \text{ ham}$$

Input = $\mathbf{20.1}$ **ha m**

Output = **35 hectares of land storing water up to 0.4 m depth**

Output = **35 x 0.4 ham = 14 ha m**

Water application efficiency,

$$(\eta_a) = \frac{\text{Output}}{\text{Input}} \times 100 = \frac{14}{20.1} \times 100 = 69.65\%$$

Example 5. At locations 25 meters apart, the depths of penetrations along a border strip were measured. They have been measured at 2.2, 1.7, 1.9, 1.6, and 1.4 meters. Calculate the water distribution efficiency.

Solution:

Observed depths of five stations are 2.2, 1.7, 1.9, 1.6, and 1.4 meters

Mean depth = D= $\frac{2.2+1.7+1.9+1.6+1.4}{5} = 1.76$

Values of deviations from the mean are $\mathbf{0.44, -0.06, 0.14, -0.16}$ **and** $\mathbf{-0.36}$

The absolute values of these deviations from the mean, are $\mathbf{0.44, 0.06, 0.14, 0.16}$ **and** $\mathbf{0.36}$

The average of these absolute values of deviations from the

Mean d= $\frac{0.44+0.06+0.14+0.16+0.36}{5} = 0.232\ meter$

Water distribution efficiency, $\left(1 - \frac{d}{D}\right) = \left[1 - \frac{0.232}{1.76}\right] = 1 - 0.1318 = 0.8681$

So, Water distribution efficiency is **86.81%.**

2.3.2 Consumptive Irrigation and Net Irrigation Requirement

It is the volume of irrigation water needed to provide the crop with the evapotranspiration it needs to develop to its maximum potential.

Hence, N.I.R = $C_u - R_e$ + losses due to percolation.

Where, C_u is consumptive use and R_e is the effective rainfall.

Consumptive use or evapotranspiration depends upon temperature, sunlight, humidity, wind, etc.

$$\mathbf{FIR} = \frac{\mathbf{NIR}}{\eta_a}$$

where,

FIR = Field irrigation requirement and η_a is the water application efficiency of field.

2.3.3 Estimation of consumptive use:

Methods proposed for the computation of evapotranspiration or consumptive use are

a. Blaney Criddle Equation

$$C_u = k \sum f$$

Where,

$$= \frac{p}{40}[1.8t + 32]$$

Here,

C_u = monthly consumptive use of water in cm

k = crop factor

t = monthly mean temperature

p = monthly annual day light hours, which occur during the period

b. Hargreaves class-A Pan method

Evapotranspiration, also known as consumptive usage, and is connected to pan evaporation by a constant k, also known as the pan evaporation coefficient.,

C_u = k E_p.

Where,

E_p = pan evaporation.

c. Penman Equation

Here, daily potential evapotranspiration (E_t) can be calculated as,

$$E_t = \frac{A\,H_n + E_a.\gamma}{A + \gamma}$$

Where,

A= Slope of the saturation vapour pressure Vs Temperature curve at the mean air temperature

H_n =Net incoming solar radiation or energy, expressed in mm of evaporable water per day.

E_a =A parameter including wind velocity and saturation deficit in mm/day

γ = Psychrometric constant= 0.49 mm of Hg/°C

The net radiation (H_n) is estimated by the equation

$$H_n = H_c(1 - r)\left(a + b.\frac{n}{N}\right) - \sigma.T_a^4(0.56 - 0.092\sqrt{e_a}) \times \left(0.10 + 0.90\frac{n}{N}\right)$$

Where,

H_c =mean incident solar radiation at the top of the atmosphere on a horizontal surface, expressed in mm of evaporable water per day.

r =reflection coefficient of the given area.

a =a constant having average value = 0.52

n =actual duration of bright sunshine in hours

N =maximum possible hours of bright sunshine (mean value).

σ =Stefan-Bolzman constant = 2.01 x 10^{-9} mm/day

K =mean air temperature in °K = 273+ °C

e_a = actual mean vapour pressure in the air in mm of Hg.

The parameter E_a of Penman's equation is estimated as:

$$E_a = 0.35\left(1 + \frac{V_2}{160}\right)(e_s - e_a)mm/day$$

Where,

V_2 = mean wind speed at 2m above the ground

e_s = mean saturation vapour pressure

e_a = actual mean vapour pressure of air

Example 6. Details about a certain crop are provided in the table below. Determine the following (i) consumptive use, (ii) consumptive irrigation demand, and (iii) field irrigation requirement using the Blaney-Criddle equation and a crop factor k = 0.75.

Month	Monthly Temp. (Average)°C	Monthly % of day time hours of the year	Useful rainfall (cm)
(1)	(2)	(3)	(4)
May	19.0	9.53	-
June	16.0	9.49	1.5
July	12.5	9.67	0.5
August	13.0	9.22	-

Solution:

Using Blaney-Criddle equation,

$$C_u = k\sum f$$

Where,

$$f = \frac{P}{40}[1.8t + 32]$$

Computation,

Month	t°c	p%	f
(1)	(2)	(3)	(4)
May	19.0	9.53	15.77
June	16.0	9.49	14.42
July	12.5	9.67	13.17
August	13.0	9.22	12.77
			$\sum f = 56.13$

$$C_u = k\sum f = 0.75 \times 56.13 = 42.09$$

$$R_e = 1.5 + 0.5 = 2.0$$

$$CIR = C_u - R_e = 42.09 - 2.0 = 40.09\ cm.$$

$$NIR = CIR\ (as\ deep\ percolation\ uses\ no\ water)$$

$$FIR = \frac{NIR}{\eta_u} = \frac{40.09}{0.7} = 57.27\ cmc$$

2.3.4 Field capacity

$$Field\ capacity = \frac{Weight\ of\ water\ retained\ in\ a\ certain\ vol.\ of\ soil}{Weight\ of\ the\ same\ volume\ of\ dry\ soil} \times 100$$

If we consider a root zone depth of d metres and a soil area of 1 m^2, the volume of soil is equal to d cubic metres. If the dry unit weight of the soil is 1 kN/m^3, then the weight of d cubic metres of soil is equal to Yd kN

Therefore,

$$F = \frac{Weight\ of\ water\ retained\ in\ unit\ area\ of\ soil}{\gamma_d . d}$$

$$Weight\ of\ water\ retained\ in\ unit\ area\ of\ soil = \gamma_d . d . F\ \text{kN/m}^2$$

Vol of water stored in unit area of soil $= \frac{\gamma_d . d . F}{\gamma_w}$ m

Where F= the field capacity moisture content.

d=depth of root zone in m

γ_w =the unit wt. of water

γ_d =the dry unit wt. of soil.

Hence, the depth of water stored in the root zone in filling the soil up to field capacity

$$= \frac{\gamma_d . d . F}{\gamma_w}\ \textbf{meters}$$

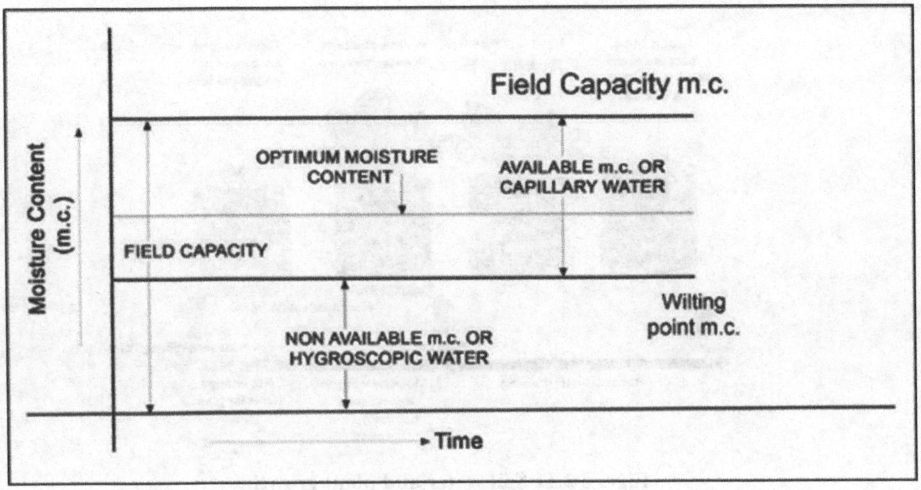

Figure 2.9 Field Capacity

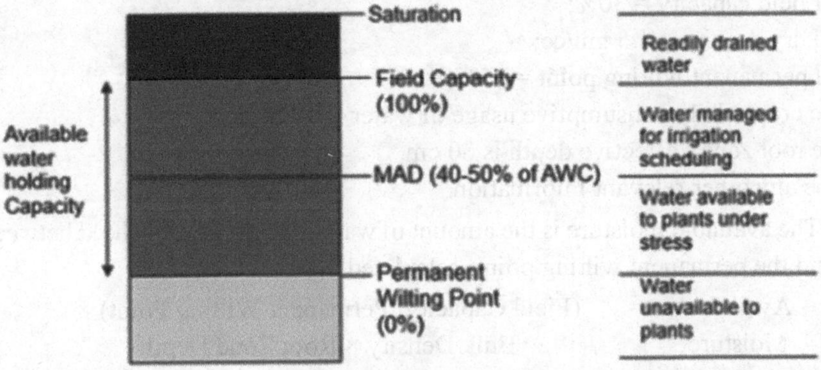

Figure 2.10 Soil Water reservoir components

Available Water Holding Capacity (AWC)

This is the maximum amount of water that the soil can store, which can be extracted by the plants. It is the water held between the range of field capacity and permanent wilting point. The total available water in the root zone for a specific crop is equal to the crop's rooting depth multiplied by the available water-holding capacity per unit depth of the soil.

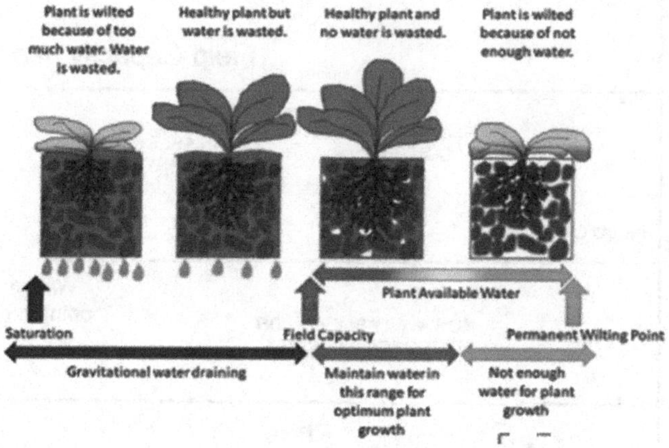

Figure 2.11 Soil water and plant growth

Example 7. If the following circumstances hold, how many days will you water the land to ensure that the crop receives enough irrigation?

(a) soil field capacity = 30%;

(b) soil dry density = 1.5 gm/cc;

(c) soil permanent wilting point = 15%;

(d) The crop's daily consumptive usage of water is 10 mm.

(e) The root zone's effective depth is 80 cm.

Assume any other relevant information.

Solution: The available moisture is the amount of water that the soil can hold between field capacity and the permanent wilting point, calculated as:

$$\text{Available Moisture (AM)} = (\text{Field Capacity} - \text{Permanent Wilting Point}) \times \text{Bulk Density} \times \text{Root Zone Depth}$$

Where,

Field Capacity = 30% = 0.30

Permanent Wilting Point = 15% = 0.15

Soil Dry Density (Bulk Density) = 1.5 gm/cc = $\mathbf{1.5\ g/cm^3 = 1500\ kg/m^3}$

Root Zone Depth = 80 cm = 0.80 m

$$\boldsymbol{AM = (0.30 - 0.15) \times 1500 \times 0.80 = 0.15 \times 1500 \times 0.80 = 180\ mm}$$

So, the available moisture in the root zone is 180 mm.

The crop consumes 10 mm of water per day (given in the problem). Thus, the irrigation frequency is determined by the time it takes for the available moisture to be depleted by the crop's daily water use.

$$\textbf{Irrigation Frequency (days)} = \frac{\textbf{Available Moisture (AM)}}{\textbf{Daily Consumptive Use}}$$

$$= \frac{\mathbf{180}\boldsymbol{mm}}{\mathbf{10}\ \boldsymbol{mm/day}} = \mathbf{18}\ \boldsymbol{days}$$

Irrigation should be applied every 18 days to ensure the crop receives enough water.

Example 8. A field with a 28% field capacity and a 14% permanent wilting point should be used to produce wheat. If the dry unit weight of the soil is 15.6 KN/m3, find the storage capacity of the soil at a depth of 60 cm. Determine the water depth needed at the root zone when the field application efficiency is 75% if the average soil moisture drops to 19%.

Solution:

Maximum storage capacity or readily available moisture = $\frac{\gamma_d . d}{\gamma_w \times 100}$ (Field capacity moisture content – wilting point moisture content) = $\frac{15.6 \times 0.6}{9.81}(0.28-0.14)$ =0.1335 m=13.35 cm

2.4 Surveys for the irrigation project

a. Examine Water Availability:
- Whether it be a barrage, weir or dam, the first thing to take into account while designing an irrigation project is the availability and presence of water. There are several kinds of availability, but before building, a thorough inspection is necessary.
- It is important to identify the type of river, whether it is an inundation or perennial, if one is present in that location.
- The water will be accessible all year round if it is perennial. Check the past yearly releases whether the river is an inundation.
- A suitable location for an irrigation project should be accessible, and the river should supply the area's water demands.

b. Investigate Topography:
- The area's topographical map is examined once the water availability is examined.
- The approximate alignment of an irrigation project may be determined more effectively with the use of this study.The conduct of agricultural areas is examined in this stage.

c. Site selection for Construction:
- The site for an irrigation project is selected when there is an abundance of water or a significant water supply.
- The project may be a barrage, weir, or dam. The following elements are taken into account while choosing a location.
- The necessary foundation depth is ascertained by the soil survey using pile testing and boring.
- There should be enough capacity and a large enough basin area to accommodate the necessary demand.
- The website need to be easy to locate. Labour and materials have to be easily accessible.

- The canal's bed slope should be kept within the permitted range.
- Key regions or lands shouldn't be submerged by the building.

2.4.1 Data collection for an irrigation project

Category: The village shall be considered as tribal and assigned code 1 if it is determined that the community has a significant number of tribal residents, as defined by the state; if not, code 2 will be assigned.

Geographical area: In accordance with village records, the whole geographical area of the village including its inhabited, agricultural, and non-agricultural areas will be documented.

Cultivable Area: The whole area of the village that can be used for farming at any time of year is referred to as the cultivable area. It needs to be less than or equivalent to the total area of the hamlet.

Net Sown Area: Net Sown Area: This refers to the entire area in the village that has been farmed, including any crops sown during any one season of the year. If a crop is seeded on the same land throughout many seasons, it will not be included again. There will only be one count per region. The cultivable area must exceed the net planted area.

Gross area irrigated: For every crop season, a seasonally-based record of the gross area irrigated shall be kept. The same process will be used for all crops and all seasons, calculating the area irrigated under multiple crops in a single year as many times as the number of crops cultivated and irrigated. Any area seeded and irrigated with a crop during a given season will be counted for that season. The gross area irrigated should not be more than the net area seeded during any given season.

Net Irrigated Area: This is defined as the area that was farmed and irrigated for any one season or crop at least once during the reference year. A single count will be performed on every irrigated and farmed area used for multiple crops.

Average Groundwater level: For the reference year, the village's pre- and post-monsoon groundwater levels will be recorded independently in metres. The average groundwater level in the village should be taken into account both before and after the monsoon, both before and after the agricultural year.

2.4.2 Reservoir planning

Introduction: Reservoir planning is a methodical process that begins with the definition of a project's goal and ends with an ultimate determination of the optimal course of action. Building dams over rivers creates artificial lakes known as reservoirs, or storage. They function to store excess water at high flow times and use it during dry spells or periods of higher demand. You will have a thorough grasp of the major reservoir components and related aspects by completing this session. The main functions of reservoirs are flood control and water conservation. During the rainy season, when demand is reduced, a conservation storage reservoir is built to gather and store extra water. When river flow is less than the demand for water during the dry season, this stored water is subsequently released.

Objectives:

a. To categorise and explain the reservoir's function
b. To calculate the reservoir's capacity using a mass curve
c. To estimate the reservoir's sedimentation and trap efficiency
d. To evaluate the reservoir's impacts

Purpose:

The storage could be used for any of the following purposes:

a. Domestic and industrial water supply
b. Water for the city
c. Irrigation
d. Hydroelectric power
e. Navigation
f. Recreation
g. Wild-life and Aquatic life Conservation

Classification of Reservoirs: *Storage or conservation reservoirs: These reservoirs are* primarily used to ensure a minimum water supply during times of low river discharge for a variety of uses, including agriculture, the production of hydroelectric power, home and industrial water supply systems, and more. The discharge from the river varies daily and seasonally. Even if too much water is wasted during severe flooding, it could not be enough to provide basic necessities in the dry months. Storage reservoirs are made to hold excess floodwater and release it gradually as needed in order to remedy this.

2.5 Area capacity curve

Area-capacity curves are commonly utilized to establish the relationship between reservoir elevation and its corresponding water surface area and capacity. These curves play a crucial role in various aspects, such as assessing reservoir classification, understanding sediment distribution, facilitating flood routing, and guiding reservoir operation.

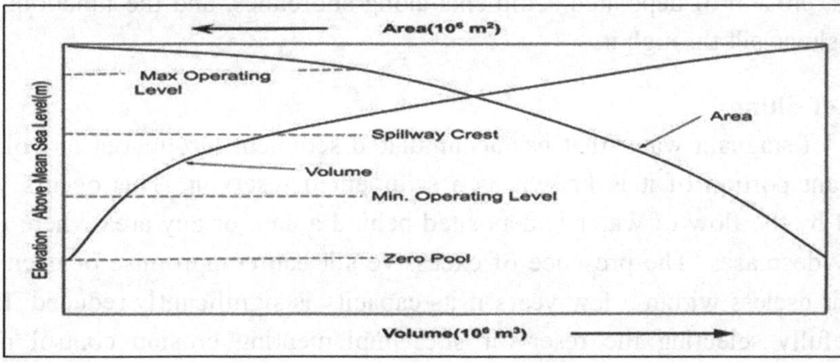

Figure 2.12 Area capacity curve

2.6 Silting of the reservoir

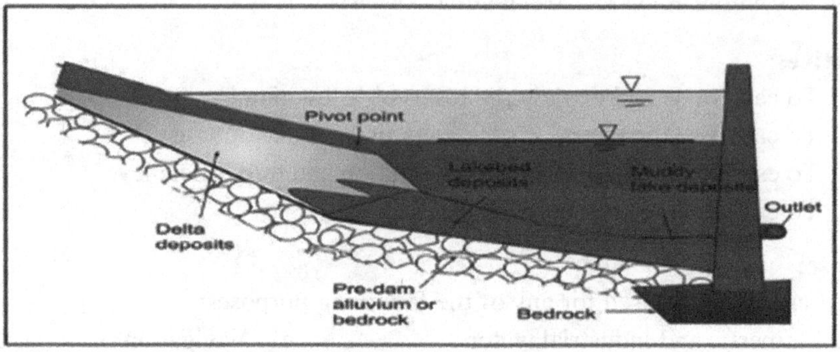

Figure 2.13 Sediment deposit in a reservoir

Increased sediment transport into an area can result from land erosion caused by water or wind forces. When a river flows into a reservoir, it carries solid particles along with it. These particles settle in the reservoir over time, leading to sedimentation. This process reduces the operational capacity of the reservoir and exerts additional pressure on the dam. To prevent this, dams are equipped with bottom drains that can be opened to release water and sediments. However, caution must be exercised to avoid negative impacts on downstream ecology and river morphology, as well as potential damage to the drain system. Reservoir design should account for sediment deposition, especially in the live storage area used for irrigation and electricity production. The knowledge of sediment distribution patterns in existing reservoirs greatly informs the planning and design process.

The vast variety in the many impacting elements makes the sedimentation processes in reservoirs highly complex. The four most important ones are (1) changes in water and sediment input caused by hydrology; (2) variations in the size of sediment particles; (3) changes in reservoir operation; and (4) physical controls, such the size and form of the reservoir. Other elements that could be highly significant for particular reservoirs include the development of vegetation in the upper reaches, turbulence and density currents, erosion of deposited sediments along shorelines, and the functioning of the dam to sluice silt through it.

2.6.1 Rate of silting

A body of stagnant water that has accumulated sediment throughout its volume or a significant portion of it is known as a sedimented reservoir. This occurs when silt brought by the flow of water is deposited behind a dam or any area where the water velocity decreases. The presence of excessive silt can compromise or even render a reservoir useless within a few years if its capacity is significantly reduced. However, by carefully selecting the reservoir site, implementing erosion control measures, managing reservoir operations, and conducting regular desilting activities, the impact of sedimentation can be minimized. Ideally, the reservoir should be located away from the main channel in a basin where heavily silt-laden water can be diverted around it, or it can be positioned on a stream with minimal silt content. It is advisable to choose a drainage area as small as possible for reservoir placement. In the context of Indian conditions, the rate of silting typically ranges from 0.1 to 0.2 hectare-meters per year per square kilometre.

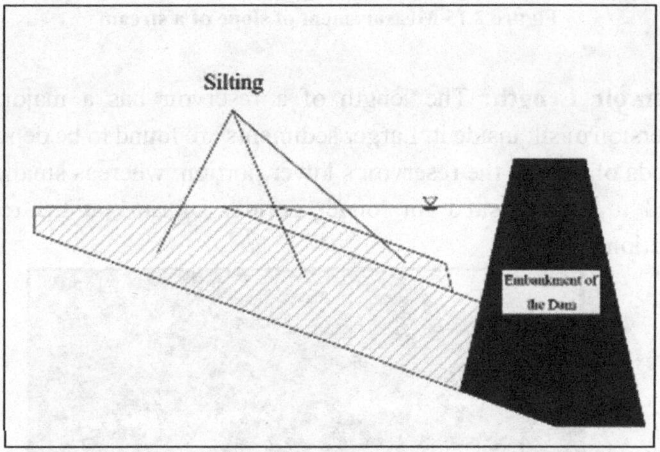

Figure 2.14 Rate of silting

2.6.2 Factors affecting silting

Sedimentation is the natural process of gravitational settling of suspended particles in water. These particles, such as clay or silt, become suspended in water and settle when the water velocity decreases below a certain threshold. Gravity causes the particles to be pulled out of the water flow when they can no longer remain suspended. Reservoir sedimentation is influenced by various factors, including the following commonly considered categories:

a. **Slope of Stream:** Unlike the higher elevation of the reservoir, which is constructed on a stream with a steeper slope and a longer reach, sediment deposition takes place in the lower elevation of the reservoir, which is built on a stream with a flatter slope. The slope of a stream is defined as the vertical decrease in height over a certain horizontal length. Knowing the slope of your stream may help you make decisions about maintenance and control of streams, as well as provide a better understanding of how and why your stream behaves.

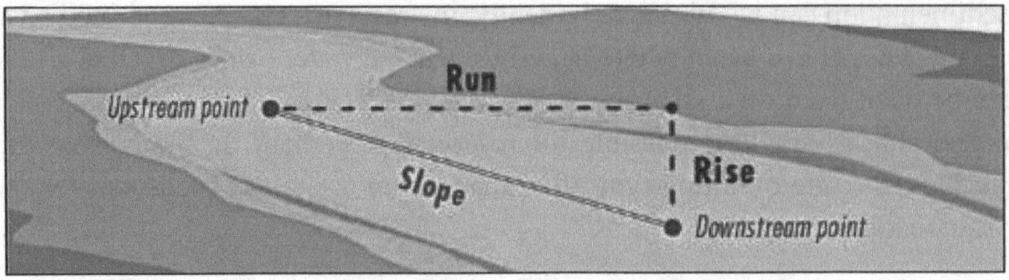

Figure 2.15 Measurement of slope of a stream

b. **Reservoir Length:** The length of a reservoir has a major impact on the dispersion of silt inside it. Larger sediments are found to be deposited for shorter periods of time in the reservoir's lower portion, whereas smaller sediments are found to be deposited for longer periods of time at the reservoir's higher elevations.

Figure 2.16 Reservoir length

(**Source:** *https://commons.wikimedia.org/wiki/File:Kurobe_Dam_survey.jpg*)

c. **Sediment Size:** The sedimentation process is greatly impacted by the characteristics of particle size and type. Due to their higher density, sand and silt particles can be rapidly removed from the flow. As the stream enters the reservoir, its velocity decreases, causing most of the gravel and grit to settle under the influence of gravity.

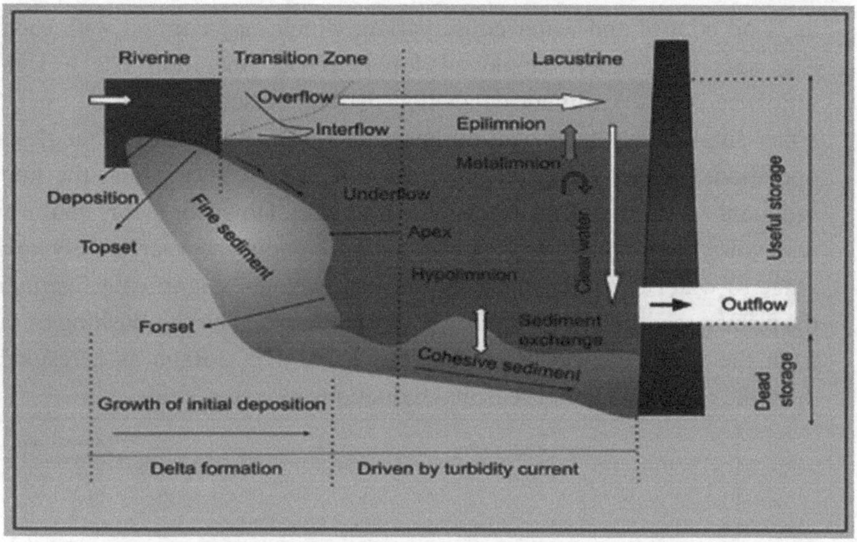

Figure 2.17 Reservoir Sedimentation and Stratification Process

d. **Inflow capacity:** Within a reservoir, the pattern of sediment dispersion is mostly determined by the inflow capacity. Most of the smaller particles are swept downstream by the influx of bigger rivers into tiny lakes, where they have little time to settle. On the other hand, in large reservoirs where water is held for a longer duration, suspended sediments tend to completely settle. Together with the demand curve, the mass inflow curve which shows the cumulative inflow over time is used to calculate the reservoir capacity that corresponds to a given yield. Reflecting the cumulative input, the mass inflow curve rises gradually and stays level until there is no inflow. The mass inflow curve abruptly ascends during high flood times, suggesting a rapid rate of influx.

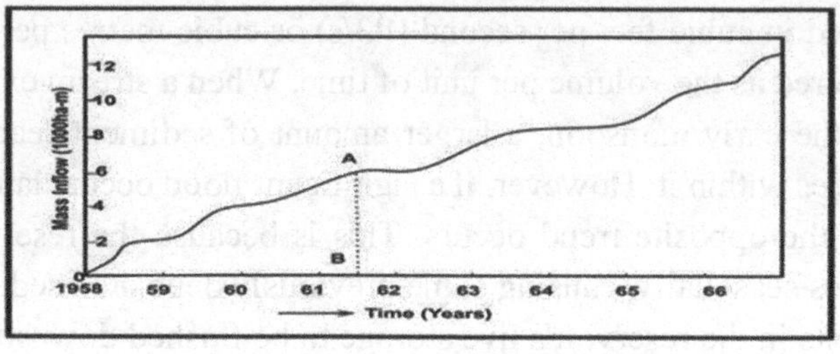

Figure 2.18 Mass Inflow Curve

e. **Vegetation:** The patchwork of different plant species spread out across the terrain is known as vegetation. It contains a wide range of organisms, including mosses, grasses, trees, shrubs, and other non-vascular plants. The amount of silt that reaches the reservoir is influenced by the vegetation around and upstream from the reservoir, which serves to trap sediments.

f. **Operation of Reservoirs:** Operating a reservoir, especially multi-purpose ones, can be a complex task as it involves balancing different objectives such as flood control and water conservation, which may conflict with each other. The specific method employed for reservoir operation has a significant influence on the sediment deposition pattern. Reservoirs can be operated for either single-purpose or dual-purpose functions. In the case of single-purpose operations, where the water level remains relatively constant, the impact on sediment deposition patterns is minimal. However, for multi-purpose reservoirs, the operation is carried out throughout the year, involving a wide range of water elevations to meet diverse demands. Significant fluctuations in the primary sediment distribution pattern are caused by the flushing of material from the upper elevations of the reservoir's live storage as a result of this dynamic functioning and seasonal reductions in water levels.

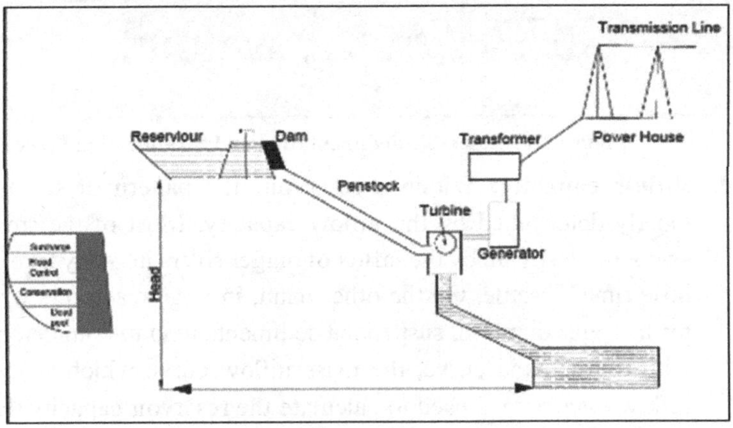

Figure 2.19 Operation of Multipurpose Reservoir

g. **Stream Inflow Patterns:** The amount of water released in a stream or channel, which fluctuates both in space and time, is referred to as streamflow. Usually expressed in cubic feet per second (ft3/s) or cubic metres per second (m3/s), it is measured as the volume per unit of time. When a stream experience flooding during the early monsoon, a larger amount of sediment reaches the reservoir and settles within it. However, if a significant flood occurs later in the monsoon season, the opposite trend occurs. This is because the reservoir's water level decreases seasonally, causing some previously deposited sediment from higher elevations in the reservoir's live storage to be flushed downstream.

h. **Sediment Load in River Flow:** The quantity and quality of the sediment load carried by river flow vary greatly depending on the features of the watershed, such as climate and land use. Sediment entrapment is further aided by the retention period, which is shorter as the reservoir ages. The reservoir's sedimentation pattern is significantly impacted by these variances. Typically, water discharge and sediment concentration are measured and represented as mass per unit of time, such as tonnes per year (tons/year), to determine a river's sediment load.

i. **Shape of Reservoirs:** The dispersion of sediment is significantly impacted by a reservoir's form. Suspended silt tends to settle uniformly along the bed in the direction of flow in a regularly shaped reservoir; the depth decreases with increasing distance from the dam. There will be a significant variance in the depth of sediment deposition at the bottom of a reservoir with an uneven form.

j. **Sediment-reservoir Volume Ratio:** The reservoir's ability to hold water for an extended period of time is compromised when the intake of silt and water surpasses its capacity. As a result of the shorter retention time, there will be less silt deposited as a percentage of the inflow. Reservoir sedimentation is the term used to describe this ongoing buildup of river silt, which presents serious difficulties for water management, flood control, and energy generation in many parts of the world. The ability of reservoirs to store energy is thought to be declining globally by 0.5% to 1.0% each year.

k. **Outlets:** The density current will quickly evaporate if the reservoir's outflow is situated at a lower elevation and has sufficient capacity. Consequently, the silt that has accumulated and combined with the density current in the vicinity of the reservoir dam is efficiently eliminated.

2.6.3 Silt control measures

The following preventive measures can be used to limit the amount of silt that enters the reservoir.

a. Selecting the right reservoir site is crucial.
b. Soft catchment soil leads to increased silting as it is easily carried by runoff.
c. Steep slopes in the catchment result in more silting due to higher runoff velocity and soil erosion.
d. Install check bunds upstream of tributaries with heavy silt loads to reduce silt entry.
e. Check bunds allow sedimentation of silt, enabling relatively clear water to enter the main reservoir.
f. Small reservoirs behind check bunds supply water to the main reservoir during low tributary flows.
g. Promoting vegetation growth on the catchment reduces silt entry into the reservoir.
h. Proper operation of sluice gates minimizes silt deposition and allows for scouring of already deposited silt.
i. Regular dredging is required to remove deposited silt.
j. Constructing the dam in stages with initial lower height and gradually increasing it helps minimize silting.

k. This technique reduces capacity and inflow rate while maintaining trap efficiency.

2.7 Control devices in the reservoir

Water reservoirs are typically controlled using four primary regulating devices: Vertical Lift Gates, Radial Gates, Drum Gates, and Flashboards and Stop-Logs.

1. **Vertical Lift Gates:** These rectangular steel gates are positioned between guide grooves in supporting piers and move vertically. The gates are operated using an overhead hoist, allowing water to be released through an undershot orifice. These gates experience high sliding friction due to water pressure, which necessitates the use of a powerful hoist. However, wheels on either side of the gate can reduce this friction, allowing for a smaller hoist. Vertical lift gates are commonly used for spans up to 20 meters and heights around 15 meters. For taller structures, an elevated operating platform becomes necessary.

2. **Radial (Tainter) Gates:** Radial gates are composed of steel plates shaped like a segment of a cylinder. They are attached to supporting bearings via radial arms, keeping the cylindrical plate concentric with the pins. This design allows the water thrust to pass directly through the pins, minimizing the moment that needs to be overcome. As a result, the hoisting load is limited to the gate's weight, sliding friction, and pin friction. Radial gates require minimal hoisting effort, making manual operation feasible in smaller installations. They also need less headroom than vertical lift gates, making them a more versatile option.

3. **Drum Gates:** Drum gates are buoyant, triangular structures made from steel plates. They are hinged at the upstream lip of a hydraulic chamber where they float. By adjusting the water in the hydraulic chamber, the gate moves up or down. Controls located near the chambers manage water flow into or out of the chamber, regulating the gate's movement.

4. **Flashboards and Stop-Logs:** These devices are used to raise the water level above a fixed spillway crest when flood releases are not required. Flashboards consist of hinged boards or panels supported by struts, while stop-logs are beams stacked to form a bulkhead. To increase spillway capacity, flashboards or stop-logs are removed before flooding. They may also be designed for easy removal while overtopped. While these devices are simple and cost-effective, they have several drawbacks:

i. Failure to remove them in time can lead to flooding, especially in small reservoir areas prone to flash floods.

ii. They require manual removal unless designed to fall automatically.

iii. They are difficult to restore while water is flowing over the crest.

iv. If designed to fail at a certain water stage, they may release large, sudden outflows, creating uncertainty in operation.

v. Frequent spillway use can make replacing flashboards costly.

2.7.1 Storage Zones and Control Levels of Reservoir

Fixing the different elements of a reservoir's design capacity at a specific site requires the following facts and information:

a) Records of precipitation, runoff, and silt;
b) Information on upstream catchment erosion features and sediment yield estimation;
c) Capacity curves for sediment areas;
d) Efficiency of traps;
e) Losses in reservoirs;
f) Requirements for water from the reservoir;
g) Current and planned upstream applications;
h) Project performance standards;
i) The position of outlets and density's present features;
j) Information pertaining to economic analysis;
k) The geological and engineering aspects.

2.7.2 Different Control Levels of a Reservoir

Full Reservoir Level (FRL): Flood storage is included in FRL along with both active and inactive storage. In the absence of spillways, it is the highest reservoir level that can be kept.

Minimum Draw-down Level (MDDL): The minimal head needed for power plants is maintained by not drawing water below the MDDL level.

Dead Storage Level (DSL): The level known as DSL is when there are no exits to allow gravity to empty the reservoir's water. During the design lifetime, silt will build below this level.

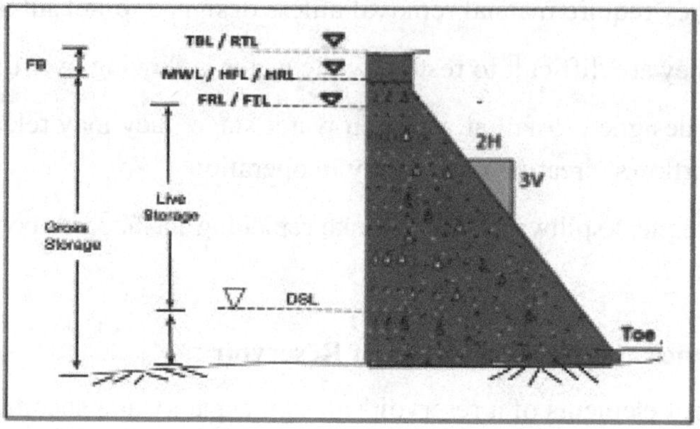

Figure 2.20 Storage Zones and Control Levels of Reservoir

Maximum Water Level (MWL): The greatest possible level expected to occur during the projected flood, high flood level (HFL), or high reservoir level (HRL) is known as the maximum water level (MWL). Tank Bund Level (TBL) is also the Road Top Level (RTL).

2.7.3 Different Storage Zones of a Reservoir

Live Storage (LS): The amount of water that is accessible at any given moment between the dead storage level and the Full Reservoir Level (FRL) is known as live storage, or LS.

Dead Storage (DS): Dead Storage (DS): The total amount of storage below the lowest discharge outlet's inverted level. Under typical operating conditions, dead storage is still non-functional and has no use.

Outlet Surcharge or Flood Storage: The amount of storage required between the highest water level and the Full Reservoir Level (FRL) is known as the flood storage or, outlet surcharge, and it is intended to control flood peaks that would surpass the storage capacity beneath the FRL.

Buffer Storage: The storage margin immediately above the dead storage level down to the minimal draw-down level is referred to as buffer storage. When the weather is dry, this reserve is drawn upon only to meet necessities. The inactive storage is made up of buffer storage and dead storage taken together.

Example 10. Fix the control levels for DSL, FRL, HFL & TBL from following data:

i.) Effective storage required 3000 ha. m
ii.) Carry over allowances (≤ tank losses) is 25% of effective storage
iii.) Dead storage = 10% of gross storage

Contour RL (m)	**580**	**582**	**584**	**610**	**612**	**614**
Storage (M m³)	**30**	**45**	**60**	**30**	**40**	**50**

Assume flood lift as 1.5 m and free board as 2.5 m.

Solution: Gross Storage = Live Storage + Dead storage

Dead storage = 10% of Gross storage

Live Storage = effective storage + carryover allowances

= 3000 + 25% (3000)

= 3750 ha.m

= 37.5 M. m^3

Gross Storage = (10% of Gross Storage) + 37.5

Gross Storage = $[\frac{10}{100}]\mathbf{Gross\ Storage + 37.5}$

Gross Storage – 0.1 $\boldsymbol{Gross\ Storage}$ = 37.5

0.9 x Gross Storage = 37.5

Gross Storage = $\frac{37.5}{0.9}$

= 41.66 M m^3

FRL = $\mathbf{612} + \frac{(614-612)(41{\cdot}66-40)}{50-40}$

= 612.332 m

Dead Storage = 10% of Gross Storage

= $\frac{10}{100} \times \mathbf{41 \cdot 66}$

= 4.166 Mm^3

DSL = $\mathbf{680} + \frac{(682-680)(4.166-3.0)}{4.5-3}$ (By interpolation)

= 681.554 m

HFL = RFL + Flood Lift

= 612.332 + 1.5

= 613.832 m

TBL = HFL + Free board

= 613.8332 + 2.5

= 616.3332 m

Example 11. Fix FRL of a dam from the following data:

i.) Effective live storage = 8000 m^3

ii.) Tank losses = 1500 m^3

iii.) Dead Storage Level = 110 m

Contour RL (m)	**110**	**112**	**114**	**116**	**118**	**120**
Capacity (m^3)	**1000**	**3000**	**5000**	**6000**	**9000**	**12000**

Solution:

We know,

Gross Storage = Live Storage + Dead storage

Total live storage = (Effective live storage + Tank Losses)

= (8000 m^3+1500 m^3) = 9500 m^3

Dead storage = 1000 m^3 (Corresponding to RL 110 m)

Hence, Gross storage = 9500 m^3 +1000 m^3 =10500 m^3

From contour RL and Capacity data, Gross storage 10500 m^3 is available between RL 118 and 120

FRL = $\mathbf{118} + \frac{(120-118)(10500-9000)}{(12000-9000)}$ (By interpolation) = [118+1] = 119 m RL

∴ FRL is fixed at RL = 119 m

Corresponding to Gross storage of 10500 m^3

Assume flood lift = 3 m

HFL = FRL + H = 119 + 3 = 122 m

Assume free board = 3 m

TBL = HFL + Free board = 122 + 3 = 125 m

Example 12. Fix FRL, TBL and HFL of dam from the following data:

i.) Effective storage required 8000 m^3

ii.) Tank losses = 1500 m^3

iii.) Dead Storage Level = 110 m

iv.) Maximum flood discharge = 400 m^3/Sec

v.) Length of waste weir = 100 m

vi.) Francis formula $Q = 1.8LH^{3/2}$

vii.) 1.5 m

Contour RL (m)	**110**	**112**	**114**	**116**	**118**	**120**
Capacity (m^3)	**1000**	**3000**	**5000**	**6000**	**9000**	**12000**

Solution:

We know,

Gross Storage = Total Live Storage + Dead storage = TLS +DS

But, Total live storage = Effective live storage + Tank Losses

= 8000+1500

= 9500 m^3

Dead storage = 1000 m^3 (Corresponding to RL 110)

Again,

Hence, Gross storage = TLS +DS =9500 m^3 +1000 m^3 = 10500 m^3

From contour RL and Capacity data, Gross storage 10500 $m^3$is available between RL 118 and RL 120

Hence, FRL $= \mathbf{118} + \frac{(120-118)(10500-9000)}{(12000-9000)}$ (By interpolation)

= 118+1

= 119 m

∴ FRL = 119 m

Corresponding to Gross storage of 10500 m^3

For fixing HFL, calculate flood lift from Francis formula

$Q = 1.8\ LH^{3/2}$

$400 = 1.8 \times 100\ H^{3/2}$

H = 1.70 m

Hence, HFL = FRL + Flood lift

= 119 m + 1.70 m = 120.70 m

TBL = HFL + Free board

= $120.70\ m + 1.5\ m$ = **122.20 m**

UNIT SUMMARY

Crop water requirements

- **Delta:** Depth of water required to raise a crop.
- **Duty:** Area of land that can be irrigated with the unit volume of irrigation water.
- **Base period:** The duration between the first watering (after sowing) to the last watering (before harvesting) represented in days.

Crop period is the duration between sowing to harvesting represented in days. In calculation, we assume crop period and base period as the same.

Relationship between Duty and Delta of a crop

$$\Delta = \mathbf{8.64}\frac{B}{D}\ \text{m}$$

Where, Δ is the Delta of the crop; B is the Base period of the crop expressed in number of days; and D is the Duty of water expressed in hectare per cubic meter per second.

- **Kor watering:** The supply of water when the plant is still in the young or earlier stage.
- **Paleo Irrigation:** Before the complete growth of the plant if the amount of moisture in the soil gets reduced/ dried, we resupply the water to a field, known as paleo irrigation.
- **Gross Command area (GCA):** It is the total area that can be irrigated by the canal.

- **Culturable command area(CCA):** Actual area of land that can be irrigated in the GCA is called the CCA.

Area capacity curve:
Reservoir elevation-area-capacity is important for planning and operation purposes. The knowledge of the distribution of sediment in a reservoir is necessary for fixing sill elevation of the outlets and the penstock gate elevation to avoid premature loss of services when sediment load is a significant factor. The distribution pattern in a reservoir depends on many factors such as the valley slope, length of the reservoir, particle size in suspended sediment, capacity inflow ratio and the most important of all the reservoir operation. The sediment deposit is not necessarily confined to the lower storage increments of the reservoir but is distributed below the normal water surface. Sedimentation is a process whereby soil particles are eroded and transported by flowing water or other transporting media and deposited as layers of solid particles in water bodies such as reservoirs and rivers.

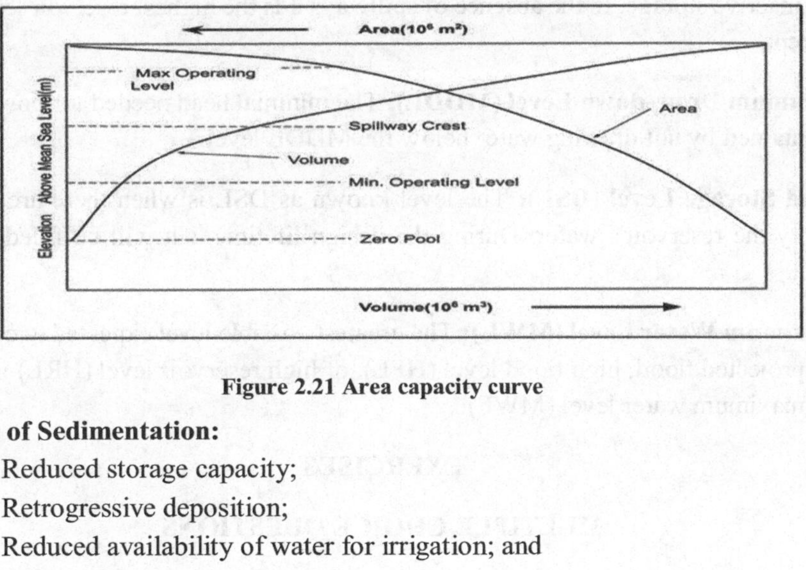

Figure 2.21 Area capacity curve

Effects of Sedimentation:

- Reduced storage capacity;
- Retrogressive deposition;
- Reduced availability of water for irrigation; and
- Shortening of life of a reservoir

In order to curb erosion and sedimentation in rivers and reservoirs, there is need to develop and implement an integrated water resources management plan by all stakeholders.

Control of Sedimentation of a reservoir: In order to increase the life of a reservoir, it is necessary to control the deposition of sediments. Various measures are undertaken in order to achieve this aim. The various methods which are adopted can be divided into two parts:

Pre-construction measures:

- Selection of Dam Site. The silting depends upon the amount of erosion from the catchment. If the catchment is less erodible, the silting will be less.
- Construction of dam in Stages.
- Construction of Check Dams.
- Growing the vegetation screens.
- Construction of Under-sluices in the dam below the Dead Storage Level.

Post-construction measures:

- Removal of Post Flood Water.
- Mechanical stirring of the Sediment.
- Adopting Erosion Control and Soil Conservation Measures in the Catchment Area.

Different Control Levels of a Reservoir

Full Reservoir Level (FRL): Flood storage is included in FRL along with both active and inactive storage. In the absence of spillways it is the highest reservoir level that can be kept.

Minimum Draw-down Level (MDDL): The minimal head needed for power plants is maintained by not drawing water below the MDDL level.

Dead Storage Level (DSL): The level known as DSL is when there are no exits to empty the reservoir's water. During the design lifetime, silt will be filled below this level.

Maximum Water Level (MWL): The greatest possible level expected to occur during the projected flood, high flood level (HFL), or high reservoir level (HRL) is known as the maximum water level (MWL).

EXERCISES

MULTIPLE CHOICE QUESTIONS

1. Alternative name of perennial irrigation is
a) Direct Irrigation
b) Controlled Irrigation
c) Flood Irrigation
d) Storage Irrigation

2. Irrigation method that utilizes supply borders, ditch and ridges is
a) Drip Irrigation Method
b) Basin Flooding
c) Check Flooding

d) Border Flooding

3. Annual Intensity of irrigation defines
a) Cultivable Command Area/Gross Irrigated Area
b) Cultivable Command Area/Net Irrigated Area
c) Net Irrigated Area/Cultivable Command Area
d) Gross Irrigated Area/Cultivable Command Area

4. Time interval between the sowing and harvesting of a crop is known as :
(a) Base period
(b) Kor period
(c) Crop period
(d) Season period

5. Superfluous water is also known as _______
(a) capillary water
(b) hydroscopic water
(c) Gravitational water
(d) saturation capacity

6. Proposition 1: When the soil moisture is just above the wilting point ,the plant expends extra energy to receive the water and hence plant will not grow healthy.
Proposition 2: Too much water supply retards the plant growth.
(a) Proposition 1 is correct
(b) Proposition 2 is correct
(c) None of the Propositions are correct
(d) both the propositions are correct.

7. A canal is to be designed for supplying water to rabi crop, khariff crop and sugarcane. Which one of the following is correct? The canal capacity should be equal to or greater than the water requirement of
(a) Rabi or khariff
(b) Rabi and sugarcane or Khariff and Sugar cane
(c) Rabi and khariff or sugarcane
(d) rabi or Khariff or Sugarcane

8. The depth of water required to bring the water content of a given soil upto field capacity is called

(a) Hydroscopic Water

(b) Soil moisture Deficiency

(c) Equivalent Moisture

(d) Pellicular water

9. Which one of the following areas is largest compared to others?

(a) Gross Commanded Area (G.C.A)

(b) Culturable Commanded Area (C.C.A)

(c) Culturable Uncultivated Area

(d) Culturable cultivated Area

10. If a crop has a net irrigation demand of 14.9 centimeters and an application efficiency of 80% and a water conveyance efficiency of 70%, how much irrigation would the crop require overall?

a) 26.6 cm

b) 21.5 cm

c) 17.6 cm

d) 18.5 cm

(Hints: GIR= NIR/η_a η_c)

11. The root zone depth of a crop can be determined based on a clayey soil with a field capacity at 35% and a permanent wilting point at 20%, having a specific weight of 12.75 kN/m³ in a soil depth of 0.8 cm. Which of the following depths represents the root zone?

a) 17.6 cm

b) 15.6 cm

c) 28.6 cm

d) 20.5 cm

Hints: $\frac{\gamma_d . d . (F-PWP)}{\gamma_w}$

Answers

1	2	3	4	5	6	7	8	9	10	11
b	d	d	c	c	d	b	b	a	a	b

SHORT AND LONG ANSWER TYPE QUESTIONS

Category – I

1. Elaborate on the concepts of 'duty' and 'delta' and establish a relationship between these two terms.

2. Calculate the delta for rice, given that rice necessitates 10 cm of water over 10 days, and its crop period extends to 120 days.

3. Explain:
   a. G.C.A
   b. Kor depth
   c. Outlet factor
   d. Capacity factor
   e. Nominal duty
   f. Open discharge
   g. Rabi and Kharif crops.

4. Explain various methodologies used to assess irrigation water.

5. A canal has culturable commanded area of 5000 hectares. The intensities of irrigation for gram and wheat are 30% and 50% respectively. Gram has a kor period of 18 days, and kor depth of 12 cm, while wheat has a kor period of 18 days with a kor depth of 15 cm. Calculate the discharge required in the canal to supply water to the command area during kor period.

Category - II

1. A tube well has a discharge capacity of 120 m3/hour. Based on the premise that this tube-well will operate for 3200 hours annually, determine the culturable area that it can command. 48 cm is the average crop depth throughout the Rabi and Kharif seasons, and 50% of the crop is irrigated.

2. A water stream irrigates 800 hectares of land. This area receives 50% intensity irrigation for rice. A rice crop is transplanted over the course of 15 days, requiring a total of 60 cm of water for the crop, as the soil receives 15 cm of rain during this time. You can observe that the crop on the field during transplanting is responsible for irrigation water at the top of the distributary. 20% water loss along the water channel is assumed. Compute the necessary discharge for the water route as well.

3. Fix the dam's FRL, TDL, and HFL of a dam using the information below:

    i. 9500 m3 of effective storage are needed.

    ii. 2500 m3 of tank losses.

    iii. The dead storage level is 205 metres.

    iv. The maximum flood discharge is 500 metres per sec.

    v. The waste weir is 130 metres long.

    vi. The Francis formula, Q = 1.75 LH3/2.

    vii. 2.5 metres.

Contour RL (m)	120	1212	124	126	128	130
Capacity (m^3)	1500	2000	3000	4000	6500	9500

PRACTICAL

EXPERIMENT 1

Aim of the Experiment

Estimation of water requirement of a chosen crop (Let us choose Wheat) from the given data.

Apparatus / Data Required

- Crop coefficients from FAO Publication No.24
- Calculator.

Theory

Consumptive use (CU), or Evapotranspiration (ET), is the sum of two terms: (a) Transpiration: Water entering plant roots and used to build plant tissue or being passed through leaves of the plant into the atmosphere and (b) Evaporation: Water evaporating from adjacent soil, water surfaces, and surfaces of leaves of the plant or intercepted precipitation. Factors affecting CU or ET are: Degree of saturation of soil surface; Temperature of air and soil; Humidity; Wind velocity; Extent of vegetative cover etc. which affect evaporation process and Transpiration is affected by: Climate factors such as Temperature; Humidity; Wind speed; Duration & intensity of light and Atmospheric vapor pressure. The Soil factors affecting Transpiration are: Soil Texture, Structure, Moisture content, and Hydraulic conductivity. Plant factors are: Efficiency of rooting systems in moisture absorption; The Leaf arrangement and structure and Stomatal behaviour.

The Blaney Criddle Equation will be used for calculating the Crop water requirement with the example crop.

Blaney Criddle Equation

$$C_u = k \sum f$$

Where,

$$= \frac{p}{40}[1.8t + 32]$$

Here,

C_u= monthly consumptive use of water in cm
k = crop factor. [k values are to be read from FAO Publication No.24]
t = monthly mean temperature
p = monthly annual day light hours, which occur during the period

Procedure

- Collect data for the period of different crop growth stages;
- compute ETo for different stages;
- take k, for the periods of initial, mid-season and late season stages of the selected crop from FAO Publication;
- plot Kc on the Y-axis and stages on the X-axis;
- interpolate crop development stage;
- read K, values for each stage corresponding to mid point of stage;
- compute ETc for each stage and also the entire growth period.

In the present case let us work out with the data provided to us for the calculation. This is to have a feel of the experiment.

Results and Discussion

Let us choose Wheat which is to be grown at a certain place, the useful climatological conditions of which are :

Month	Monthly temperature (C) averaged over the last 5 years	Monthly percent of day time hour of the year computed from the Sun-shine	Useful rainfall in cm averaged over the last 5 years
November	18.0	7.20	1.7
December	15.0	7.15	1.42
January	13.5	7.30	3.01
February	14.5	7.10	2.75

Determine the evapo-transpiration and consumptive irrigation requirement of wheat crop. Also determine the field irrigation requirement if the water application efficiency is 80%. Use Blaney-Criddle equation. Adopt crop factor of 0.8.

Let's calculate in the following table:

Month	t (C)	p (hour)	R (cm)	f= P/40(1.8t + 32) (cm)
November	18.0	7.20	1.7	11.6
December	15.0	7.15	1.42	10.5
January	13.5	7.30	3.01	10.3
February	14.5	7.10	2.75	10.3
			=8.38	= 42.7

$Cu = k. \Sigma f = 0.8 \times 42.7 = 34.16$ cm

Hence, Consumptive use, Cu = 34.16 cm

Consumptive irrigation requirement, C.I.R = Cu – Re = 34.16 – 8.38 = 25.78 cm

Field irrigation requirement, F.I.R = C.I.R/ ηa = 25.78/0.8 = 32.23 cm

Conclusions

Hence the crop water requirement is 34.16cm and irrigation water to be supplied to the field is 32.23cm

Precautions to be taken

A thorough practice of getting the crop coefficients is required before adopting this in the field.

If no measured data on pan evaporation are available locally, a theoretical method, i.e. the Blaney-Criddle method can be used to calculate the reference crop evapotranspiration ETo. There are a large number of theoretical methods to determine the ETo. Many of them have been determined and tested locally. If such local formulae are available, they should be used. If such local formulae are not available one of the general theoretical methods has to be used.

The most commonly used theoretical method is the modified Penman method which is described in detail in FAO Irrigation and Drainage Paper 24. This method, however, is rather complicated and beyond the scope of this manual.

Here only the Blaney-Criddle method is given. The Blaney-Criddle method is simple, using measured data on temperature only. It should be noted, however, that this method is not very accurate; it provides a rough estimate or "order of magnitude" only. Especially under "extreme" climatic conditions the Blaney-Criddle method is inaccurate: in windy, dry, sunny areas, the ETo is underestimated (up to some 60 percent), while in calm, humid, clouded areas, the ETo is overestimated (up to some 40 percent).

EXPERIMENT 2

Aim of the Experiment

Crop water requirement and Irrigation water need for a single crop, i.e., Potato crop.

Let's prepare the table and enter the available data.

The Concept:

The relationship between the reference grass crop and the crop actually grown is given by the crop factor, Kc, as shown in the following formula:

ETo × Kc = ET crop

with ET crop =_____ crop evapotranspiration or crop water need (mm/day)

Kc =_________ crop factor

ETo =________ reference evapotranspiration (mm/day)

Both ET crop and ETo are expressed in the same unit: usually in mm/day (as an average for a period of one month) or in mm/month.

$$ET_0 \times K_c = ET_{Crop}$$

The crop factor, Kc, mainly depends on:

- The type of crop
- The growth stage of the crop
- The climate

Kc and the type of crop

Fully developed maize, with its large leaf area will be able to transpire, and thus use, more water than the reference grass crop: Kc, maize is higher than 1. Cucumber, also fully developed, will use less water than the reference grass crop: Kc, cucumber is less than 1.

Kc and the growth stage of the crop

A certain crop will use more water once it is fully developed, compared to a crop which has just recently been planted.

Kc and the climate

The climate influences the duration of the total growing period and the various growth stages. In a cool climate a certain crop will grow slower than in a warm climate.

Thus, to determine the crop factor Kc, it is necessary, for each crop, to know the total length of the growing season and the lengths of the various growth stages.

Pe is the effective precipitation;

IN is the irrigation needed.= ETc - Pe

Calculation:

Crop: Potatoes Planting date: 1 October

	Jan	Feb	Mar	Apr	May	Jun	Jul	Aug	Sep	Oct	Nov	Dec
ETo (mm/day)	4.7								5.2	4.7	4.6	
Growth stages	Late s.st.								Ini. st	crop dev.st.	Mid s.st.	
Kc per gr. st.	0.65								0.45	0.75	1.15	
Kc per month	0.4								0.5	0.35	1.15	

	Jan	Feb	Mar	Apr	May	Jun	Jul	Aug	Sep	Oct	Nov	Dec
ET crop (mm/day)	4.2								2.6	3.5	5.3	
ET crop (mm/month)	126								78	105	159	
P (mm/mo)	19								28	19	5	
Pe (mm/mo)	1								7	1	0	
IN (mm/a)	125								71	104	159	
IN (mm/day)	4.2								2.4	3.5	5.3	

Notes:

ET crop (mm/day) = Kc (per month) x ETo (mm/day)

ET crop (mm/month) = 30 x ET crop (mm/day)

Pe = 0.6 P - 10 if P < 75 mm/month

Pe = 0.8 P - 25 if P > 75 mm/month

IN (mm/month) = ET crop (mm/month) - Pe (mm/month)

IN (mm/day) = IN (mm/month) / 30

Results and Discussion

The Evapo-transpiration , i.e. Consumptive use or Crop water requirement of the potato crop works out to be ….. and irrigation water to be supplied to the crop field are ….. for the months of ….

Conclusions

As per the above results obtained for potato, the irrigation water is to be supplied to the crop field keeping an eye on the month of the year.

Critical Comments

The tabular for is a very convenient way to calculate the irrigation water need of a crop.

Precautions to be taken

We should be careful while taking observations, filling the data. Most importantly, when multiple crops are to be cultivated in a given season in the command area, the crop water need for eac crop is to be calculated separately and them added.

EXPERIMENT 3

Aim of the Experiment

Estimation of capacity of the canal for the given data.

Data Given

Let us determine the capacity of a canal to which water required to be diverted from the head works to irrigate area of 5000 ha using the data given in the table below. Assume 80 % as the effective precipitation to take care of the consumptive use of the crop. Also assume 50 % efficiency of water application in the field and 75 % as the conveyance efficiency of canal.

Month	Temp (°F)	% hours of sunshine	Rainfall (mm)	Consumptive coefficient or Crop factor (k)
June	70.8	9.90	75	0.80
July	74.4	10.20	108	0.85
August	72.8	9.60	130	0.85
September	71.6	8.40	115	0.85
October	69.3	7.86	105	0.65
November	55.2	7.25	25	0.65
December	47.1	6.42	0	0.60
January	48.8	8.62	0	0.60
February	53.9	9.95	0	0.65
March	60.0	8.84	0	0.70
April	62.5	8.86	0	0.70
May	67.4	9.84	0	0.75

Method of Calculation

Month	Temp (°F)	% hours of sunshine	Rainfall (cm)	Crop factor (k)	Cu = kf * (P - Pe) / 40 (cm)
June	70.8	9.90	7.5	0.80	14.02
July	74.4	10.20	10.8	0.85	16.13
August	72.8	9.60	13.0	0.85	14.85
September	71.6	8.40	11.5	0.85	12.78
October	69.3	7.86	10.5	0.65	8.85
November	55.2	7.25	2.5	0.65	6.50
December	47.1	6.42	0	0.60	4.54
January	48.8	8.62	0	0.60	6.31
February	53.9	9.95	0	0.65	8.71
March	60.0	8.84	0	0.70	9.28
April	62.5	8.86	0	0.70	9.68
May	67.4	9.84	0	0.75	12.44
Total or Average			55.8		124.09 cm

Total consumptive use = 124.09 cm

Useful rainfall = 80 % of total precipitation (given) = (0.80 × 55.8) cm = 44.64 cm

Net irrigation requirement, N.I.R = (Consumptive use of crop – Effective Rainfall)

= (Cu – Re) = (124.09cm – 44.64cm) = 79.45 cm

Field irrigation requirement, F.I.R = N.I.R/η_a = [79.45cm/(50%)] = [79.45cm/0.5] = 158.9 cm

η_c = conveyance efficiency of the canal = 75 % = 0.75

Gross irrigation requirement, G.I.R = F.I.R/η_c = 158.9/0.75 = 211.87 cm

Volume of water requirement for 5000 hectares area = 2.1187 m × (5000×104 m^2)

= 105.93 × 106 m^3

Let the Canal runs for 300 days in a year.

The carrying capacity of the canal = [105.93 × 106 m3]/[300x24x60x60] = 4.075m^3/s

Conclusions

Hence the capacity of the canal to carry irrigation water works out to be 4.1 m^3/s

Critical Comments

To make the calculation simple, especially for Beginners, we have taken only one crop to be grown in the command area. This is an over simplification of the case.

Precautions to be taken

While adopting for a real field, different crops to be grown in the command area are to be taken with other related data. Also, the conveyance efficiency of different canal are different, and hence they are to be assessed before taking a venture to apply.

EXPERIMENT 4

Aim of the Experiment

Estimation of capacity of reservoir for irrigating a command area.

The base periode, intensity of irrigation and duty of various crops under a cannal system are given in the Table below. Find the reservoir capacity if the canal losses are 20% and reservoir losses are 12%.

Crop	Base period (days)	Duty at the field (hectares/ cumec)	Areas under the crop (hectares)
Wheat	120	1800	4800

Sugar-cane	360	800	5600
Cotton	200	1400	2400
Rice	120	900	3200
Vegetables	120	700	1400

Water Discharge and Volume Requirements

(i) Wheat

Discharge required = 4800 cumecs

Volume of water required = 4800 / 1800 ×120 = 320 cumec-days.

(ii) Sugar-cane

Discharge required = 5600 cumecs

Volume of water required = 5600 / 800 = 7 cumec

Therefore, Volume of water required = 7 x 360 = 2520 cumec-days.

(iii) Cotton

Discharge required = 2400 cumecs

Volume of water required = 2400 / 1400 x 200 = 343 cumec-days.

(iv) Rice

Discharge required = 3200 cumecs

Volume of water required = 3200 / 900 x 120 = 427 cumec-days.

(v) Vegetables

Discharge required = 1400 cumecs

Volume of water required = 1400 / 700 = 2 cumec

Calculation of Water Volume Required for Crops

Volume of water required = 2 x 120 = 240 cumec-days.

Hence, total volume of water required on the field for all crops

= 320 + 2520 + 343 + 427 + 240

= 3850 cumec-days.

Now 1 cumec-day = 1 cumec flowing for the whole day = (1 x 24 x 60 x 60) m³

1 hectare-metre = 1 x 104 m³

Hence 1 cumec-day = (1 x 24 x 60 x 60) / (1 x 104) = 8.64 hectare-metres

.: Total volume of water required on the field

= 3850 x 8.64 hectare-metres.= 33264 hect-m.

Since losses in the canal system are 20% the volume of water required at the head of the canal

= 33264 x 100 / 80 = 41580 hect-m.

Allowing 12% reservoir losses, the storage capacity of the reservoir

= 41580 x 100 / 88 = 47250 hectare-metres.

Results and Discussion:

The storage capacity of the reservoir works out to be ______ha.m

Critical Comments

The above capacity of a reservoir is calculated to serve a command area without considering the inflow patterns. While considering a real life project, a part of the water requirement is met by rainfall and the reservoir receives water from monsoon runoff, stores it for use in monsoon and non-monsoon seasons.

Precautions to be taken

Sufficient care should be taken to adopt the above method only to calculate the reservoir capacity required to meet the crop water need, without considering the inflow of water into the reservoir.

EXPERIMENT 5

Aim of the Experiment

Fixing the control levels of a reservoir.

Theory

Different Control Levels of a Reservoirs

- Full Reservoir Level (FRL): Flood storage is included in FRL along with both active and inactive storage. In the absence of spillways it is the highest reservoir level that can be kept.
- Minimum Draw-down Level (MDDL): The minimal head needed for power plants is maintained by not drawing water below the MDDL level.
- Dead Storage Level (DSL): The level known as DSL is when there are no exits to allow gravity to empty the reservoir's water. During the design lifetime, silt will build below this level.

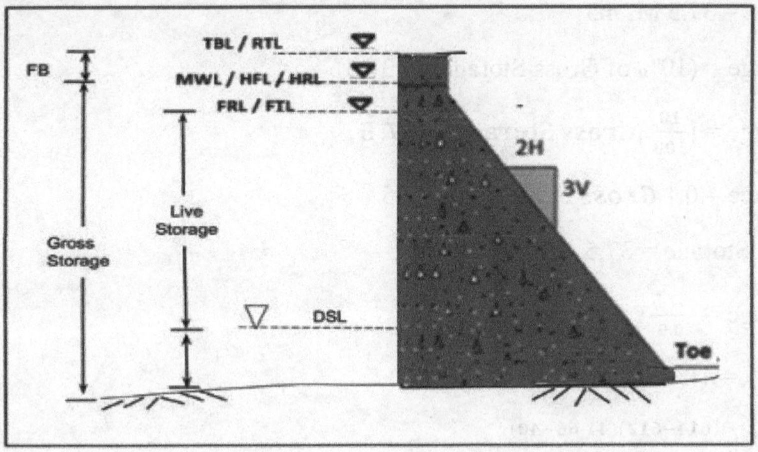

- Maximum Water Level (MWL): The greatest possible level expected to occur during the projected flood, high flood level (HFL), or high reservoir level (HRL) is known as the maximum water level (MWL).

The Experiment

Fix the control levels for DSL, FRL, HFL & TBL from following data of a Reservoir:

i. Effective storage required = 3000 ha. m

ii. Carry over allowances (≤ tank losses) is 25% of effective storage

iii. Dead storage = 10% of gross storage

Contour RL (m)	580	582	584	610	612	614
Storage (M m^3)	30	45	60	30	40	50

Assume flood lift as 1.5 m and free board as 2.5 m.

Results and Discussion

Gross Storage = Live Storage + Dead storage

Dead storage = 10% of Gross storage

Live Storage = effective storage + carryover allowances

= 3000 + 25% (3000)

= 3750 ha. m

= 37.5 M. m3

Gross Storage = (10% of Gross Storage) + 37.5

Gross Storage = $[\frac{10}{100}]\textbf{Gross Storage} + \mathbf{37.5}$

Gross Storage – 0.1 $\textbf{\textit{Gross Storage}}$ = 37.5

0.9 x Gross Storage = 37.5

Gross Storage = $\frac{37.5}{0.9}$

= 41.66 M m^3

FRL = $\mathbf{612} + \frac{(614-612)(41\cdot66-40)}{50-40}$

= 612.332 m

Dead Storage = 10% of Gross Storage

$= \frac{10}{100} \times \mathbf{41\cdot66}$

= 4.166 Mm^3

DSL = $\mathbf{680} + \frac{(682-680)(4.166-3.0)}{4.5-3}$ (By interpolation)

= 681.554 m

HFL = RFL + Flood Lift

= 612.332 + 1.5

= 613.832 m

TBL = HFL + Free board

= 613.8332 + 2.5

= 616.3332 m

Critical Comments

The above levels will help in the construction of a reservoir.

Precautions to be taken

Sufficient care should be taken to choose the value of freeboard.

EXPERIMENTS

Based on the above Example Experiments, the students should conduct Experiments choosing different data on crops, etc.; prepare the report and submit.

KNOW MORE

Activity 1: Discuss about the water requirement of Rice, Wheat, Green gram and Sugarcane. Give a comparison. Which one should be adopted in your crop field or field of a farmer you know.

Activity 2: Describe various types of irrigation efficiency and their relevance in practice.

Activity 3: Visit the nearby crop field and discuss with farmers about the crops which they like to grow and why? Give your comments on the adoption of the crops (Whether ok or not).

Activity 4: Discuss about the problem of sedimentation of a reservoir in your vicinity and based on your study propose how to prevent the sedimentation.

History and Origin of Crop Water Requirement and Reservoir Planning: References to irrigation practices can be traced back to the Rigveda, where chapters such as 1.55, 1.85, 1.105, 7.9, 8.69, and 10.101 describe the use of wells (kupa and avata) that are always filled with water. These wells employed ropes (varatra) and wheels (cakra) to draw water (kosa) up, which was then directed into wide channels (surmi susira) and from there into diversion channels (khanitrima) to irrigate fields.

The concept of river water utilization for irrigation was further mentioned by the 4th-century BCE scholar Pāṇini, who listed rivers such as the Sindhu, Suvastu, Varnu, Sarayu, Vipas, and Chandrabhaga. Additionally, Buddhist texts from the 3rd century BCE and records from the Maurya Empire era highlight the practice of irrigating crops and the state's role in generating revenue through charges for irrigation services from rivers.

Patanjali, in his 4th-century CE Yogasutra, likens a yoga technique to the method a farmer uses to divert water from an irrigation canal, illustrating the ingrained knowledge of irrigation practices by that time. In Tamil Nadu, the Grand Anicut (canal) constructed across the Kaveri river in the 3rd century CE showcases the long-standing application of sophisticated irrigation designs still relevant today.

A significant expansion of irrigation systems in India occurred during the medieval period, led by Sultanate rulers. Firoz Shah Tughlaq, ruling from 1309 to 1388, developed a comprehensive canal irrigation system in the Indo-Gangetic doab and the regions west of the Yamuna River in the 14th century. These canals not only augmented agricultural output in northern India but also supplied water to both urban and rural areas. Successive rulers, including the Mughals until the early 18th century, expanded these irrigation projects. The British later built upon these medieval canal networks, creating extensive colonial canal systems.

Ancient Egyptians: As early as 3000 BC, Egyptians relied on the Nile River's annual floods for irrigation, developing intricate canals and basins to distribute water and grow crops. They also understood the importance of soil moisture and drainage, laying the foundation for later water management practices.

Mesopotamian civilizations: In Mesopotamia (present-day Iraq), Sumerians and Babylonians established complex irrigation systems around 5000 BC, using dikes, canals, and reservoirs to support agriculture. They also developed rudimentary methods for measuring water flow and calculating crop water needs.

Asian civilizations: In China, the Indus Valley civilization, and other parts of Asia, early societies employed diverse water management techniques, including terracing, waterwheels, and simple storage structures. These practices aimed to capture and utilize seasonal rainfall for irrigation.

Development of Scientific Understanding: 18th and 19th centuries: During this period, scientists began to quantify the relationship between plant growth, water availability, and environmental factors like temperature and humidity. Pioneering work by Jean-Baptiste de Lamarck and others laid the foundation for modern evapotranspiration (ET) calculations, a key metric for estimating crop water requirements.
20th century: The 20th century saw significant advancements in agricultural hydrology and irrigation engineering. The development of lysimeters (instruments measuring ET) and advancements in soil science improved the accuracy of water requirement estimations. Additionally, large-scale reservoir projects worldwide aimed to regulate water flow and ensure reliable irrigation supplies.

Modern Era and Technological Advancements: Remote sensing and GIS: Today, remote sensing technologies like satellite imagery and Geographic Information Systems (GIS) provide sophisticated tools for mapping crop types, assessing water needs, and monitoring reservoir levels. This allows for more precise and data-driven approaches to water management.

Modelling and prediction:: Advanced computer models are used to simulate crop growth, predict water demand under different scenarios, and optimize reservoir operations. This helps in planning for droughts, floods, and climate change impacts.

Precision agriculture: Precision agriculture utilizes sensors, real-time data, and variable-rate irrigation systems to apply water more efficiently and precisely to each field based on specific needs. This minimizes water waste and optimizes crop yields.

Interesting facts

India possesses close to 4% of the global water resources, highlighted by the highest aggregate of river discharge and rainfall, measured at 2,000 million cubic meters and 4,500 millimeters, respectively. This surpasses the combined water resources of the entire European continent, underscoring India's significant endowment in terms of freshwater availability.

Mohenjodaro and Harappa: India's history of water management extends far back, predating the formation of many civilizations into organized societies. The ancient cities of Mohenjodaro and Harappa stood out for their highly developed urban planning, characterized by their organized layouts and robust infrastructure, including advanced drainage, well systems, and water storage facilities. Their sophisticated use of brick and stone in construction set a precedent unmatched by their contemporaries.

Located strategically along water bodies like rivers or seas, these early civilizations leveraged their positions to ensure a steady water supply vital for agriculture, irrigation, and daily life. Waterways played a crucial role in transportation, serving as vital arteries for trade and commerce, further underlining the importance of water in the socioeconomic fabric of these societies. Remarkably, about 5000 years ago, structures such as water tanks, canals, and bunds were constructed in Harappa and Mohenjodaro, with every village in the Sindhu-Saraswati basin boasting a water storage tank. Some of these edifices have withstood the test of time, bearing testimony to those prosperous epochs. Notably, the urban planning ensured that all homes, even those on the city outskirts, were connected to the central drainage network.

The Indus Valley Civilization, flourishing along the Indus River and its environs, was renowned for its unparalleled urban water supply and sewage disposal systems. This civilization exemplified high sanitation and hygiene standards, with enclosed drains running beneath street level, showcasing their advanced understanding and implementation of water management and urban planning.

Lothal: In Gujarat, the Harappan city of Dholavira, unearthed by the Archaeological Survey of India in 1989, showcases a civilization that flourished well before 3000 B.C., extending over a millennium. Dholavira presents key insights into the evolution and sophistication of ancient urban planning and water management systems. Its hallmark is a highly advanced water conservation mechanism consisting of stone-built channels and reservoirs, the earliest and most sophisticated of their kind globally. These structures captured rainwater and diverted stream flow, a critical innovation prompted by the arid conditions of the Kutch region, where droughts were common.

In similar ingenuity, homes in parts of Rajasthan incorporated rooftop water harvesting systems to channel rainwater into subterranean tanks, adapting to the region's sparse rainfall. This practice underscores the ancient societal emphasis on water conservation, highlighting a deep-rooted understanding of sustainable living in response to environmental challenges.

About 80 kilometers from Ahmedabad in Gujarat lies Lothal, an ancient Harappan city. Despite its current arid landscape and seemingly desolate conditions, Lothal was a bustling port and a key player in the Indus Valley Civilization 4,000 years ago. Contrary to its literal meaning in Gujarati, "the mound of the dead," Lothal was a center of innovation, especially in environmental design and urban planning.

Lothal's inhabitants pioneered a remarkable "terraquaculture system," integrating land and water use based on lunar farming cycles and leveraging seasonal floods. This advanced approach included creating waterways for internal transport, canals for irrigation, and wells for drinking water, demonstrating a sophisticated understanding of hydrology and environmental management. Furthermore, Lothal featured elaborate drainage systems and advanced water purification methods using brick cisterns with aeration chambers and natural filters. This integration of water management with the city's infrastructure and its economy, including industries situated along waterways for efficient transport and resource use, exemplifies the ancient civilization's foresight and ingenuity in sustainable living.

Dholavira: The Harappan city of Dholavira, located in Gujarat, was unearthed by the Archaeological Survey of India in 1989. This ancient settlement, with origins dating back to before 3000 B.C., thrived for over a thousand years, shedding light on the civilization's evolution and lifestyle. Dholavira is renowned for its advanced water management system, featuring an elaborate network of channels and reservoirs crafted entirely from stone. Recognized as the earliest of its kind globally, this system was essential for harvesting rainwater and channeling water from nearby streams, a necessity in the arid and unpredictable climate of the Kutch region, where droughts were common.

The inhabitants of Dholavira were keenly aware of the importance of water conservation, implementing measures to ensure its efficient use despite their sophisticated water infrastructure. This practice of water conservation is a testament to the ingenuity and foresight of this ancient society.

Similarly, in Rajasthan, a region known for its limited rainfall, ancient homes were equipped with rooftop water harvesting systems. This ingenious solution allowed rainwater to be collected and funneled into underground tanks, demonstrating early efforts to adapt to and mitigate the challenges posed by dry climates.

Naneghat: In Maharashtra, archaeological digs have unearthed ancient irrigation systems and methods for collecting and distributing water, tracing back to 1600 BC. An inscription on a stone pillar by Skanda Gupta in 456 AD at Junagadh recounts the refurbishment of Sudarshan Lake, constructed three centuries earlier. The Kanheri caves from the 1st century

AD, along with other Buddhist caves, feature techniques for capturing and distributing water, still operational today. Moreover, historical records indicate the presence of numerous water collection systems across the nation, supported by both governing authorities and local communities.

In the era following India's independence, Visvesvarayya, an engineer, advocated for the nation to harness its aquatic resources efficiently. He pioneered the invention of automatic sluice gates, first deployed in 1903 at the Khadakvasla reservoir near Pune, enhancing the reservoir's flood storage capacity without jeopardizing the dam's integrity. He also devised flood defense mechanisms for Hyderabad. Drawing inspiration from ancient practices, Visvesvarayya is celebrated as a pioneer in modern Indian water management.

However, over the past two centuries, India has witnessed the decline of numerous traditional water conservation structures. For example, Delhi has seen nearly 274 Mughal-era stepwells fall into disuse. Recently, the National Water Development Agency proposed the creation of canals to interlink river basins, aiming to bolster food production and improve water efficiency in existing irrigation areas.

The fort complex featured two rainwater collection systems; one aimed at ensuring water self-sufficiency for its inhabitants, while the other supplied water to the surrounding moat. Both the fort and moat have since deteriorated. Nearby, a granite hill facilitates the accumulation of rainwater into a vast reservoir at its base, holding up to 2.6 million gallons. The reservoir's thoughtful design includes surrounding trees to reduce evaporation and lotus plants for water purification. The Chandragiri Fort's design incorporates a water collection system from steep hillsides, preventing settlement expansion due to the terrain's incline, ensuring water purity.

Naneghat, near Pune, hosts one of the oldest water conservation systems in the world, featuring rock-hewn tanks to supply water to ancient trade route travelers. The area is dotted with cisterns, ponds, and wells for water collection, and ancient earthen pipes ensured water delivery to distant locales like Burhanpur, Golconda, Bijapur, and Aurangabad. The practice of water purification has deep roots in the region, with ancient texts and scientific studies endorsing the use of brass vessels for storing drinking water to prevent diseases. Varahmihira's Brihat Samhita and the writings of Sushruta, an Indian physician, detail methods for groundwater purification and the treatment of turbid water using natural remedies, sunlight, and heat.

Chandragiri Fort in Andhra Pradesh(10th century): In this location, there were two key systems for capturing rainwater. One system aimed at ensuring water self-sufficiency for the inhabitants, while the other provided water to the surrounding moat of the fort, both of which are now in a state of neglect. Nestled near a granite hill, nearly all the rainfall is directed into a large, open reservoir with a capacity of 2.6 million gallons, situated at the base of the hill.

The design of this system was the result of considerable scientific planning and intent. To reduce water evaporation, the area around the reservoir is encircled with trees, and lotus plants within the water body are believed to help purify the water. Specifically, at Chandragiri Fort, the design strategy was to utilize the runoff from steep hill slopes for water collection, ensuring the water's cleanliness. This method was particularly effective due to the steepness of the terrain, which prevented settlement expansion in these areas, unlike flatter regions.

Inamgaon: In Maharashtra, archaeological digs have uncovered evidence of ancient water management systems, including irrigation canals and methods for collecting and distributing water, that date as far back as 1600 BC. A notable inscription on a rock pillar by Skanda Gupta from 456 AD in Junagadh mentions the renovation of Sudarshan Lake, constructed three centuries earlier. The Kanheri caves from the 1st century AD, along with other Buddhist cave sites, showcase sophisticated water collection and distribution technologies that remain functional today. Moreover, historical records indicate the existence of thousands of water conservation systems across India, which were supported by both governing authorities and local communities.

In the era following India's independence, the engineer Visvesvarayya recognized the critical need for the country to optimize its water resources. He innovated the design of automatic weir water floodgates, first implemented in 1903 at the Khadakvasla reservoir near Pune. These gates enabled the maximization of water storage levels in the reservoir without risking damage to the dam. Furthermore, Visvesvarayya developed a flood mitigation strategy to safeguard Hyderabad against flooding, drawing inspiration from India's rich heritage of water management.

Over the past two centuries, India has witnessed the neglect and loss of many of its traditional water harvesting structures. For example, Delhi has seen nearly 274 stepwells from the Mughal era fall into disrepair and abandonment.

However, recent initiatives by the National Water Development Agency (NWDA) suggest a resurgence in water management efforts. The agency has proposed creating inter-basin transfer canals, a project that aims to enhance food production and water availability, along with boosting productivity in areas currently under irrigation.

REFERENCES & SUGGESTED READINGS

- Asawa, G.L. 2005. Irrigation and water resource Engineering, New Age Publishers
- Basak, N.N.1999. Irrigation Engineering, McGraw Hill Education
- Brouwer, C. and M. Heibloem. 1986. Irrigation Water Management: Irrigation Water Needs, Training manual no. 3. Food and Agriculture Organization of the United Nations, Via delle Terme di Caracalla, 00100 Rome, Italy.
- Dahigaonkar, J.G.2006. Text Book of Irrigation Engineering, Asian Book Pvt. Ltd., New Delhi.
- FAO. 1984. Crop water requirements. By: J. Doorenbos and W.O. Pruitt. FAO Irrigation and Drainage Paper 24. Rome, Italy.

- FAO. 1986. Yield response to water. By: J. Doorenbos and A.H. Kassam. FAO Irrigation and Drainage Paper 33. Rome, Italy.
- FAO. 1992. CROPWAT: A computer program for irrigation planning and management. Developed by: Martin Smith. FAO Irrigation and Drainage Paper 46. Rome, Italy.
- FAO. 1993. CLIMWAT for CROPWAT: A climatic database for irrigation planning and management. Developed by: Martin Smith. FAO Irrigation and Drainage Paper 49. Rome, Italy.
- FAO. 1998a. Crop evapotranspiration: Guidelines for computing crop water requirements. By: Richard Allen, Luis Pereira, Dirk Raes and Martin Smith. FAO Irrigation and Drainage Paper 56. Rome, Italy.
- FAO. 1998b. Guidelines for investigation, design, construction and management of irrigation schemes. Prepared by: FAO TCP/BOT/4451 and FAO UTF/BOT/010/BOT.
- Garg, S K. 2023. Irrigation Engineering and Hydraulic Structures, 38th Edition, Khanna Publishers, Delhi
- Patra, K.C. 2001. Hydrology and Water Resources Engineering, CRC Press.
- Punmia, B.C., Pande, B, Lal., Jain, A. K. and Jan, A.K. 2009. Irrigation and Water Power Engineering, Laxmi Publications, New Delhi
- Sharma, S.K. 2017. Irrigation Engineering and Hydraulic Structures, S.Chand Publishing

Dynamic QR Code for Further Reading

Crop Water Requirement by IIT Kharagpur	

3 DAMS & SPILLWAYS

परिचयः ॥
Introduction

Dams and spillways are vital elements of water management systems, crucial for regulating, storing, and safely releasing water. These structures serve multiple purposes, such as flood control, water supply, irrigation, hydroelectric power generation, and recreational activities. Knowledge of the design, operation, and maintenance of dams and spillways is essential to ensure their safety and effectiveness. Understanding their roles and functions is essential for the sustainable and safe utilization of water resources.

"जलमेव जीवनम्। यत्र जलं तत्र जीवनम्।"

"Water is life. Where there is water, there is life."

UNIT SPECIFICS

The following aspects will be discussed elaborately in this unit.

- Classification of Dams
- Construction of Earthen Dams
- Modes of failure of earthen dams and preventive measures
- Design of Gravity dams
- Classification of spillways
- Types of Energy Dissipators

This chapter will introduce the practical uses of the subjects covered to enhance curiosity, creativity, and problem-solving abilities. It features a vast array of multiple-choice and both short and long-answer questions, organized into two levels according to Bloom's taxonomy's lower and higher orders. Additionally, learners are provided with numerical assignments, along with a compilation of references and recommended readings for further practice.

To enrich the learning experience with more in-depth information on selected topics, QR codes are strategically placed throughout the text. These codes lead to additional supportive material upon scanning.

Following the practical exercises, the chapter introduces a "Know More" segment, carefully crafted to offer extra information that is of great value to readers. This segment focuses on the foundational activities, intriguing facts, analogies, and the historical progression of the subject, emphasizing key observations and discoveries. It outlines the timeline of the subject's evolution to present times and discusses its application in everyday life and various industries. Case studies are included to give the reader a real life experience. The purpose is to stimulate curiosity and inquisitiveness about the topics discussed in the unit, enriching the reader's understanding.

RATIONALE

This introductory course on is designed to build students' knowledge and skills in the field. By the end of the course, students will have a solid foundation on "Dams and Spillways", which they will be able to apply specifically in civil engineering context. They will possess the capability to employ techniques for selection of sites, layout, planning and execution of dams spillways and energy dissipators.

A reservoir has a certain capacity to store water. If the reservoir is full of water and then flood water enters it, the reservoir level goes up and may eventually result in over-topping of the dam. To avoid this situation, the flood water is to be released downstream. This is done by providing a spillway which draws water from the top portion of the reservoir. Then comes the role of energy dissipators, which are constructed downstream of hydraulic structures to dissipate high energy of the turbulent high energy water flowing downstream of them.

PRE-REQUISITES

Science: Fundamentals of Intermediate Science

Mathematics: Fundamentals of Intermediate Mathematics

UNIT OUTCOMES

At the end of the course, the student will be able to:

U3-O1: Differentiate various types of Dams and choose a given type for a section of a stream.

U3-O2: Select site, give layout and construct the earth dams

U3-O3: Analyze and design the gravity dams and execute their construction

U3-O4: Choose a befitting spillway for a site and execute its construction.

U3-O5: Select a given type of Energy Dissipator for a hydraulic structure

ALIGNMENT WITH COURSE OBJECTIVE

UNIT OUTCOMES	EXPECTED ALIGNMENT WITH COURSE OUTCOMES (1: Low Correlation; 2: Moderate Correlation; 3: High Correlation)				
	CO:1	CO:2	CO:3	CO:4	CO:5
U3-O1	-	-	3	2	2
U3-O2	-	-	3	2	2
U3-O3	-	-	3	2	2
U3-O4	-	-	3	2	2
U3-O5	-	-	3	2	2

3.1 Dams and their classification

3.1.1 Introduction

Water is crucial for the survival of humans, animals, and plants. In the preceding chapter, we explored the availability and duration of precipitation. Rainfall not only varies across different locations but also changes over time. This variability in both space and time has led humans to consider the necessity of storing water for future use, especially in the absence of rainfall. Consequently, the concept of building a barrier to collect and store precipitation water emerged in ancient and prehistoric times. This barrier, constructed across a river or water flow to create a reservoir, is known as a "dam."

The region where water accumulates to create a reservoir is termed as the upstream side, while the opposite part of the dam is referred as the downstream side. Water stored in the reservoir serves various purposes, including recreational activities, drinking water supply, and irrigation. Additionally, the energy harnessed from the reservoir can be employed to rotate a turbine for electricity generation. During periods of flooding, the dam acts as a regulatory structure, safeguarding villages, cities, and other downstream areas. Moreover, dams find applications in municipal water supply, industrial water provision, and navigation.

Prehistoric and ancient eras reveal that the earliest known manmade dam dates back approximately 3000-5000 years. This ancient dam had a primary purpose of irrigation and was crafted from materials such as logs, tree branches, mud, and stones. Aside from facilitating irrigation, it played a crucial role in preventing silt from entering cultivated fields.

When the Aswan Dam was constructed in Egypt in 1902 on the Nile River, it was a major turning point in the history of modern dam construction. This dam is regarded as the first modern dam, built mainly for irrigation and flood control. After that, in 1911, the United States' Roosevelt Dam on the Salt River was finished and gained international acclaim. The Roosevelt Dam was built with concrete blocks, in contrast to the Aswan Dam, which was built with stone.

In the context of India's post-independence era, the Hirakud Dam holds historical significance as the first major dam. Situated on the powerful Mahanadi River near Burla town in the Sambalpur district, the Hirakud Dam played a crucial role in India's developmental efforts.

3.1.2 Classification of Dams

3.1.2.1 Based on Materials of Construction

a. Earthen dams: This is the oldest form of dam, typically constructed in regions with insufficient soil foundation to support the weight of concrete and where soil is readily accessible. These dams are not completely impermeable and are less expensive to build, as they do not demand highly skilled labor. However, a notable drawback is their limitation in terms of height, and hence they cannot be constructed for greater heights.

b. Concrete dams: These kinds of dams are constructed using either reinforced concrete or regular cement concrete. They can be designed as buttress dams, arch dams, gravity dams, or in a variety of other ways.

c. Masonry dams: This dam variant is constructed using stone masonry and cement mortar. Typically, these dams belong to the gravity type category, with rare instances of employing steel or timber dams.

d. Rock-fill dams: This type of dam is constructed by using rocks and boulders as construction materials. An impervious layer made up of concrete or earth fill is laid on the upstream of the dam as only rock can't check the flow of water. Now days these are not in use.

3.1.2.2 Based on the flow over its Top

a. Over flow dam: In this case, the water flows over the top of the dam; e.g. Spillways and weirs. This type of dam is mainly made up of plain concrete and masonry.

b. Non overflow dam: In this instance, the dam's top was consistently higher than the maximum anticipated flood level. It is forbidden for water to flow over the dam's top.

3.1.2.3 Based on the use of the dam

a. Storage dam: This dam type is usually built to reserve surplus water during floods on the upstream side. The stored water is then utilized during periods of water scarcity, fulfilling needs such as irrigation, hydropower generation, and navigation.

b. Diversion dam: This type of dam is generally constructed to divert water in to the canal. These arc usually of lower heights. Examples of such dams are weirs, and barrages.

c. Detention dam: The goal of building this kind of dam is to control flooding. It temporarily reduces the river's floodwater flow, and then when the flood subsides, the water is released downstream.

3.1.2.4 Based on structure and design

a. Embankment Dams: An embankment dam is a large artificial barrier that is often built by building up and compressing a complex semi-plastic heap formed of various combinations of rock, sand, silt, or clay. It has a compact, watertight core and a surface covered in a somewhat porous, waterproof natural covering.

b. Earth-fill dams: Built from a simple mound of compacted earth, earth-fill dams are often referred to as earthen dams, rolled-earth dams, or just earth dams. A drainage layer to collect leaking water may be included, but a homogenous rolled-earth dam is constructed entirely of one type of material.

c. Rock-Fills Dams: Rock-fill dams are embankments made of granular earth that has been compacted and easily drains, with a part that is waterproof. This type of earth usually has a high percentage of big particles, thus the term "rock-fill."

d. Concrete-face rock-fill dams: One kind of rock-fill dam with concrete slabs running upstream is called a concrete-face rock-fill dam (CFRD). This arrangement provides a design that is unaffected by uplift pressure and makes use of the concrete slab as a barrier that keeps leaks out.

e. Gravity Dam: The only way that gravity dams, which are composed of stone or concrete masonry, can withstand the horizontal force of water pressing on them is by their own weight and resistance to the foundation. They are designed to ensure that every section of the dam functions independently of the others and is stable.

f. Arch Dam: A concrete dam with a curving shape that bends upstream is called an arch dam. The force that the water applies to it, known as hydrostatic pressure, helps the dam's construction by enabling the arch to somewhat straighten. This strengthens the dam as it presses against the foundation or abutments. This kind of dam works particularly well in small gorges or canyons with sturdy, steep rock walls that can hold the weight of the dam and its pressures.

g. Arch-Gravity Dam: This dam is a hybrid of an arch dam and a gravity dam. As it curves upstream in a shrinking arc, it sends the majority of the water pressure against the canyon's rock walls. The lateral, or horizontal, stresses acting on the dam are lessened by the internal pressure of the water.
h. Buttress Dam: The dam which consists of number of buttresses (piers or props) is called Buttress dam. It supports a slab on its upstream face.

Two primary types of dams, namely earthen dams and gravity dams (constructed from masonry or concrete), which enjoy widespread acceptance and global construction, are outlined below.

3.2 Earthen dams

3.2.1 Introduction

These dams represent the most ancient type and can be built using readily available natural resources. Gravel, sand, and silts are fundamental materials which are physically combined in different proportions, and with the process of rolling, and tamping to create these structures. The main advantages of earth dams are:

a. Easy availability of earth material on dam site.
b. Earth can easily be excavated, transported, compacted and can be handled and moved with least number of machinery.
c. Earth dam can be constructed even on compressible foundations where a masonry dam can't be built due to structural reason.
d. The most important advantage is its cheaper construction cost. It requires less skilled laborers and natural cheap materials for its construction.

Examples of three major earthen dams in India

Located in the Indian state of Orissa, roughly 15 km away from Sambalpur, the ***Hirakud Dam***, constructed in 1957 to control the flow of the Mahanadi River, stands as the world's longest earthen dam, stretching close to 26 kilometres. Representing a significant landmark, it was among the first large-scale multipurpose river valley endeavors undertaken following India's independence.

Nestled between Mettupalayam and Sathyamangalam in Tamil Nadu's Erode District, in the southern part of India, the ***Bhavanisagar Dam*** and ***Reservoir adorn the Bhavani River***. Famous for its dimensions, the dam is celebrated as one of the biggest earthen dams within India.

Located in the Western Ghats of Kerala's Wayanad District, about 21 kilometres from Kalpetta, the ***Banasura Sagar Dam*** holds the title of the second-largest earthen dam in Asia and the largest in India.

3.2.2 Types of Earthen dams

a. Homogeneous embankment type Earth Dam: This represents the simplest approach to dam construction, employing just one kind of soil material. For improved water tightness and stability, a layer of comparatively less permeable material might be incorporated on the upstream side. Such embankments are typically built when only one type of material is readily accessible in the local area. They are well-suited for constructing dams of low to moderately high heights, as well as for levees.

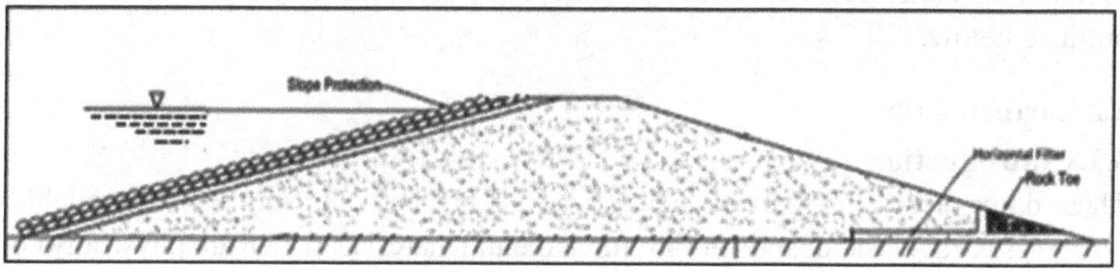

Figure 3.1 Homogeneous embankment type Earth Dam

b. Zoned embankment type Earth Dam: This kind of earth dam has an exterior permeable zone that is further encircled by an intermediate zone with relative permeability and an impermeable core in the centre. Seepage issues are successfully resolved by the central core, and possible seepage through cracks in the core is prevented by the intermediate transition zone. The outer zone helps the dam stay stable by distributing the weight across a wider area. This design is widely used because it allows for flexibility in the selection of materials for various zones according to availability.

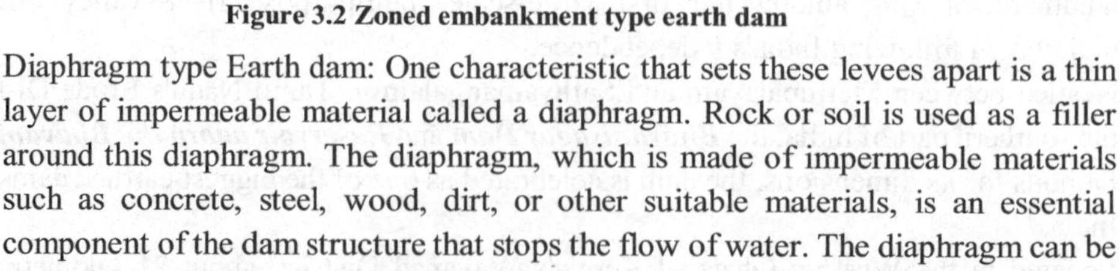

Figure 3.2 Zoned embankment type earth dam

c. Diaphragm type Earth dam: One characteristic that sets these levees apart is a thin layer of impermeable material called a diaphragm. Rock or soil is used as a filler around this diaphragm. The diaphragm, which is made of impermeable materials such as concrete, steel, wood, dirt, or other suitable materials, is an essential component of the dam structure that stops the flow of water. The diaphragm can be placed either as a protective layer on the upstream surface or as a vertical core in the middle. To minimize excessive leakage through the foundation, it's essential to ensure it is securely connected to the bedrock or a non-permeable base.

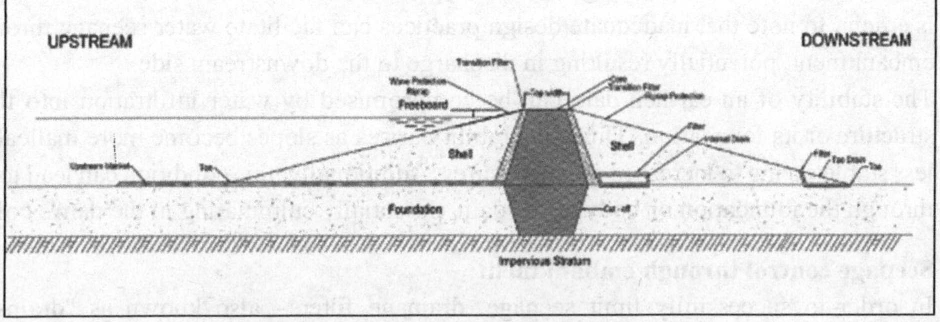

Figure 3.3 Diaphragm type embankment dam

3.2.3 Components with function of earthen dam

There are three basic components of an earth dam. They are foundation, Inner core and outer shell.

a. Foundation: This component, comprising either earth or stone, serves as a foundational support for the embankment. It plays a crucial role in withstanding both horizontal and vertical forces exerted on the dam and acts as a barrier against the seepage of water beneath the structure.

b. Inner core: The core is situated either in the center or slightly upstream from the center of the dam. To combat under-seepage, the core is extended deep into the foundation to form a watertight barrier. This downward extension of the core is known as a cut-off.

c. Outer shell: This component provides essential support to the core, ensuring that the load is distributed uniformly across the foundation. In the construction of dams, a transition filter is placed between the core and the shell to prevent the movement of fine-grained materials from the core into the larger spaces within the coarser shell material. Should the particle size discrepancy between the core and shell be slight, the need for a transition filter might be bypassed. Yet, in situations where there is clay cover paired with a gravel shell, incorporating a transition filter becomes crucial.

A downstream internal drain is positioned strategically to limit seepage through the core and prevent rains from flooding the upper portion of the downstream shell. Moreover, a top drain is installed on the shell's downstream surface. To reduce erosion and damage from waves, riprap protects the upstream side. A berm is also included to facilitate slope protection observations and to meet maintenance and repair needs.

3.2.4 Seepage through earth dam and its control

Seepage in dams is predominantly influenced by certain soil properties, including the plasticity of the soil, gradation, degree of compaction, and others. Soil with a plasticity index less than 15, especially when well compacted, is generally more susceptible to seepage. Additionally, poorly graded soil typically exhibits lower resistance to seepage. It is crucial to note that inadequate design practices can facilitate water seepage through the embankment, potentially resulting in discharge to the downstream side.

The stability of an earthen dam can be compromised by water infiltration into the dam structure or its foundation. This vulnerability arises as slopes become more malleable and less stable owing to increased pore pressures. Additionally, this condition can lead to piping through the foundation or body of the dam, potentially culminating in the dam's collapse.

Seepage control through embankment:

In order to successfully limit seepage, drainage filters—also known as "drains"—are integrated into embankments in a variety of forms, including rock toe, horizontal blanket, chimney drain, and others. These filters are essential in lowering pore pressure along the dam's downstream section, which enhances the structure's overall stability. Moreover, by limiting particle movement, they serve as a prophylactic strategy against piping. These drains, which are usually made of graded coarse materials, effectively collect seepage water and enable its safe release.

Various types of drains are described below:

a. Rock toe: The downstream toe of the dam is home to the carefully placed stones that make up the rock toe. These stones are usually 15 to 20 cm in size. As seen in the following figure, these stones are arranged in graded strata that include gravel, fine sand, and coarse sand. In most cases, the rock toe height is maintained between 25 and 30 percent of the reservoir head.

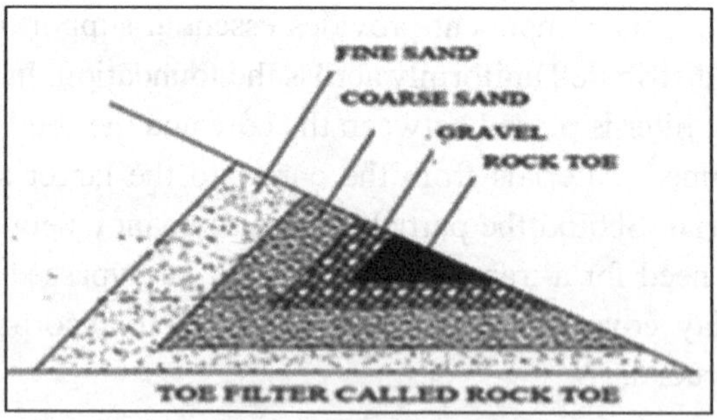

Figure 3.4 Rock toe to facilitate drainage

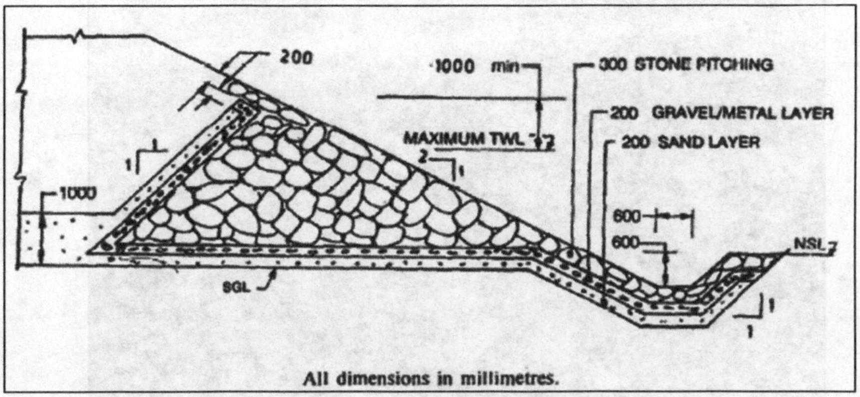

Figure 3.5 Details of Rock Toe Protection with Toe Drain Where Tail Water Level (TWL) is higher than Stripped Ground Level (SGL)

(Reproduced from Indian Standard IS 9429 : 1999 DRAINAGE SYSTEM FOR EARTH ROCKFILL DAMS - CODE OF PRACTICE (First Revision).

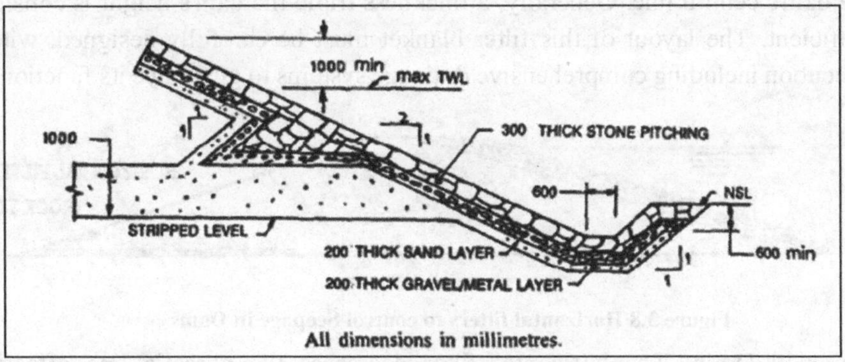

Figure 3.6 Downstream Toe Protection When SGL is Above Maximum TWL

(Reproduced from Indian Standard IS 9429 : 1999 DRAINAGE SYSTEM FOR EARTH ROCKFILL DAMS - CODE OF PRACTICE (First Revision).

Figure 3.7 Downstream pitching, Rock toe, and toe drain in right dyke of Hirakud Reservoir

b. Horizontal blanket: The horizontal filter stretches inward from the downstream side or toe of the dam, covering distances from 25% to 100% of the way from the toe to the dam's central line. Generally, a thickness triple the dam's height is considered sufficient. The layout of this filter blanket must be carefully designed, with the execution including comprehensive drainage systems to guarantee its functionality.

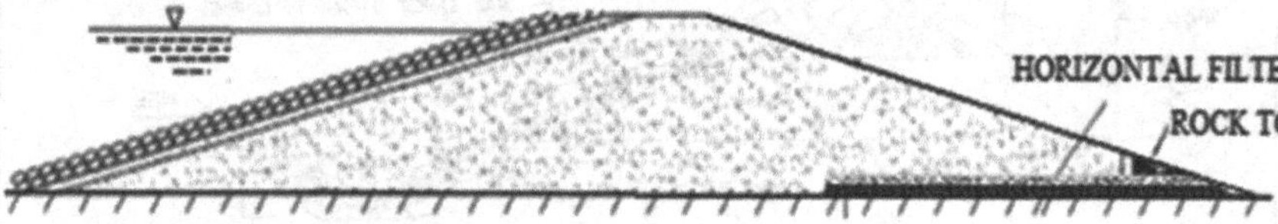

Figure 3.8 Horizontal filters to control Seepage in Dams

c. Chimney Drain: The horizontal filter decreases the phreatic line effectively, although it can cause problems with horizontal stratification on a larger scale. As seen in the picture, seepage is effectively managed by adding a vertical filter in addition to the horizontal filter to prevent stratification of soil in the dam body. The term "chimney drain" refers to this combination design.

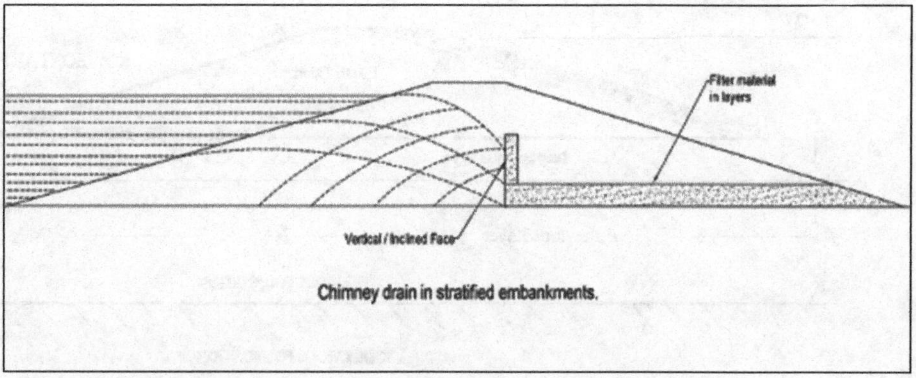

Figure 3.9 Chimney drain to Control Seepage in Earthen Dams

Seepage control through foundation:

a. **Impervious cutoffs:** It is often located at the heel or upstream end of the earth fill dam, as indicated in the figure below, and is made of sheet pile or concrete. In order to successfully limit seepage, these cutoffs are often built across the porous foundation. Typically, 50% cutoff results in a 25% reduction in seepage, while a 90% cutoff can reduce seepage through the foundation by 65%.

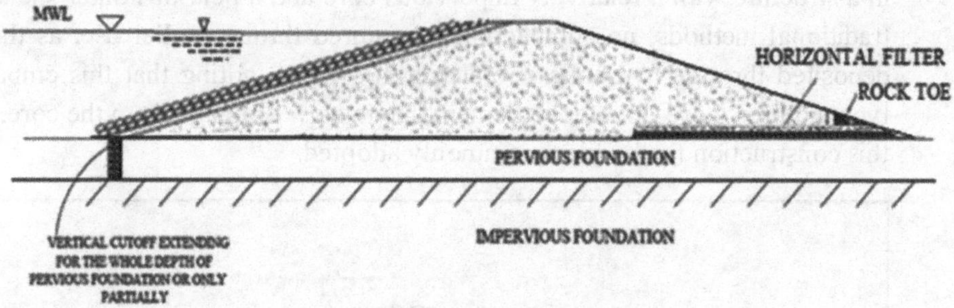

Figure 3.10 Impervious cutoff to Control Seepage

b. **Relief wells and Drain trenches**: There is a chance that water will boil close to the dam's toe if seepage through a permeable foundation that is covered in a less compacted pervious layer occurs in substantial quantities. Relief wells and drain trenches can be built through the foundation's upper impermeable layer to allay this worry.

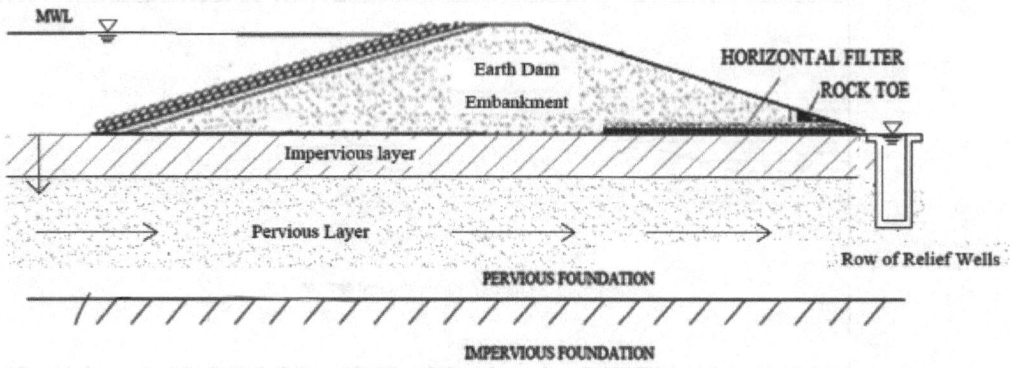

Figure 3.11 Impervious cutoff to Control Seepage

3.2.5 Methods of construction of earthen dam

a. Hydraulic fill method: In this approach, the necessary quantity of soil is excavated and thoroughly blended with water using various puddling techniques. Subsequently, the mixture is transported to the designated location for constructing the earth dam. The soil-water mixture, or slush, is discharged through these pipes at appropriate intervals along their length. The coarse particles settle near the pipe exit, while the finer particles are carried toward the middle of the section, resulting in a structure with a relatively impervious core and a pervious outer shell. Unlike traditional methods, no compaction is required through roller use, as the soil is deposited through hydraulic operations. It's worth noting that this embankment type requires more time for settlement due to slow drainage from the core, making this construction method less commonly adopted.

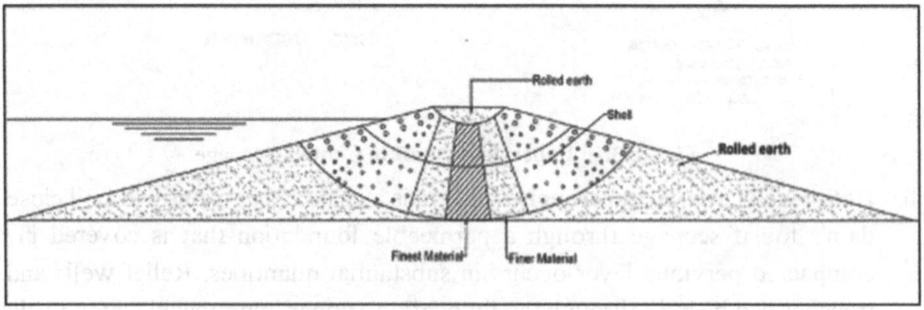

Figure 3.12 Hydraulic fill earth dam

b. Rolled fill method: In this construction method, layers of soil materials, each approximately 20cm thick, are carefully placed and compacted using power-operated rollers. This process allows for effective control of moisture content. It is a widely favored and popular approach for the construction of earthen dams.

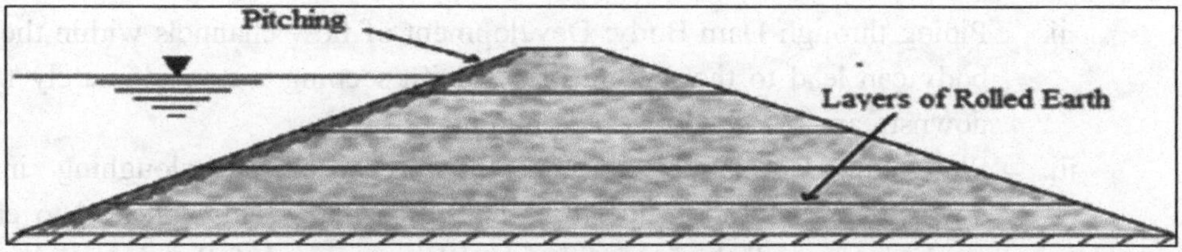

Figure 3.13 Rolled fill earth dam

3.2.6 Types of failure in earthen dams and preventive measures

a. Hydraulic failure

i. Overtopping: This situation arises when the spillway lacks adequate capacity, the design flood level is underestimated, or the spillway gates fail to close correctly during flood conditions. To address this issue effectively, it is crucial to ensure sufficient freeboard is provided.

ii. Erosion of Upstream Face: Soil from the dam's upstream face may become loose or shift as a result of wave erosion. It is advised to use riprap or stone pitching upstream as a prophylactic step to counteract this.

iii. Cracking Due to Frost Action: Frost can cause the upstream face to heave and break, which could lead to seepage and eventual failure. It is advisable to include preventive measures, such as offering freeboard up to 1.5 metres, to avoid these problems.

iv. Gulling: On the downstream face, heavy rains may cause gulling action, which increases the risk of erosion and dam failure. Careful management procedures, such as berm installation at the proper heights, grassing slopes, and filling in cuts prior to the rainy season, help prevent this. In addition, effective rainfall removal depends on having proper drainage in place.

v. Toe Erosion: Cross currents produced by spillway buckets or erosion from tail water are the causes of these phenomena. Implementing riprap or downstream slope pitching to a height above the average tail water level will help to mitigate this. In order to stop cross-current flow, spillway sides must also be sufficiently long and high.

b. Seepage failure

Uncontrolled seepage through a dam's foundation or body can cause sloughing or piping, which can lead to dam failure. In contrast, controlled seepage is usually harmless. This particular reason is responsible for more than 33% of dam failures.

i. Piping through Foundation: Water flow through the foundation can loosen the soil, weakening its strength and potentially causing catastrophic failures. This is often the result of highly permeable cavities, fissures, or coarse sand strata in the foundation.

ii. Piping through Dam Body: Development of flow channels within the dam's body can lead to the mixing of soil with seeping water, ultimately flowing downstream and resulting in dam failure.

iii. Sloughing: Similar to piping, failure caused by sloughing involves downstream saturation due to extensive seepage. This can lead to erosion, producing a small slump or slide when the reservoir is full. Adopting improved construction and maintenance methods for the embankment can help address and mitigate the causes of seepage.

c. **Structural failure**

i. Foundation Slide: When soft soils, like fine silt or soft clay, make up the foundation, the likelihood of a dam failing rises. Under such circumstances, especially if there is fractured rock underneath, the entire dam may experience sliding over the foundation.

ii. Slide in Embankments: Steep embankment slopes exceeding the strength of the soil can lead to sliding, causing dam failure. Sudden drawdown of the reservoir can result in upstream slope slide, while a full reservoir can lead to downstream slope failure. Downstream failure is considered more severe than upstream failure, with higher pore pressure being a key factor in slope failure, whether upstream or downstream.

Example 1. For a uniform earth dam that is 52 meters tall with a 2-meter freeboard, a flow net analysis yielded the following data: there are 25 potential drops and 4 flow channels. The dam includes a 50-meter-long horizontal filter at its downstream end. Determine the discharge per meter length of the dam section, given the dam material's coefficient is 3×10^{-3} cm/sec.

Solution:

The discharge per unit length is given by

$$q = k\,H\,\frac{N_f}{N_d}$$

Hence, H=water depth=52-2=50

$k = 3\times10^{-3}$ cm/sec $= 3\times10^{-5}$ m/sec

$N_f = 4$

$N_d = 25$

$q = 3\times10^{-5} \times 50 \times \frac{4}{25} = 24\times10^{-5}$ m³/sec/m

= 0.00024 cumec/meter length

Example 2. For a homogeneous earthen dam with a height of 54 meters and a freeboard of 4 meters, a flow net analysis produced the following findings: there are 25 potential drops and 5 flow channels. The dam has a 50-meter-long horizontal filter at its downstream end.

Determine the discharge per meter length of the dam section, given that the coefficient of permeability for the dam material is 3×10^{-3} cm/sec.

Solution:

The discharge per unit length is given by

$$q = k\,H\,\frac{N_f}{N_d}$$

Hence, H=water depth=54-4=50

$k = 3\times10^{-3}$ cm/sec$=3\times10^{-5}$ m/sec

$N_f = 5$

$N_d = 20$

$$q = 3\times10^{-5} \times 50 \times \frac{5}{25} = 30\times\mathbf{10^{-5}}\ \text{m}^3/\text{sec/m}$$

$= 0.0003$cumec/meter length

3.3 Gravity Dams

3.3.1 Introduction

Compared to other dam types, gravity dams are more stable and independent. They can be constructed on various sites, provided the natural foundation is strong enough to support the dam's substantial weight. Typically, straight in plan, gravity dams may have a slight curve, and their base width-to-height ratio is generally less than 1:1.

Here are examples of three gravity dams to illustrate this type:

a) Located in Himachal Pradesh and Punjab, India, the Bhakra Nangal Dam is a concrete gravity dam. With a height of 225 meters, it ranks as the tallest dam in India. Additionally, it crosses the Sutlej River, making it the second-largest dam in Asia.

b) The Sardar Sarovar Dam, located in Gujarat, India, stands as the most significant structure within the Narmada River Valley Project. This gravity dam, rising to a height of 163 meters, is positioned on the Narmada River.

c) Boasting an impressive height of 284 meters, the Dixen Dam in Switzerland holds the title of the world's tallest dam. This engineering marvel is a gravity dam constructed from concrete.

3.3.2 Cross-section of gravity dam

The upstream face of a gravity dam is typically vertical. However it occasionally has a slight splay / slanted towards upstream side at the lower portion. A drainage tunnel built into the dam's framework reduces uplift pressure caused by seepage. The theoretical and practical profiles of the concrete gravity dam are discussed as follows.

a. Theoretical and Practical Profiles of Gravity Dam

Imagine a right-angled triangle representing the elementary or theoretical profile of a gravity dam's cross-section, designed under the influence of three principal forces: its own weight, the pressure from water, and uplift pressure. This simplified model visualizes the dam in an empty reservoir state, featuring a top width that is essentially zero. Yet, in reality, an actual gravity dam incorporates a minimum top width and a freeboard to account for factors such as wave action, and it also endures more forces than those three foundational ones considered in the elementary profile's design. This conceptual figure serves as a basic starting point for understanding the structural considerations in dam design before additional complexities are added for practical application.

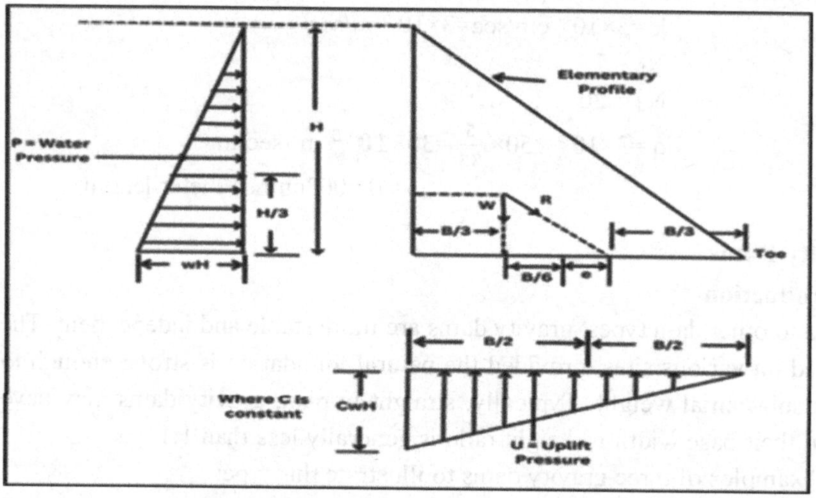

Figure 3.14 Elementary Profile or Theoretical Profile of a Gravity dam

Yet, in reality, an actual gravity dam incorporates a minimum top width and a freeboard to account for factors such as wave action, and it also endures more forces than those three foundational ones considered in the elementary profile's design. This conceptual figure serves as a basic starting point for understanding the structural considerations in dam design before additional complexities are added for practical application.

b. Practical Profile of a Gravity Dam

Elementary profile of a given dam is only theoretical profile. Certain changes have to be made in this profile to cater the practical needs.

They are as follows:

(i) Provision of top width for the construction of a road.

(ii) Provision of free-board to prevent over topping of water from upstream side.

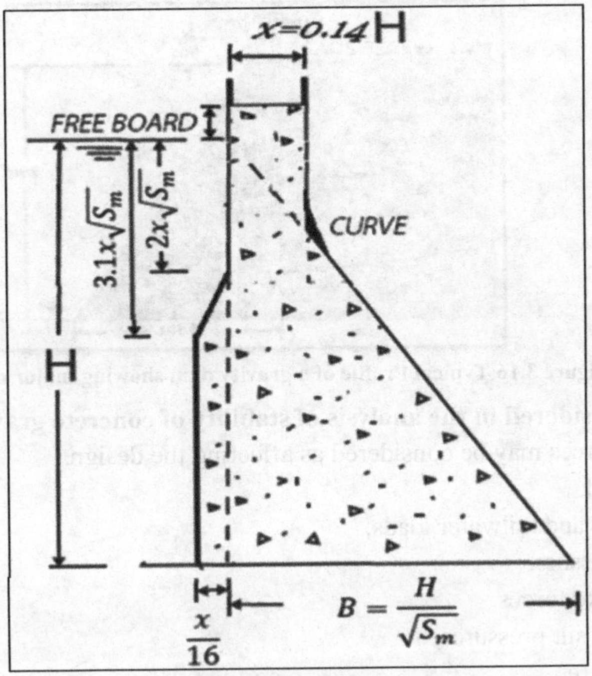

Figure 3.15 Practical Profile of a gravity dam

- Due to the provisions for practical utility of the dam, the resultant shifts more towards the heel, thereby crossing the inner middle third point and consequently, the tension will develop.
- Hance, to avoid tension, some additional mass of masonry or concrete is to be added on the up-stream side. This is required for a low gravity dam.
- If required, foundation gallery and / or drainage gallery are to be provided to reduce uplift pressure.
- Final shape and dimensions are decided after the stability check of the dam.

The approximate / typical practical profile of a low gravity dam is presented above in Figure 3.12 for ready reference. Typical section of a gravity dam with major details is presented below to have feel of the dimensions and details of the dam. The figure shows the drainage gallery, upstream slanting portion, roadway width, Maximum Water Level, Tow of the dam, Heel of the dam, typical dimensions.

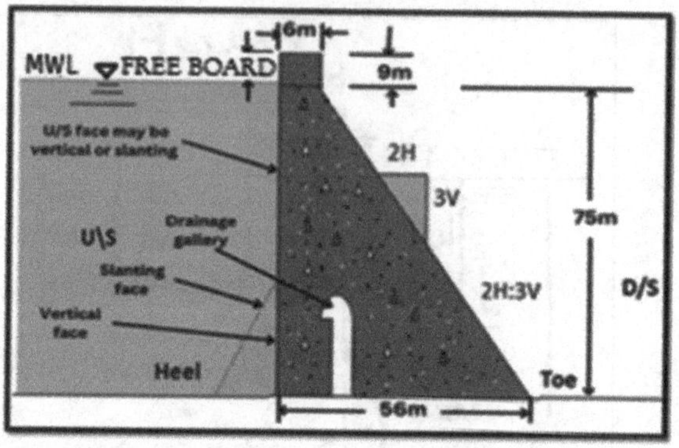

Figure 3.16 Typical Profile of a gravity dam showing major details

3.3.3 Forces considered in the analysis of stability of concrete gravity dams.

The following forces may be considered as affecting the design:

a) Dead load,
b) Reservoir and tailwater loads,
c) Uplift pressure,
d) Earthquake forces,
e) Earth and silt pressures,
f) Ice pressure,
g) Wind pressure,
h) Wave pressure, and
i) Thermal loads.

[Ref.: IS: 6512 - 1984 Indian Standard CRITERIA FOR DESIGN OF SOLID GRAVITY DAMS (First Revision)]

The forces to be resisted by a gravity dam fall into two categories as given below:

a. Forces, such as weight of the dam and water pressure, which are directly calculable from the unit weights of the materials and properties of fluid pressures; and
b. Forces, such as uplift, earthquake loads, silt pressure and ice pressure, which can only be assumed on the basis of assumption of varying degree of reliability.

It is in the estimating of the second category of the forces that special care has to be taken and reliance placed on available data, experience, and judgement".

The major forces considered to be acting on the elementary profile are as follows:

a. **Self-Weight of the Dam:**

The formula for calculating the weight (***W***) of the dam is given as

$$\boldsymbol{W = 21 \times B \times H \times G \times w}$$

where ***G*** represents the specific gravity of the dam material, commonly taken as 2.4 for concrete. The term w stands for the specific weight of water, which is $\boldsymbol{9.81 kN/m^3}$. B and H denote the base width and height of the dam, respectively. The weight (***W***) exerts a vertical force through the centroid of the triangle, positioned at a distance of B/3 from the heel.

b. Water Pressure:

Water pressure is the major external force acting on a gravity dam.

When the dam is vertical the water pressure acts horizontally with intensity of pressure, p being directly proportional to the depth of water from free surface, h. The relationship is as follows:

$$p = wh$$

Hence the variation is triangular in shape.

The resultant water pressure can be resolved into horizontal component as well as vertical component.

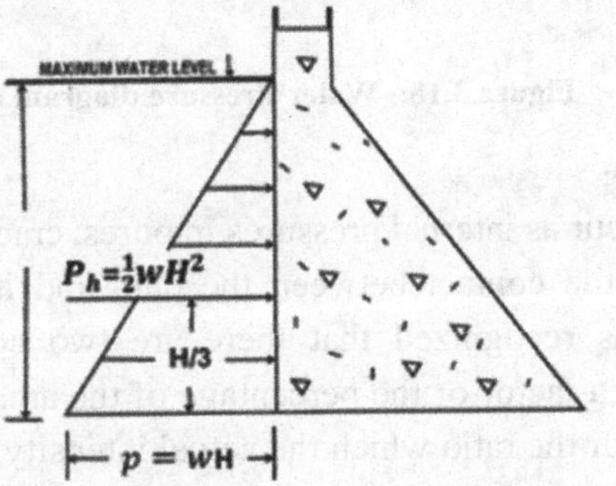

Figure 3.17: Water Pressure diagram at upstream side (u/s)

The horizontal component is P_h, and vertical component P_v which is acting due to the weight of the water supported by the inclined face.

The horizontal component $P_h = (\frac{1}{2})\ wH^2$ acts at a height of $\frac{H}{3}$ from the base of the gravity dam, i.e. $\frac{2}{3}H$ from the surface of water in the upstream pool or reservoir. Here w =unit weight of water.

The horizontal component is only considered when the upstream face of the gravity dam is vertical.

When there is an inclined upstream surface, the weight of water on this inclined portion is considered as the vertical force.

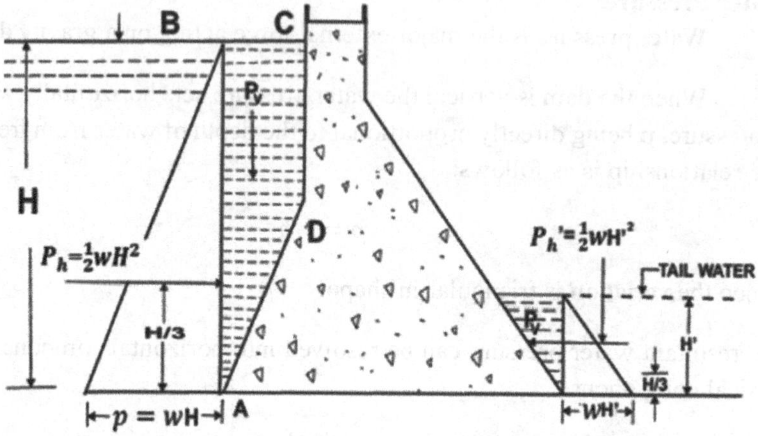

Figure 3.18: Water Pressure diagram at u/s and d/s

c. **Uplift Pressure:**

Uplift forces occur as internal pressures in pores, cracks and seams within the body of the dam, at the contact between the dam and its foundation and within the foundation. It is recognized that there are two constituent elements in uplift pressure; the area factor or the percentage of the area on which uplift acts and the intensity factor or the ratio which the actual intensity of uplift pressure bears to the intensity gradient extending from head water to tailwater at various points *(IS : 6512 – 1984).*

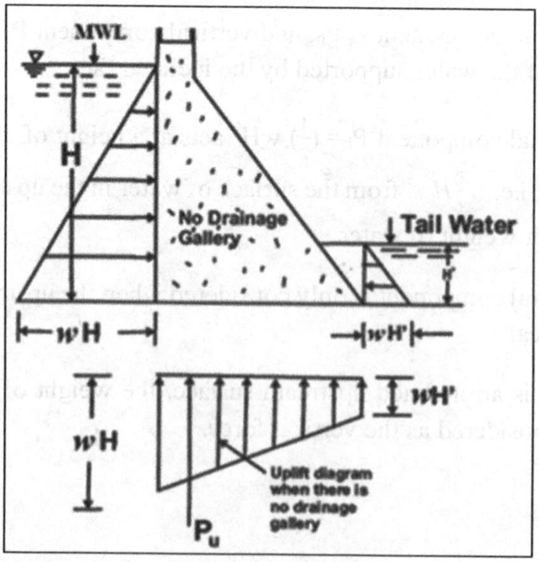

Figure 3.19: Uplift Pressure Diagram when there is no drainage gallery provided in the dam

i. The uplift force virtually reduces the downward weight of the body of the dam and hence acts against the dam stability.

ii. United States Bureau of Reclamation (U.S.B.R) suggest the following-
   - The uplift pressure at heel=WH
   - Uplift pressure at toe=WH'
   - Uplift pressure at drainage gallery $w\left[H' + \frac{1}{3}(H - H')\right]$

Some of the techniques by which uplift pressure can be controlled are:

i. by constructing cut-off walls under the upstream face,

ii. by constructing drainage channels between the dam and its foundation and

iii. by pressure grouting the foundation.

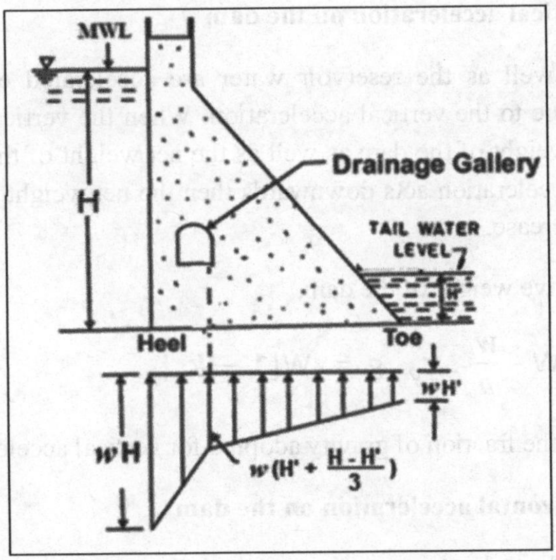

Figure 3.20: Distribution of Uplift Pressure when drainage gallery is provided in the gravity dam

Force on the dam due to earthquake

If the dam is to be located in an earthquake prone region, then allowance must be made for the stresses generated by the earthquakes. The effect of earthquake forces depends on the following:

- The magnitude and severity of earthquake
- The mass of the structure and its elasticity.
- The earthquake effects on the load of the water

Earthquake wave may travel in any direction as it has the capacity of shaking the earth on which dam is being constructed. The knowledge of earthquake acceleration or intensity is useful for the estimation of earthquake load.

- For design purpose earthquake acceleration has to be resolved in horizontal as well as vertical components.
- The horizontal acceleration is α_h and vertical acceleration is α_v which are generally expressed in relation to acceleration due to gravity.
- According to IS 1893:2002, India is divided into four seismic zones II, III, IV, V and zone V being the most serious one which covers the Himalayan and north regions of India.

Effect of vertical acceleration on the dam

The dam as well as the reservoir water are accelerated either vertically upwards or downwards due to the vertical acceleration. When the vertical acceleration acts upwards then the net weight of the dam as well as the net weight of the water will increase. When the vertical acceleration acts downwards then the net weight of the dam as well as of the water will decrease.

The net effective weight of the dam,

$$W - \frac{W}{g} \cdot k_v \cdot g = W\lfloor 1 - k_v \rfloor$$

Where k_v is the fraction of gravity adopted for vertical acceleration such as 0.1 or 0.2 etc.

Effect of horizontal acceleration on the dam

The horizontal acceleration may be caused due to:

- Inertia force in the body of the dam.
- Hydrodynamic pressure of the water.

a. Inertia force in the body of the dam

- Inertia force is the product of mass and acceleration and it acts opposite in the direction of the ground motion.
- For stability analysis we have to choose the direction of this force in such a way that it produces most unfavourable effects under the considered conditions.

- The stability analysis for reservoir empty condition may be carried out only on the basis of weight of the dam and by ignoring the earthquake forces.

- The horizontal inertia force

$$= \frac{W}{g} \times \alpha_h = \frac{W}{g} \times k_h \times g = W \times k_h$$

Where k_h is the fraction of gravity adopted for horizontal acceleration such as 0.1 or 0.2 etc.

b. Hydrodynamic pressure of the water

- The momentary increase in water pressure is due to the horizontal acceleration of the dam and foundation towards the reservoir.

- The additional water pressure above the static water pressure is known as hydrodynamic pressure.

- According to Von-Karman, the amount of this hydrodynamic force (P_e) is given by,

$$P_e = 0.555 \,.\, k_h w H^2$$

And it acts at a height of $\frac{4H}{3\pi}$ above the base.

Where k_h is the fraction of gravity adopted for horizontal acceleration such as 0.1 or 0.2 etc.

w = unit weight of water

Moment of this force about the base,

$$= M_e = P_e\left(\frac{4H}{3\pi}\right) = 0.424\, P_e \,.\, H$$

- Zanger gave the formula for computing the hydrodynamic force exerted on the vertical and sloping face of the dam.

The formula was based on electrical analogy and on the assumption that water is incompressible and here the pressure variation is elliptical cum parabolic.

According to Zanger,

$$P_e = 0.726\, p_e \,.\, H$$

Where $p_e = C_m\, k_h\, w\, H$

Thus, $P_e = 0.726\; C_m\, k_h\, w H^2$

Where, C_m = Maximum value of pressure coefficient for a given constant slope $=0.735\left[\frac{\theta}{90}\right]$, where θ= angle in degrees which the upstream face of the dam makes with the horizontal. k_h is the fraction of gravity adopted for horizontal acceleration such as 0.1 or 0.2 etc. w = unit weight of water.

The moment of this force about the base is given by $M_e = 0.412\ P_e$ H

Ice Pressure

- The force due to ice pressure is to be considered for dams in cold countries.
- Due to temperature variation, ice formed on the surface of the reservoir is subjected to expansion and contraction.
- The dam face has to resist the force due to the expansion of ice.

Silt Pressure

The construction of the dam across the river carrying sediment results in reservoir sedimentation which causes additional force on the upstream face of the dam.

$$P_{silt} = \frac{1}{2} \cdot \gamma_{sub} \cdot h^2 \cdot K_a \text{ which acts as } \frac{h}{3} \text{ from the base.}$$

Wave Pressure

- Waves are generated on the surface of the reservoir by the blowing winds which causes a pressure additional to the static water pressure towards the downstream side.
- Wave pressure depends on the height of the waves developed.
- Wave height can be calculated using the following relation-
- For F< 32 km,

$$h_w = 0.032\sqrt{V} \cdot \sqrt{F} + 0.763 - 0.271\, F^{\frac{3}{4}}$$

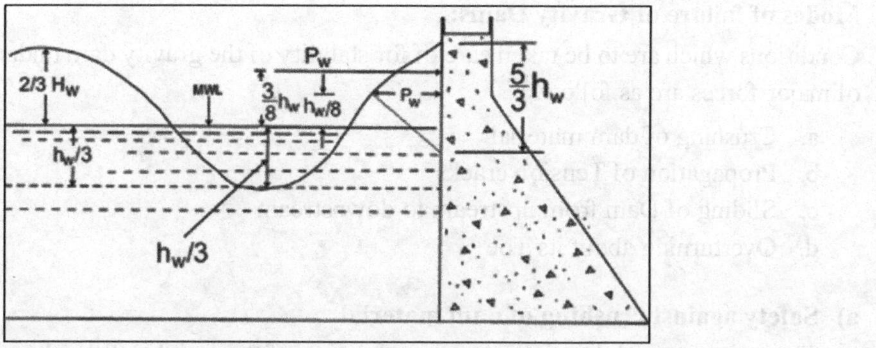

Figure 3.21: Wave pressure diagram

For F> 32 km,

$$h_w = 0.032\ \sqrt{V}\ .\ \sqrt{F}$$

Where, h_w = height of water waves in meters between crest and trough.

V = wind velocity in km/hr and F = fetch or straight length of water expanse in km.

Free Board - Free board is the vertical distance between the top of the dam and still water level. The free board shall be wind set-up plus 14 times wave height above normal pool elevation or above maximum reservoir level corresponding to the design flood, whichever gives higher crest elevation for the dam. The free board shall not, however, be less than 1.0 m above mean water level (MWL) corresponding to the design flood. If design flood is not same as probable maximum flood (PMF) than the top of dam shall not be lower than MWL corresponding to PIMF. Notwithstanding the above requirement, 1.0 m high solid parapet shall be provided on the upstream side above the top of the dam in all cases (*IS : 6512 – 1984).*

Thermal Loads - Measures for temperature control of concrete in solid gravity dams are adopted during construction. Yet it is noticed that stresses in the dam are affected due to temperature variation in the dam on the basis of data recorded from the thermometer embedded in the body of the dam. The cyclic variation of air temperature and the solar radiation on the downstream side and the reservoir temperature on the upstream side also affect the stresses in the dam. Even the deflection of the dam is maximum in the morning and it goes on reducing toga minimum value in the evening. The magnitude of deflection is also affected depending on

whether the spillway is running or not. It is generally less when spillway is working than when it is not working. While considering the thermal load, temperature gradients are assumed (*IS : 6512 – 1984*).

Modes of failure of Gravity Dams:

Conditions which are to be taken care of for stability of the gravity dam under the influence of major forces are as follows:

a. Crushing of dam material
b. Propagation of Tension cracks
c. Sliding of Dam from upstream to downstream
d. Overturning about its Toe

a) Safety against crushing of dam material

The stress created due to the combined action of the weight of the dam as the vertical force and the horizontal force due to the water in the upstream reservoir should be less than the compressive strength of the dam material to avoid crushing.

Hence the famous middle third rule should be satisfied, i.e., the Resultant force should lie within the middle third of the base.

$$p_{max/min} = \frac{W}{B}\left(1 \pm \frac{6e}{B}\right)$$

where p is the stress created at the base of the dam due to horizontal and vertical forces; W is the weight of the dam; B is the base width of the dam, e is the eccentricity of the resultant force.

b) Propagation of Tension cracks

- When the reservoir is empty, to avoid tension within the dam, the resultant force should remain within the inner third point.
- Under full reservoir conditions, to prevent tension at the heel, the resultant force, which is the sum of all acting forces, must pass through the outer middle third point. The maximum eccentricity (*e*) value is *B*/6 when the resultant lies at the outer middle third point

By taking the moment of all forces about *B* and setting it to zero, we arrive at the equation $\boldsymbol{W.B/3 - U.B/3 - P.H/3 = 0}$. Solving this yield different base width (*B*) depending on the intensity of uplift pressure (*C*):

- If the uplift pressure intensity $\boldsymbol{C = 1}$, then $\boldsymbol{B = \frac{H}{\sqrt{(S_m - 1)}}}$
- If the uplift pressure intensity $\boldsymbol{C = 0}$, then $\boldsymbol{B = \frac{H}{\sqrt{S_m}}}$

Where $\boldsymbol{S_m}$ is the specific gravity of the dam material.

c) Sliding of Dam from upstream to downstream

The forces that cause sliding must be less than the forces that resist sliding in order to prevent sliding. These two forces should be equal and opposing in the critical condition, and to ensure safety against sliding, the force causing sliding should be less than the frictional force that opposes this sliding force. Hence, the factor of safety should be more than one.

$$\frac{\mu\Sigma V}{\Sigma H} > 1$$

where, μ is the coefficient of friction between the founding soil and the dam material.

c) Overturning of the dam

This case generally does not occur, as the dam material will fail due to crushing before it overturns about its toe.

Base Width with No Tension:

- When the reservoir is empty, to avoid tension within the dam, the resultant force should remain within the inner third point *A*.
- Under full reservoir conditions, to prevent tension at the heel, the resultant force (*R*), which is the sum of all acting forces, must pass through the outer middle third point *B*. The maximum eccentricity (*e*) value is *B*/6 when the resultant (*R*) aligns with point *B*.

By taking the moment of all forces about *B* and setting it to zero, we arrive at the equation $\boldsymbol{W.B/3 - U.B/3 - P.H/3 = 0}$. Solving this yield different base width (*B*) depending on the intensity of uplift pressure (*C*):

- If the uplift pressure intensity $\boldsymbol{C = 1}$, then $\boldsymbol{B = \frac{H}{\sqrt{(G-1)}}}$
- If the uplift pressure intensity $\boldsymbol{C = 0}$, then $\boldsymbol{B = \frac{H}{\sqrt{G}}}$

Base width for no Sliding:

The forces that cause sliding must be less than the forces that resist sliding in order to prevent sliding. These two forces should be equal and opposing in the critical condition, $\mu\Sigma V = \Sigma H$

where, u is the coefficient of friction.

$$\mu\,(W-U) = P \quad \text{or} \quad P = \mu\,(W-U)\ \frac{1}{2}wH^2 = \mu\left(\frac{1}{2}\mathbf{BHGw} - \frac{1}{2}\mathbf{BCwH}\right)$$

$$\text{or} \quad H^2 = \mu(BHG - BHC)$$

$$\text{or} \quad H = \mu B(G - C)$$

$$\textbf{or} \quad \mathbf{B} = \frac{H}{\mu(G-C)}$$

3.3.4 Drainage gallery of gravity dam

Horizontal and sloping openings also known as passages in the body of the dam are known as galleries. These are generally provided to collect seepage water from the foundation and body of the dam. They may run parallel and normal to dam axis. Most galleries are related to one another. The magnitude of the dam and the gallery's intended purpose are the main factors influencing its dimensions.

Foundation galleries are otherwise known as the Drainage galleries. In order to aid in the drainage of water seeping through the foundations, this specific gallery is located near to the rock foundation. It follows the dam's upstream face lengthwise. This drain's average dimensions are 1.5 × 2.2 m to 1.8 × 2.4 m. When the grouting of the foundation is complete, drain holes are bored out of the gallery floor. These holes effectively catch the most seepage. They also help with foundation drilling and grouting, which is especially useful when the work cannot be done from the dam's surface.

3.3.5 Joints in Gravity Dams

In substantial gravity dams, construction joints are a common inclusion to manage several structural needs. When dealing with particularly thick dams, longitudinal joints become essential. Their purposes include controlling potential cracking, accommodating volumetric changes due to temperature fluctuations or moisture content alterations, and simplifying the construction process. These joints are designed to effectively transfer both compressive and shear stresses across the sections of the dam and are typically grouted post-cooling to ensure durability and structural integrity, as outlined in the ICOLD (International Commission on Large Dams) bulletin 107 on concrete dams.

The necessity for construction joints stems from the impracticality of placing concrete in a continuous process throughout the entirety of a large structure's construction. These joints provide a systematic method to pause and later resume work without compromising the structure's stability or integrity. Concrete, inherently susceptible to volume changes due to shrinkage or temperature variations, requires these strategically placed joints. They serve the crucial role of alleviating tensile or compressive stresses induced within the dam structure, thereby preventing damage and preserving the dam's long-term functionality and safety.

The joints provided in the gravity dam are generally divided in to two types.

a. **Construction joints**: A dam is not concreted all at once; rather, it is done in lifts, or stages. One layer of concrete is put at a time in each lift. Each lift of a concrete dam is normally about 1.5 meters thick. Every construction joint function as a contraction joint by counteracting the stresses associated with contraction. Two adjacent joints should ideally differ as little as possible. Nevertheless, observable deviations may result from practical issues including difficulties laying concrete and the need to account for shrinkage and temperature strains.

   A construction joint is the term used to describe the horizontal joint that separates two successive lifts. Each concreting layer's lift is chosen to allow for efficient cooling of the concrete throughout the setting process by both artificial and natural methods. The lowest layer of concrete is preserved at half its thickness, or roughly 0.75 meters. Water stops or keys in construction joints are no longer nearly as necessary thanks to modern surface treatment processes before adding a new layer of concrete.

b. **Contraction joints:** Contraction joints are provided to avoid development of shrinkage cracks in the dam due to temperature changes. Cracking due to shrinkage of the concrete can be controlled to some extent by properly controlling the temperature and adopting proper methods of curing. But provision of contraction joints in dams is very essential. Construction joints may further be classified in to transverse contraction joints and longitudinal contraction joints.

   i. **Transverse contraction joints:** These joints are at right angles to the axis of the dam. The spacing of this type of joints depends on factors like topographical features, the dam location, type of cement and climatic conditions, but in general practice the spacing is restrict about to 15 m or the height of the dam whichever is small. These joints are generally extended throughout the height of the dam. To insure proper connection between adjacent parts so that stresses are properly transmitted, the joints are either filled by grouting or by leaving a slot which is filled later when shrinking ceases. The joints may not be grouted and are made water tight by introducing water stops or key ways in the joints.

   ii. **Longitudinal contraction joints:** These joints are provided mostly along the direction of the axis of dam. These joints are considered objectionable from safety point of view as they may coincide very closely with the planes of maximum shear. Longitudinal joints do not run continuously and they are staggered in plan as shown in Figure below.

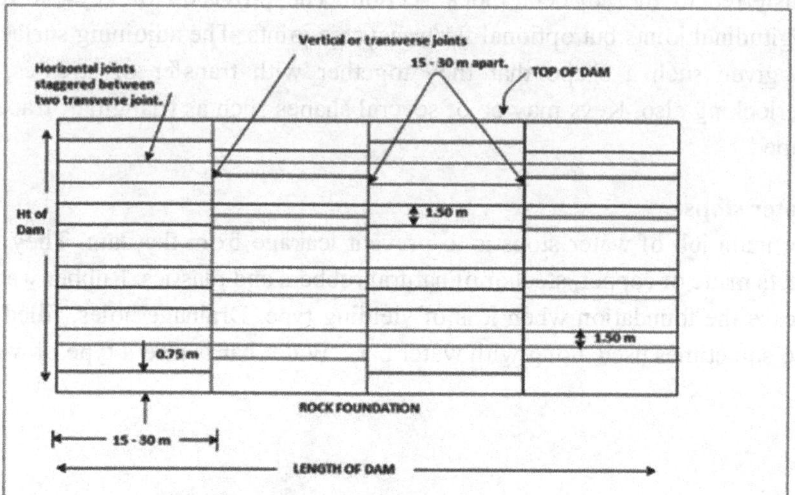

Figure 3.22: Joints in concrete gravity Dam

However, they are continuous in the vertical direction. They are laid in between two adjacent transverse joints. The spacing of these joints is also limited to about 15 m. These joints are provided with the key ways so as to transmit the principal stresses. Spacing of key ways in vertical direction is 1.5 m or one key way is to be provided in each lift.
The guidance regarding the placement of longitudinal joints in large gravity dam structures varies, with some advocating for very close spacing of these joints, around 15 meters, or even suggesting their complete omission. Specifically, the Bureau of Indian Standard Specifications, through its IS Code, recommends not incorporating longitudinal joints as a consideration for enhancing safety. This recommendation stems from a focus on ensuring the structural integrity and long-term durability of such dams, suggesting that eliminating these joints could potentially reduce weak points where cracking or failure might initiate, thus bolstering the dam's overall safety profile. "Basically, IS Code recognising the practice of dividing a monolith block into two or more blocks by introducing joints parallel to the axis of Dam as unsound. However, if necessary, a high degree of perfection has to be ensured by providing suitable shear keys and then properly grouting the joints to create a monolithic block".
IS Code:6512 on "Criteria for Design of Solid Gravity Dams" vide clause 7.1.1.1 states that "It is now being increasing accepted that better alternative is to achieve necessary temperature control by pre-cooling of concrete supplemented wherever necessary by post-cooling and avoid longitudinal joints altogether, even in case of high dams."

Keys
These are devices, by means of which shearing stresses from one block section are transferred to the adjacent block section. The provision of keys is very essential for longitudinal joints but optional for transverse joints. The adjoining surfaces of each block are given such a shape that they together with transfer of stresses, cause effective interlocking also. Keys may be of several shapes such as triangular, trapezoidal or trough shaped.

Water stops
The main job of water stops is to prevent leakage from the dam. They may be made of sheets made of copper, steel or of natural rubbers and plastics. Rubber water stops are used in case the foundation when it is of yielding type. Drainage holes, filled with asphalt are also sometimes used along with water bars. Water bar is also a type of water stops.

3.3.6 Concept of High and Low Gravity Dam

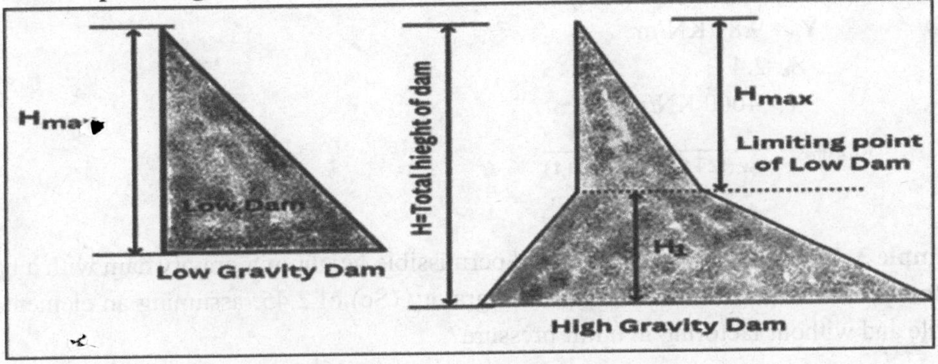

Figure 3.23: Low and High gravity dam

A gravity dam classified as low has a height that does not surpass a specified maximum value (H_{max}), whereas a high gravity dam exceeds this limit. The designation of a dam as low gravity hinges on its base width being calculated with the aim that the resulting force falls as near as possible to the outer edges of the base's middle third. Conversely, for a dam deemed high, allowing the resultant force to traverse through the middle third's point would result in surpassing the allowable stress limits.

Here $H_{max} = \dfrac{\sigma}{\gamma_w (S_c+1)}$

Where,

σ = Compressive Strength of the material of construction of the dam

γ_w = Specific weight of water

S_c= Specific gravity of dam material

Example 1. What is the vertical stress distribution at the base of the gravity dam when the reservoir is empty?

Solution: Given: $\sum V = W$, $e = \frac{B}{6}$

We know $P_{max/min} = \frac{W}{B}(1 \pm \frac{6e}{B}) = \frac{W}{B}(1 \pm \frac{6 \times B}{B \times 6})$

So $P_{max} = \frac{2W}{B}$ and $P_{min} = 0$

Hence, the maximum vertical stress equal to $\frac{2W}{B}$ act at the heel and zero at toe.

Example 2. What is the maximum height for a small concrete gravity dam built with concrete that has a strength of 4000 KN/m^2, given that Sc=2.4?

Solution: We know $H_{max} = \frac{f}{Y_w(S_c+1)}$

$Y_w = 9.81$ KN/m^2

$S_c = 2.4$

$f = 4000$ KN/m^2

So $H_{max} = \frac{f}{Y_w(S_c+1)} = \frac{4000}{9.8(2.4+1)}$

$= \mathbf{120m}$

Example 3. What would be the estimated permissible height of a gravity dam with a base width of 35 meters and a material specific gravity (Sc) of 2.45, assuming an elementary profile and without factoring in uplift pressure?

Solution: The base width at bottom is given by $B = H/S_c^{1/2}$ ($c = 0$ since uplift is not considered).

$B = 35$ m and $S_c = 2.45$

Hence, allowable height of the dam:

$H = 35 \times 2.45^{1/2} = 54.8$ m.

3.4 Spillways

A spillway serves as a critical mechanism for the controlled release of excess water from a reservoir to the downstream area. Once the reservoir reaches its normal pool level, water begins to overflow across the spillway crest and descends back into the main course of the Parent River. The water level can escalate beyond the spillway crest but should not surpass the maximum reservoir level. Thus, the spillway stands as the sole structure tasked with managing surplus water, ensuring it does not exceed the reservoir's capacity. Without such a facility, the dam could face catastrophic failure due to water breaching the maximum allowable level. Therefore, the spillway acts as an indispensable safety feature within a dam's design.

3.4.1 Functions of a spillway:

Spillways, which either form a part of a dam's structure or are situated adjacent to one, play a crucial role when a reservoir reaches full capacity. Their purpose is to facilitate the safe and regulated passage of floodwaters over the dam, directing the excess water back into the originating river. Once the dam's reservoir hits the normal pool level, water begins to overflow the spillway crest. The water's ascent to the maximum reservoir level, determined through flood routing, is managed by the spillway—the sole structure capable of handling such overflow without letting the water exceed the dam's maximum capacity. In the absence of a spillway, floodwaters might surpass the dam's freeboard, potentially causing overtopping and, ultimately, dam failure. Therefore, the design of an adequately proportioned spillway is vital for the dam's integrity and safety.

3.4.2 Location of a Spillway:

a. A spillway's positioning can vary significantly: it may be integrated into the dam's structure, located at either or both ends of the dam, or situated completely apart from the dam in a nearby saddle. If the terrain features a deep, narrow gorge with steep sides, set apart from a flank by a small hill whose peak is higher than the dam's crest, placing the spillway independently of the dam is often the most advantageous option.

b. In such scenarios, a dam, either concrete or earthen, can span the main valley, while the spillway is constructed separately in the saddle. At times, it's feasible to build a concrete or masonry dam complete with its spillway in the main valley and use earthen dikes or embankments to seal off the flanks. Though independent spillways are typically favoured for earthen dams to mitigate risks, the absence of suitable locations may necessitate the incorporation of a concrete spillway within or at the extremities of an earthen dam.

3.4.3 Types and Components of Spillways

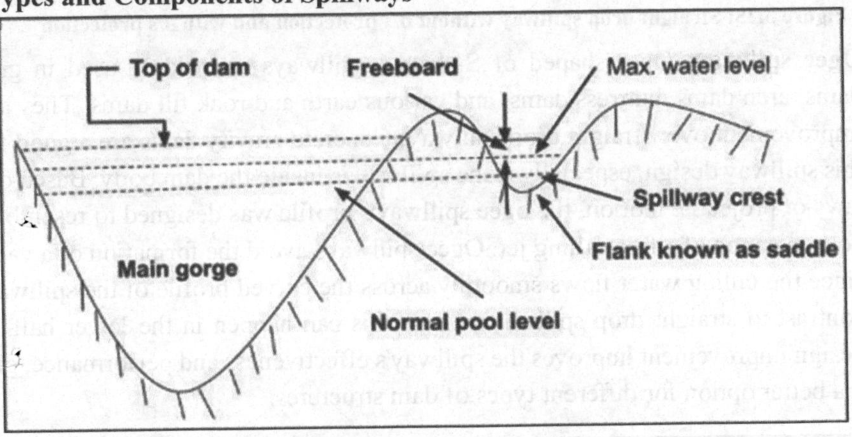

Figure 3.24: Location of spillway

The classification of spillways is primarily based on the structural form employed to manage and discharge excess water. These major types include:

a. **Straight Drop Spillway or Overfall Spillway:** The free overfall spillway stands as the most basic form of spillway. In this design, water cascades directly from the spillway's crest to the riverbed below, which can sometimes lead to scouring and the creation of pools. This spillway design is compatible with arch dams, earthen dams, and levees. Its downstream face is typically vertical or slightly sloped, allowing water to drop freely under gravity's influence. The formation of vacuums under the water jet is a possibility, necessitating adequate ventilation beneath the nappe to mitigate the pulsating and fluctuating effects on the water jet. To safeguard against the erosion (scouring) of the downstream bed caused by the impact of the falling water jet, an engineered pool equipped with a concrete apron and a smaller, secondary dam may be constructed downstream. Ensuring proper ventilation under the falling jet is crucial to avoid the aforementioned pulsating effects. Occasionally, an extended lip is added to the weir's crest to block small volumes of water from flowing down the weir wall's face.

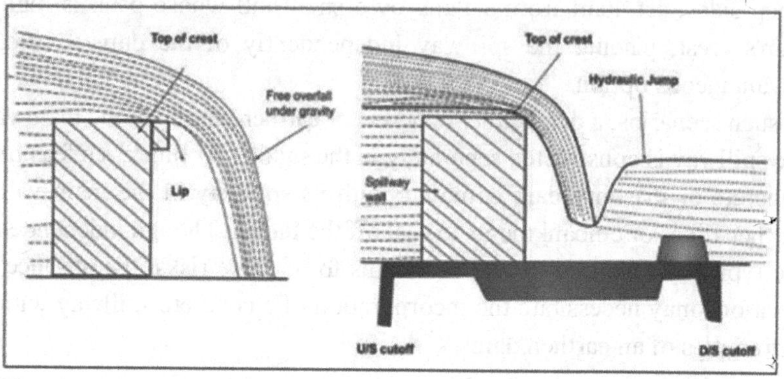

Figure 3.25: Straight drop spillway without d/s protection and with d/s protection

b. **Ogee spillway:** Ogee-shaped or S-shaped spillways are widely used in gravity dams, arch dams, buttress dams, and various earth and rock fill dams. They are an improvement over straight drop spillway. Concrete gravity dams are a good fit for this spillway design, especially if the spillway is inside the dam body. Based on the laws of projectile motion, the ogee spillway's profile was designed to resemble the bottom nappe of a free-falling jet. Ogee spillways avoid the formation of a vacuum since the falling water flows smoothly across the curved profile of the spillway, in contrast to straight drop spillways where this can happen in the lower half. This design improvement improves the spillway's effectiveness and performance, giving it a better option for different types of dam structures.

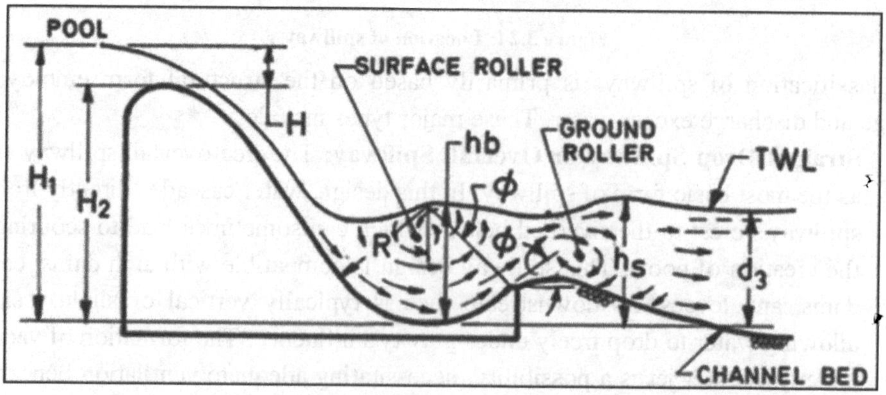

Figure 3.26: Ogee spillway with energy dissipator at downstream

(Source: *https://www.researchgate.net/figure/Solid-bucket-Bhavan-and-Shahzafar-2010-d-3-height-of-tailwater-above-bucket_fig3_343278067*)

Figure 3.27: Ogee spillway (Cidra Dam)
(**Source:** *https://energyeducation.ca/encyclopedia/Spillway*)

c. **Chute Spillway:** A chute spillway, also known as a trough spillway, is typically constructed in a flank or saddle area distinct from the main valley where the dam is located. This design is especially favoured for earthen and rock fill dams. In addition, because the main valley is narrow, chute spillways are frequently required for gravity dams. The simplest kind of spillway is this one, which can be installed separately with ease and at a reasonable cost.

Figure 3.28: Chute spillway (Benmore Earth Dam)
(**Source:** *https://pespk.com/portfolio/diversion-weir-of-kabul-weir/*)

The chute spillway's slope was thoughtfully planned to guarantee that the flow would always remain in a supercritical state. Energy dissipaters can be installed on the chute spillway's bed to disperse the energy from the falling water. In relation to earthen and rock fill dams, this design works well for controlling high-velocity water flow. The purpose of chute spillways is to transport supercritical flow in an open channel down a steep slope. The entrance, the steeply sloped channel, the outflow, and the vertical curve section which is frequently shaped like an ogee curve—are the four main parts of a chute spillway. The spillway's slope needs to be steep enough to guarantee that the flow stays in the supercritical state as it descends in order to avoid hydraulic jumps. In order to keeps the chute spillway functioning effectively and efficiently for controlling high-velocity water flow, this is an essential design element.

d. **Side Channel Spillway**: The fundamental difference between a chute spillway and a side channel spillway is where the crest is positioned. The crest of a chute spillway is located between the side walls, while the crest of a side channel spillway is located on one of its sides. Stated differently, water in a chute spillway flows over the weir crest at a straight angle. On the other hand, with a side channel spillway, the water flows parallel to the crest after turning 90 degrees to spill from the crest.

Figure 3.29: Side Channel spillway

(**Source:** *https://odishabytes.com/youth-falls-into-power-channel-in-odishas-sambalpur/*)

When there is not enough width on the flanks, side channel spillways are usually preferred over chute spillways, usually to prevent significant excavation. It is possible to change the angle at which the water flow turns from 0 to 90 degrees once it passes the weir crest

e. **Shaft Spillway or Morning Glory Spillway**: With this spillway design, the reservoir water first enters a vertical shaft and then travels via a horizontal tunnel before emptying into the riverbed downstream. Common materials utilised in the construction of small-height shaft spillways include metal, concrete, and clay tiles. However, reinforced cement concrete is the material of choice for projects that are taller. The "morning glory" inlet, a flared inlet, is frequently included in large-height spillway projects to improve the inlet design. Smaller shaft spillways normally do not require this design.

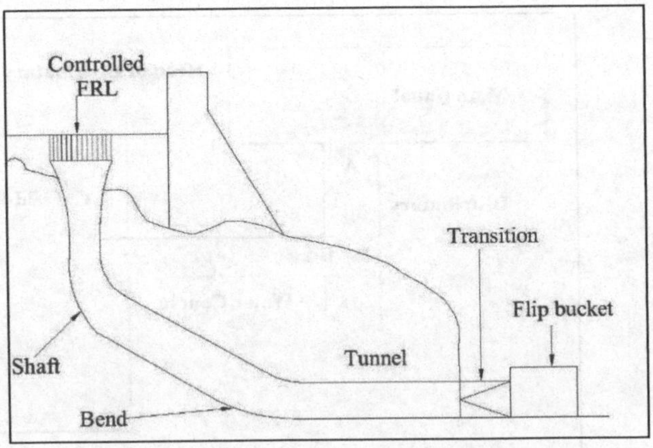

Figure 3.30: Components of a Shaft spillway

Figure 3.31: Shaft Spillway of Tehri Dam on River Ganga

f. **Siphon Spillway**: As its name implies, this spillway operates on the basis of a symphonic action. It is made consisting of a syphon pipe, the end of which should always be on the reservoir's upstream side while the other end releases water onto the downstream side. Two types of installation of siphon are shown below:

i. Tilted outlet type: This kind of outlet may have an air vent and is created by inserting a syphon pipe inside the dam's structural body. In order to keep ice and debris out of the dam, the air vent's opening is usually placed lower. To stop air from entering, the pipe's outlet side is submerged in the downstream side. When the water level of the dam is higher than the average pool level, symphonic action takes place.

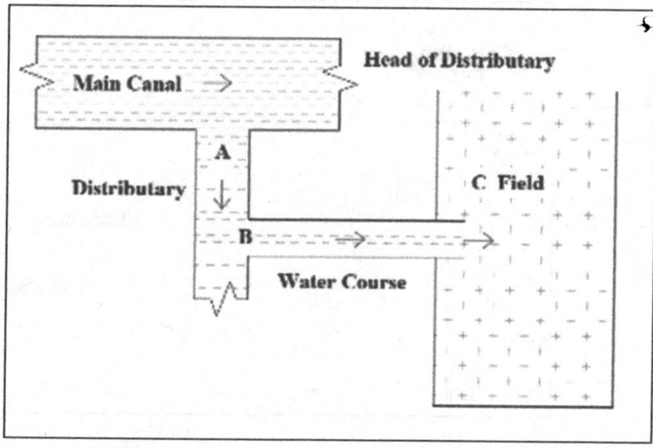

Figure 3.32: Components of siphon Spillway of tilted outlet type

Figure 3.33: Siphon Spillway releasing excess water from the Power channel

This power channel leads water from tail race of the Power house of Hirakud Dam, near Burla town, Sambalpur to the Reservoir upstream of the Power house at Chiplima, near Sambalpur, Odisha for second phase of power generation.

Figure 3.34: Siphon spillway (Chopyeong Dam)

ii. Hooded type: This explains a syphon spillway, a form of spillway that is commonly used. This design places a reinforced concrete cover over the gravity dam's flow section. To keep ice and debris out, the hood's entrance is kept below water. Above the primary hood, there is also a deprimer hood, and an air vent connects the two. Normal circumstances cause the water to rise to the dam's crest when it reaches the reservoir's full level.
The entire above two type siphon spillways are called Saddle Siphon type spillway. In India another type known as Volute Siphon Type spillway was designed by Ganesh Iyer.

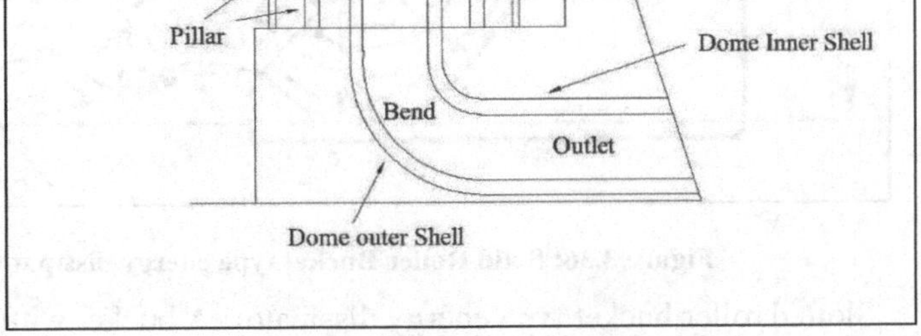

Figure 3.35: Volute Siphon type spillway

3.4.4 Energy Dissipators:

Water flowing down a spillway gains a lot of kinetic energy, especially as it approaches the spillway's toe. Significant scouring on the downstream side of the dam, both close to the toe and farther away, is possible in the absence of appropriate measures for the dissipation of this significant kinetic energy and the decrease in water velocity.

Energy dissipaters are structures or systems that are used to deal with this problem and disperse extra kinetic energy. Their goal is to stop erosion and other possible problems brought on by the flow over the spillway Various types of energy dissipators generally adopted for dissipating energy of water downstream of hydraulic structures are mentioned below:

Bucket type energy dissipaters

Due to formation of hydraulic jump on flip bucket at the base of a spillway and it deflect water upward direction which ultimately falls on the water cushion available at the downstream, leading to energy dissipation.

These may be of following types:

i. Solid roller bucket type energy dissipator: An upturned solid bucket is utilized in scenarios where the depth of the tail water significantly exceeds the sequent depth, leading to a substantial portion of energy dissipation through the creation of two complementary elliptical rollers. These rollers form due to the unique shape and orientation of the bucket. The first roller, known as the surface roller, occurs within the bucket itself and rotates in an anticlockwise direction when the flow is from left to right. The second, called the ground roller, forms downstream of the bucket and rotates in a clockwise direction. This configuration is particularly effective in dissipating the energy of the water jet, thereby reducing erosion and potential damage downstream of the spillway.

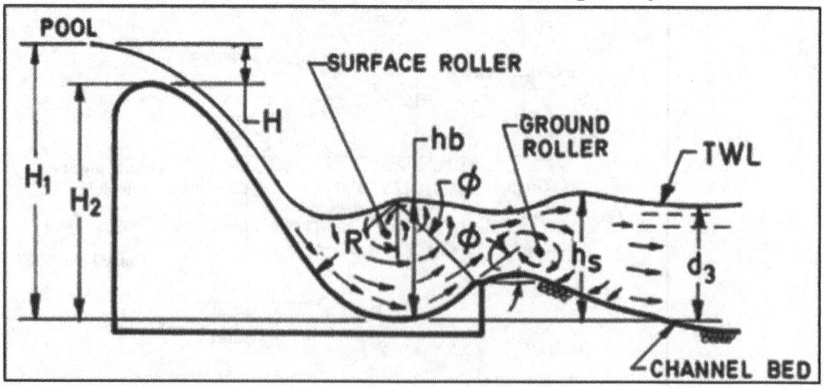

Figure 3.36: Solid Roller Bucket type energy dissipator

ii. Slotted roller bucket type energy dissipator: A bucket with teeth, turned upwards, is employed in situations where the depth of the downstream water significantly surpasses the subsequent depth. Here, energy dissipation is achieved through the sideward expansion of the jet that moves through the bucket's slots, coupled with the creation of two supplementary rollers, similar to those seen in a solid bucket.

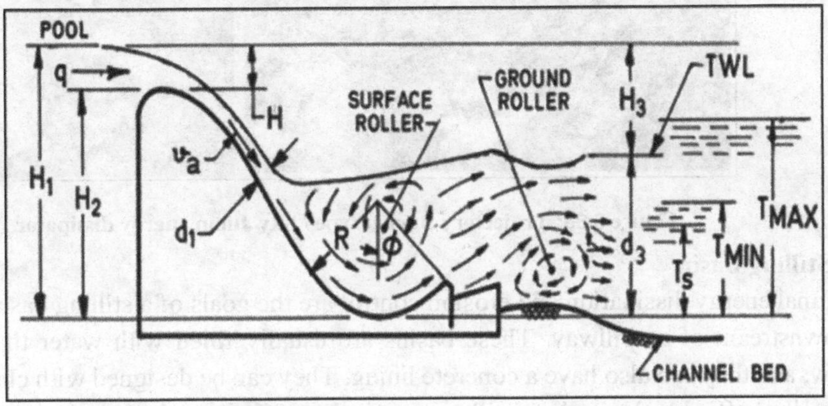

Figure 3.37: Slotted Roller Bucket type energy dissipator

iii. Trajectory Bucket/ Flip Bucket / Sky Jump Energy Dissipator: The ski jump is a type of energy dissipater that propels water into the air via a trajectory bucket, leading to its impact on the plunge pool. This impact disrupts the momentum, significantly lowering the flow velocity. In contrast, an upturned solid bucket is utilized when the depth of water downstream (tailwater) is too shallow for a hydraulic jump to form. This method is suitable when the riverbed downstream is composed of robust rock that can withstand the jet's high velocity without substantial erosion. The water flowing over the spillway is catapulted away from the dam's base, traveling a considerable distance downstream as a freely discharged, upward-facing jet before it directly enters the channel. This technique minimally dissipates energy within the bucket. Its primary purpose is to extend the distance between the structure and the point where the high-velocity jet contacts the riverbed, thereby minimizing the risk of severe erosion just downstream of the spillway.

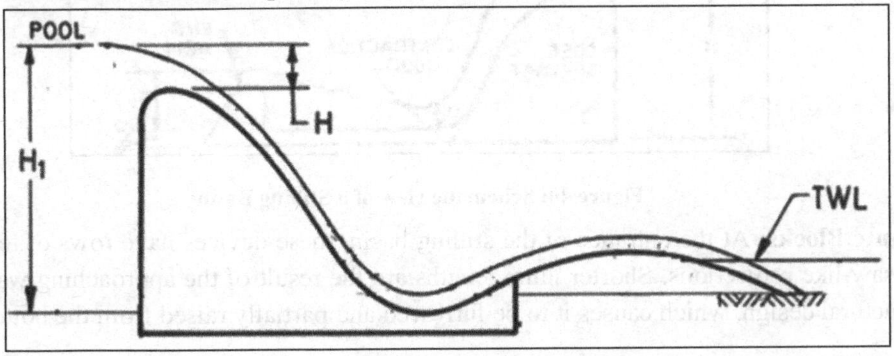

Figure 3.38: Trajectory Bucket type / Sky Jump energy dissipator

3.4.5 Stilling basin

Additional energy dissipation and erosion control are the goals of a stilling basin placed at the downstream of a spillway. These basins are usually filled with water that is rather shallow, and they can also have a concrete lining. They can be designed with chute blocks, wing walls, baffle blocks, and end sills, among other velocity-reducing elements.

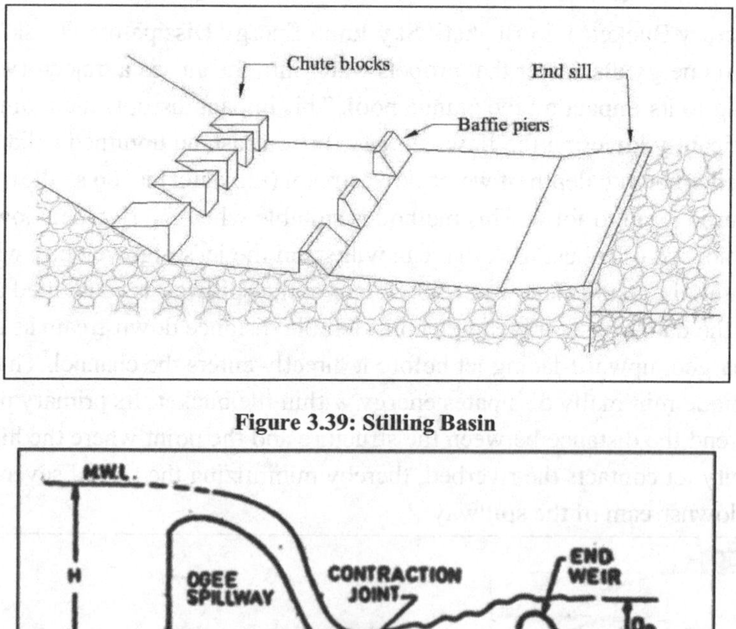

Figure 3.39: Stilling Basin

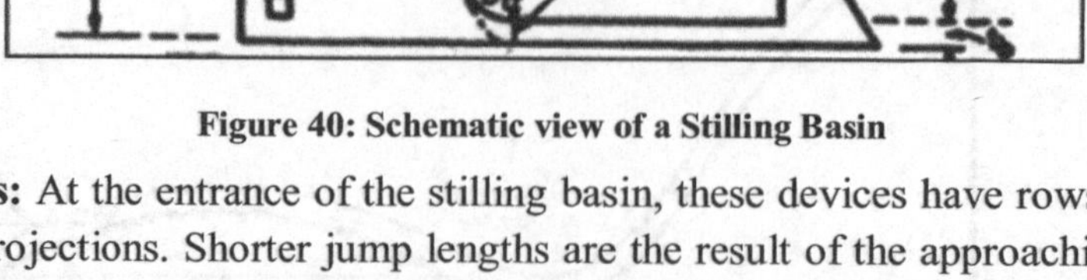

Figure 40: Schematic view of a Stilling Basin

Chute Blocks: At the entrance of the stilling basin, these devices have rows of teeth-like or saw-like projections. Shorter jump lengths are the result of the approaching water jet's structural design, which causes it to be furrowed and partially raised from the bottom.

Sill and Dentated Sills: These structures are usually erected at the end of a stilling basin. By acting as sills, the remaining part of the high-velocity jet is kept from reaching the basin's end. As a result, they help to shorten the jump distance and assist in releasing any stored energy.

Baffle Piers (or Basin Blocks): These are little bricks that are placed on the structure's basin floor with purpose. They function to disperse energy and lessen the flow. Known by another name, friction blocks, these piers are very useful in smaller constructions such as spillways and weirs. They can cause cavitation, although they perform well in huge works, especially when high-velocity jets are present.

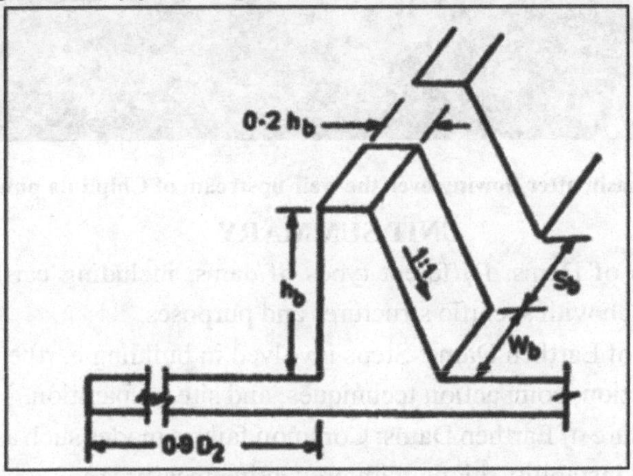

Figure 3.41: Baffle Block or Basin Block

(hb = height of basin block, Sb = spacing between the blocks. Wb = width of block, and D2= conjugate depth.)

Figure 3.42: Stilling basin (View during Maintenance work) at downstream of the weir at Chiplima power house

Figure 3.43: Stilling basin after flowing over the weir upstream of Chiplima power house, Odisha

UNIT SUMMARY

- Classification of Dams: Different types of dams, including earthen, gravity, and arch dams, each with specific structures and purposes.
- Construction of Earthen Dams: Steps involved in building earthen dams, including material selection, compaction techniques, and site preparation.
- Modes of Failure of Earthen Dams: Common failure modes such as seepage, piping, and structural instability, along with preventive measures.
- Design Principles for Gravity Dams: Key design principles, including stability analysis, material requirements, and structural calculations.
- Classification and Function of Spillways: Different types of spillways, their design criteria, and how they manage water discharge to protect dam structures.
- Types of Energy Dissipators: Various energy dissipators like stilling basins and baffle blocks, which reduce the kinetic energy of discharged water.

EXCERCISE

MULTIPLE CHOICE QUESTIONS

1. In comparison to a earth dam, gravity dams are generally:
   a. Less prone to failure
   b. More expensive
   c. Less demanding of skilled labor
   d. Dependent on solid rock foundations

2. The most appropriate material for constructing the impermeable core of a zoned type earthen dam is:
   a. Coarse sand
   b. Clay

c. Clay mixed with fine sand

d. Silty clay

3. To control seepage through the embankment of an earthen dam, one should utilize:

   a. Relief wells

   b. Drain trenches

   c. Drainage filters

   d. Downstream berms

4. Controlling seepage through the foundation of an earthen dam can be achieved by installing:

   a. Chimney Drain

   b. Horizontal blanket

   c. Impervious cutoff

   d. Rock Toe

5. Essential components of an earthen dam are:

   a. Shell

   b. Core

   c. The foundation

   d. All of these

6. The failure mechanisms for earthen dams are:

   a. Seepage failure

   b. Structural failure

   c. Hydraulic failure

   d. All of these

7. Which type of earthen dam is only appropriate for impervious foundation?

   a) Homogenous embankment type

   b) Diaphragm type

   c) Non-homogenous type

   d) Zoned embankment type

8. For which type of embankment is the thickness of the diaphragm less than 10 meters or the height of the embankment above the corresponding elevation?

   a) Zoned type dam

   b) Non-homogenous earth dam

   c) Homogenous earth dam

   d) Diaphragm type dam

9. The blanket in an earthen dam is provided:
   a) At ground level on the down-stream side
   b) At ground level on the upstream side
   c) At the ground level of the downstream side of the dam
   d) On the downstream slope of the earth dam

10. During the construction of an earthen dam by the hydraulic fill method, the development of pore water pressure is a concern in:
    a) Central impervious core
    b) Pervious outer shell
    c) Transition zone
    d) Both the central core and outer shell

11. The process of laying and compacting earth in layers using power rollers at optimal moisture content for the construction of earthen dams is known as:
    a) OMC method
    b) Hydraulic fill method
    c) Rolledfill method
    d) Compaction

12. What force is taken into account when analyzing the basic profile of a gravity dam when the reservoir is empty?
    a. Water pressure
    b. Self-weight
    c. Uplift pressure
    d. Pressure due to earthquake

13. For a gravity dam with a vertical upstream face, how does the intensity of water pressure at the water's surface compare to that at the base?
    a. 0 and wH^2
    b. $wH^2/2$ and $wH^2/3$
    c. wH and 0
    d. 0 and wH

14. In the scenario of a fully filled reservoir behind a gravity dam, which combination of vertical and horizontal earthquake accelerations is critical for stability assessment?
    a) vertically upward and horizontally downstream
    b) vertically downward and horizontally downstream
    c) vertically upward and horizontally upstream
    d) vertically downward and horizontally upstream

15. How can uplift pressure on a gravity dam be mitigated?
    a. Constructing cutoff under upstream face
    b. Constructing drainage channels between dam and its foundation
    c. By pressure grouting in foundation
    d. All of these

16. The uplift pressure in a dam's drainage gallery is considered as which of the following?
    a. Hydrostatic pressure at toe
    b. Average of hydrostatic pressure at toe and heel
    c. Two third of hydrostatic pressure at the toe plus one third of hydrostatic pressure at the heel
    d. None of these

17. What is the primary force that a gravity dam resists?
    a. Water pressure
    b. Wave pressure
    c. Self-weight of dam
    d. Uplift pressure

18. Horizontal earthquake acceleration results in what type of pressure in a gravity dam?
    a. Hydrodynamic pressure
    b. Inertia force into the body of the dam
    c. Both (a) and (b)
    d. None of the above

19. At what height does hydrodynamic pressure from an earthquake act?
    a. $3H/4\pi$ above the base
    b. $3H/4\pi$ below the water surface
    c. $4H/3\pi$ above the base
    d. $4H/3\pi$ below the water surface

20. Where does the total force from wave action on a gravity dam act?
    a. $h_w/2$ above the reservoir surface
    b. $5h_w/4$ above the reservoir surface
    c. $3h_w/8$ above the reservoir surface
    d. $2h_w/8$ above the reservoir surface

21. What shape does the basic profile of a dam typically have?
    a. A rectangle
    b. A trapezoid
    c. An equilateral triangle

d. A right-angled triangle

22. What is the maximum allowable eccentricity for preventing tension at the base of a gravity dam?
    a. B/2
    b. B/3
    c. B/4
    d. B/6

23. What formula determines the highest safe height for a gravity dam with a basic profile?
    a. $\frac{f}{w\sqrt{G+1}}$
    b. $\frac{f}{w\sqrt{G}}$
    c. $\frac{f}{w(G+1)}$
    d. $\frac{f}{w\sqrt{G-1}}$

    Where f = allowable stress on dam material, G = specific gravity of dam material, and w = unit weight of water.

24. Given that the effective length of a spillway crest is denoted as L, and the total head on the spillway crest, including velocity head, is H, how is the discharge through an ogee spillway calculated?
    a. $CLH^{3/2}$
    b. $CHL^{3/2}$
    c. $CLH^{5/2}$
    d. $CLH^{1/2}$

25. Which type of spillway is considered the least appropriate for use with an earthen dam?
    a. Ogee spillway
    b. Chute spillway
    c. Side channel spillway
    d. Shaft spillway

26. What is the typical flow condition in a chute spillway?
    a. Uniform
    b. Subcritical
    c. Critical
    d. Super critical

27. When there is a limitation of space due to the surrounding topography, which spillway design is most preferred?
    a. Straight drop spillway
    b. Shaft spillway
    c. Chute spillway
    d. Ogee spillway

28. How is the discharge coefficient of an ogee spillway affected?
    a. Depends on depth of approach and U/S slope
    b. Depends on D/S apron interference and D/s submergence
    c. Remains constant
    d. Both (a) and (b)

29. How does water flow after passing over the weir crest in both chute spillways and side channel spillways?
    a. At right angle and parallel to weir crest
    b. Parallel and right angle to weir crest
    c. Parallel to weir crest in both
    d. Right angle to weir crest in both

Answers

1	2	3	4	5	6	7	8	9	10
b	b	c	c	d	d	a	d	b	d

11	12	13	14	15	16	17	18	19	20
c	b	d	b	d	c	a	c	b	a

21	22	23	24	25	26	27	28	29
b	d	d	a	a	d	b	d	a

SHORT ANSWER TYPE QUESTIONS

1. Enumerate are the main advantages of earthen dam?
2. Mention the difference between Homogeneous embankment type and Zoned embankment type of earth dams.
3. Write down the components of an earthen dam?
4. Give your idea about the control of seepage through Chimney. drains in earthen dams.
5. Write the difference between hydraulic fill method and roll filled method of construction of an earth dam.
6. Explain the concept of hydraulic failure of an earthen dam.

7. What is seepage failure? Explain with examples.
8. Why is the name "gravity dam"?
9. In which site condition gravity dam construction is preferred?
10. Name different forces acting on the gravity dam.
11. Draw the elementary profile of a gravity dam.
12. Differentiate between a "high" and a "low" gravity dam.
13. Write short notes on earthquake forces acting on gravity dam.
14. What are different types of spillways?
15. Sketch an Ogee profile. Why is the name "Ogee"?
16. What is a spillway?
17. Differentiate between main spillway and subsidiary spillway.
18. What is a chute spillway?

LONG ANSWER TYPE QUESTIONS

1. Mention the types of earthen dams with illustrations.
2. Illustrate the phenomenon of seepage through earth dam and methods to control it.
3. Mention the methods of construction of earth dam with neat figures.
4. What are various types of failure of earthen dams? Mention the preventive measures.
5. Out of two different methods of construction of earth dam, which method is preferable to you and why?
6. Explain in detail about various forces acting on gravity dam for its stability. Explain with a neat labelled figure.
7. Describe about theoretical and practical profiles of a gravity dam.
8. Why are the joints provided in a gravity dam?
9. What are the benefits and drawbacks of using a gravity dam compared to an earthen dam?
10. What does the term "concrete gravity dams" refer to? Illustrate with a detailed diagram the cross-sectional view of such a dam. Provide an extensive description of the world's longest earthen dam, the largest by volume, the tallest gravity dam, the tallest arch dam, and the tallest rock fill dam. Additionally, include information about such dams located within India.
11. 'Spillway is the safety valve of a dam'- Briefly discuss on this statement.

12. What are spillways and where are they provided in a dam?
13. Briefly describe an Ogee spillway and give its discharge formula. Give two real life examples.
14. What is a syphon spillway? Describe its component parts. Substantiate your answer with a neat labeled sketch.
15. Enumerate the benefits of energy dissipators. Illustrate your answer with three real life examples with details.

PRACTICAL

Experiment 1: Draw a labelled sketch of the given masonry/earthen dam section. Write down the need of each part.

Experiment 2: Draw the theoretical and practical profile of a concrete gravity dam section. Why should there be a difference between them?

Experiment 3: Draw the profiles of the overflow section and non-overflow section of the concrete gravity dam of your choice, existing in any part of India. Mention the major differences between them.

KNOW MORE

Activity 1: Visit a Dam (either Earth Dam / Gravity Dam) in the vicinity of your place. Study the details of the dam and collect the data in line with the subject taught to you in this unit. Prepare a report, give critical comments on the usefulness of the dam, satisfaction level of the beneficiaries, improvements needed.

Activity 2: Visit a Dam (either Earth Dam / Gravity Dam) in the vicinity of your place. Study the details of the spillway of the dam and collect the data in line with the subject taught to you in this unit. Classify the spillway. Prepare a report, give critical comments on the usefulness of spillway, and if there is any improvement needed.

Activity 3: Study the details of the energy dissipator provided downstream of any hydraulic structure e.g. Spillway, or Weir and collect the data in line with the subject taught to you in this unit. Classify the energy dissipator you visited. Prepare a report, give critical comments on the usefulness of the energy dissipator and any improvement required.

Interesting Facts

Timelines

Throughout history, from the 8th century BC to the 6th century AD, stepped chute spillways have been used in various applications, including dam spillways, urban water supply channels, and drainage systems. The Kallanai dam, constructed by the Chola Dynasty around 100 BC on the Kaveri River in Tamil Nadu's Thanjavur district, stands as the oldest dam in India. In 1838, the East India Company built the Mukkombu dam on the Kaveri River in Tamil Nadu's Jeeyapuram village. By 1896, James Mahsergh had

introduced the Morning Glory spillway for England's Blackton reservoir. In 1898, Henry Bazin highlighted the significance of head geometry in spillway design.
The 1930s saw the construction of the first side channel spillway on the Hoover Dam. In 1953, a straight drop spillway was established at the Antony Falls Hydraulic Laboratory, University of Minnesota, Minneapolis, by the Agriculture Research Service Staff. The Bhavani Sagar Dam was erected on the Bhavani River in Tamil Nadu's Sathyamangalam district in 1955, becoming the largest earthen dam in India and South Asia, and the second largest globally. In 1957, the Hirakud dam was constructed on the Mahanadi River near Odisha's Sambalpur District, marking one of India's first major multipurpose river valley projects post-independence and the world's longest earthen dam.
The Rihand Dam, built in 1962 on Uttar Pradesh's Rihand River, became India's largest dam by volume, being a concrete gravity structure. The following year, the Bhakra Nangal Dam was raised on the Sutlej River in Himachal Pradesh's Bilaspur district, becoming the third-largest reservoir in India and a significant concrete gravity dam at 741 ft in height. In 1967, the Nagarjun Sagar Dam was constructed on the Krishna River in Andhra Pradesh's Guntur district, *holding the title of the second-largest reservoir in India with a masonry* dam standing 407 ft tall.
By 1970, Fernando M.M. Abecasis of Madrid, Spain, had fully designed the Ogee crest spillway. The Indira Sagar Dam, built in 2005 on the Narmada River in Madhya Pradesh's Khandwa district, was established as a multipurpose project. In 2006, the Tehri Dam was completed on the Bhagirathi River in Uttarakhand's Teri district, recognized as the highest dam in India and among the top ten globally, being an embankment dam with a height of 855 ft and a length of 1,886 ft. Lastly, in 2017, the Sardar Sarovar Dam was erected on the Narmada River in Gujarat's Navagam district, functioning as a concrete gravity dam.

Inquisitiveness

Definition of Large Dams For Inclusion Under National Register of Large Dams, India

The International Commission on big Dams (ICOLD) has established standards that define a dam as big if it is higher than 15 meters from the deepest foundation to the crest. Furthermore, a dam that has a height ranging from 10 to 15 meters from its deepest foundation is also considered large if it meets one or more specific conditions:

a. The length of the dam's crest is equal to or greater than 500 meters,

b. The reservoir capacity formed by the dam is not less than one million cubic meters,

c. The dam faces significant challenges with its foundation, or

d. The dam features an unconventional design.

When considering the criterion of "height" to classify dams as large or not, the above definition applies to dams other than those of Earthen and Rock fill types. However, for Earthen and Rock fill dams, the definition of large dams has been derived from the "IS 12169-1987 - Criteria for Design of Small Embankment Dams" for inclusion in the National Register of Large Dams (NRLD).

Large Dam: A dam is deemed large if its height surpasses 15 meters above the lowest point of the riverbed. Should the dam's height be between 10 and 15 meters, it qualifies as large provided the volume of earthwork involved is more than 0.75 million cubic meters or if its storage capacity is over 1 million cubic meters. Furthermore, a dam within this height bracket is also considered large if it has a peak flood discharge capacity greater than 2000 cubic meters per second.

Curiosity Topics

Before the 20th century, the evolution of fixed overflow hydraulic structures was deeply influenced by their distinctive head-discharge characteristics. Initially, their design was primarily driven by economic and construction factors, with little emphasis on the shape of the spillway crest in relation to discharge characteristics, especially at lower heads. However, as the head at the spillway crest surpassed about 5 meters, the crest's geometry became crucial. This prompted a concerted effort to identify a crest shape that would optimize hydraulic performance. Despite Bazin's valuable contributions, he did not propose applying his findings to determine the shape of spillway crests.

William P. Creager
(1878-1953)
(Hager, 2017)

William Pitcher Creager was a well-known civil engineer who was born in Baltimore, Maryland, on September 21, 1878, and died in Buffalo, New York, on April 4, 1953, at the age of 75. In 1901, he graduated from Troy, New York's Rensselaer Polytechnic Institute. He started off as a provincial administrator for the Philippine government, a role he held until 1904. After that, he worked on the design of the New York State Barge Canal until 1906. Following that, Creager was employed as a draughtsman for the chief hydraulic engineer of the White Engineering Company until 1922, when he accepted a position as head engineer at the New York Power Corporation. He began providing consulting services in Baltimore, Maryland, in 1931. Moreover, Creager contributed his knowledge as a member of Princeton University's Advising Engineering Council. He was also a member of the American Institute of Consulting Engineers (AICE) and the American Society of Civil Engineers (ASCE).

Richard O. Muller was a graduate of Hannover University. He was born in Stendal, Germany, on October 17, 1881, and died in New York, NY, on June 4, 1944, at the age of

63. He was mostly interested in the steam turbine industry professionally. After starting his career in Britain at the Thompson-Houston Co. and then at the Westinghouse Co., Muller finally relocated to the United States, where he made important contributions as a consultant in Washington, DC, and as a turbine innovator in Brooklyn, NY. In addition to teaching electrical engineering at the University of Quito, he provided consulting engineering services to the Ecuadorian government. Having started in 1915, he became chief engineer of the Terry Steam Turbine Co. in Hartford, CT, in 1926, and retired from the company in 1943 because of health problems. Erroneously credited to Creager, Muller invented the design philosophy of spillways that resembled the bottom nappe profile of sharp-crested rectangular weirs. As early as 1908, when the first significant dams were being built, Muller promoted this architectural idea. His book "Hydro-electrical Engineering," published in 1921, covers a wide range of subjects related to civil and electrical engineering, including hydrology, stream measurement, canals, pipes, dams, turbines, powerhouses, transmission lines, water power projects, hydroelectric plants, and related laws. As an American Society of Mechanical Engineers (ASME) member, he was well respected.

Fernando M.M. Abecasis (Hager, 2017).

Fernando Maria Manzanares Abecasis, who passed away in Lisbon on October 12, 2003, at the age of 81, was a prominent figure in Portuguese hydraulic engineering. He was born in Madrid on August 30, 1922. After earning his civil engineering degree from Lisbon's Instituto Superior Técnico (IST), he began his illustrious career in 1948, initially heading the Hydraulic Division at the LNEC Laboratory before becoming a professor of hydraulic engineering in 1956. His career achievements, closely aligned with those of his brother, included notable contributions to hydraulic engineering through both research and consultancy.

Abecasis is celebrated for his 1955 study on the morning glory spillway, where he identified its potential to create significant under-pressure, flow instability, and cavitation damage. He advised that such structures should exclusively use free flow for the design discharge to prevent the creation of dangerous low-pressure areas. His work was crucial in improving the safety and efficiency of hydraulic structures, ensuring a smooth flow of water from reservoirs to the outlets preceding stilling basins.

In 1961, Abecasis made a significant breakthrough with a novel design for the crest geometry of standard overflow spillways to combat the issue of substantial under-pressure upstream of the crest. Introducing a three-radius approach for the upstream quadrant, he managed to raise the limit on unit discharge. This contribution highlighted his extensive expertise and dedication to the field of hydraulic engineering, aiming to improve the design and functionality of water management systems.

REFERENCES & SUGGESTED REFERENCES

- Asawa, G.L. 2008. Irrigation and Water Resources Engineering, New Age International (P) Limited, Publishers.
- Basak, N.N. 2017. Irrigation Engineering, McGraw Hill Education
- Brouwer, C. and M. Heibloem. 1986. Irrigation Water Management: Irrigation Water Needs, Training manual no. 3. Food and Agriculture Organization of the United Nations, Via delle Terme di Caracalla, 00100 Rome, Italy.
- Dahigaonkar, J.G. 2006. Text Book of Irrigation Engineering, Asian Book Pvt. Ltd., New Delhi.
- Patra, K.C. 2001. Hydrology and Water Resources Engineering, CRC Press.
- Punmia, B.C., Pande, B, Lal., Jain, A. K. and Jan, A.K. 2009. Irrigation and Water Power Engineering, Laxmi Publications, New Delhi
- Sharma, S.K. 2017. Irrigation Engineering and Hydraulic Structures, S. Chand Publishing
- Sivaraman, V, Devanathan, D and Marak, A. K. C. 2022. Water Storage and Supply System in Ancient India. Journal of Pharmaceutical Negative Results. Volume13, Special Issue 1, pp 1088-1093. DOI:10.47750/pnr.2022.13.S01.130
- Hager, W.H. and Castro-Orgaz, O. 2017. Ogee Weir Crest Definition: Historical Advance. Proceedings of the 37th IAHR World Congress August 13 – 18, 2017, Kuala Lumpur, Malaysia.

Dynamic QR Code for Further Reading

Features of some of the world's most interesting and famous dams are presented in the QR Code. Presented are few largest and most fascinating dams in the world.	
To know more about the Developments in water dams and water harvesting systems throughout history in different civilizations, please scan the QR Code.	

4 MINOR & MICRO IRRIGATION

परिचयः ॥ Introduction

Minor and micro irrigation are advanced agricultural techniques that maximize water efficiency for optimal crop production. These methods deliver water directly to the plant root zones, reducing water waste and improving irrigation effectiveness. With the growing scarcity of water resources and the increasing need for food production, minor and micro irrigation practices are crucial for achieving sustainable agriculture.

"अर्थात्, भूमेः सततं सिंचनं जीवनस्य आधारस्तु।"

"Continuous irrigation of the land is the foundation of life."

UNIT SPECIFICS

In this unit the following aspects of minor and micro-irrigation are elaborately discussed:

- Bandhara irrigation: Layout, components, construction and working
- Percolation Tanks: Need, selection of site.
- Lift irrigation Scheme: Components and their functions, Layout.
- Drip and Sprinkler Irrigation: Need, components, and Layout.
- Well irrigation: types and yield of wells, advantages and disadvantages of well irrigation.

This chapter is designed to apply theoretical knowledge to practical scenarios, fostering curiosity, creativity, and problem-solving skills. It includes a wide range of exercises, from multiple-choice questions to detailed short and long-answer queries, categorized into basic and advanced levels based on Bloom's taxonomy. To complement learning, numerical problems are provided, along with a list of references and further readings for comprehensive practice.

To deepen the learning experience, QR codes are embedded within the text, directing readers to supplementary material that supports the chapter's content. These resources offer a richer understanding of the topics discussed.

The chapter concludes with a "Know More" section, which aims to expand the reader's knowledge by exploring the fundamentals, fascinating facts, analogies, and the historical development of the subject. This segment traces the evolution of the topic up to the current day and examines its practical applications in daily life and various sectors. Additionally, case studies that consider environmental, sustainability, social, and ethical issues are presented. This approach is intended to spark interest and encourage deeper exploration of the subject matter, enhancing the learner's engagement and comprehension.

RATIONALE

Minor and micro-irrigation projects play a significant role in the expansion of global irrigation efforts. These projects, which utilize either groundwater or surface water for irrigation purposes, are defined as Minor Irrigation Schemes when they cover a Culturable Command Area of up to 2000 hectares each. In this Unit, we will specifically discuss on the Bandhara irrigation, Percolation Tanks, Lift irrigation, Drip and Sprinkler Irrigation, and Well irrigation Schemes.

This introductory course on minor and micro-irrigation is designed to build and improve students' knowledge and skills in the field. By the end of the course, students will have a solid foundation in minor irrigation, which they will be able to apply specifically in civil engineering context. They will possess the capability to employ techniques for laying out, planning, designing, and construction of various minor and micro-irrigation projects.

PRE-REQUISITES

Science: Fundamental knowledge of Science up to Intermediate level

Mathematics: Fundamental knowledge of Mathematics up to High School Level

UNIT OUTCOMES

After the completion of this module, the students will be able to:

U4-O1: Layout, and construct various Bandhara irrigation units.

U4-O2: Select proper sites for Percolation Tanks.

U4-O3: Select the site and give a layout for a Lift Irrigation Scheme.

U4-O4: Select the site and give the layout for the Drip Irrigation and Sprinkler Irrigation units.

U4-O5: Select a given type of well for a given purpose and compute the yield of wells.

ALIGNMENT WITH COURSE OBJECTIVE

UNIT OUTCOMES	EXPECTED ALIGNMENT WITH COURSE OUTCOMES (1:Low Correlation; 2: Moderate Correlation; 3: High Correlation)				
	CO:1	CO:2	CO:3	CO:4	CO:5
U4-O1	-	-	3	-	2
U4-O2	-	-	3	-	2
U4-O3	-	-	3	-	2
U4-O4	-	-	3	-	2
U4-O5	-	-	3	-	2

4.1 Bandhara Irrigation

4.1.1 Introduction

Bandhara irrigation is a minor irrigation system suitable for irrigating isolated areas up to around 500-2000 hectares. A small structure is constructed over a river or stream to slow down the flow and raise the water level upstream so that water can be diverted to a canal for irrigation. This construction is analogous to a weir, which is erected perpendicularly across a river to raise the water level on the upstream side similarly. The height of bandhara depends on the water level to be raised for irrigation purposes.

It is built with stone as well as brick masonry with an R.C.C crest. The width of the crest varies from 1 m to 2 m. The under sluices or scouring sluices are provided at the bottom of the bandhara to pass silt-free water to the canal.

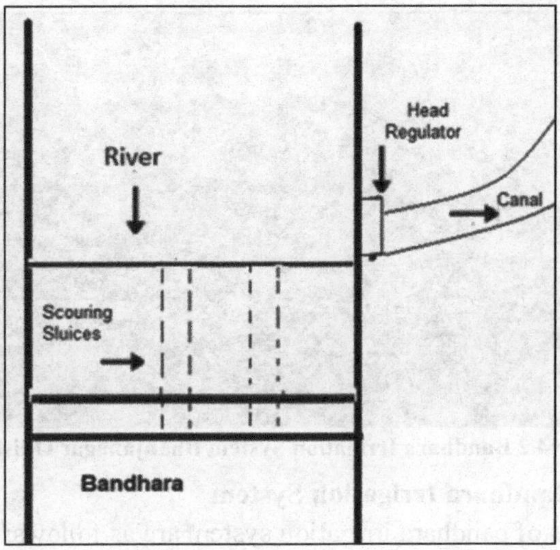

Figure 4.1 Layout of Bandhara Irrigation System

4.1.2 Site Selection for Bandhara

a. The location site should have a straight approach, be narrow, and be well-defined so the cost of construction will be minimal and can be constructed on both sides of the bank.
b. The head of the canal should be higher than the bed level of approach of bandhara to provide silt-free water into the canal.
c. The river or stream across which the bandhara will construct should be a Perennial River so sufficient water will be available entire crop period.
d. A solid foundation should be available at the location site.
e. The upstream should have a steep slope to flow water under gravity.
f. The area under the command of the canal should be adequate.
g. There must be avoidance of deep excavation for the canal on the sides of the banks.
h. Canal taking off from bandhara should not obstruct any cross drainage work across their path canal lining on the wall.

Figure 4.2 Bandhara Irrigation System Bhanjanagar Odisha

4.1.3 Components of Bandhara Irrigation System

The various components of bandhara irrigation system are as follows:

a. Bandhara
b. Scour Hole
c. Screen Wall & Outlet
d. Embankment
e. Off Taking Canal with Lining Wall

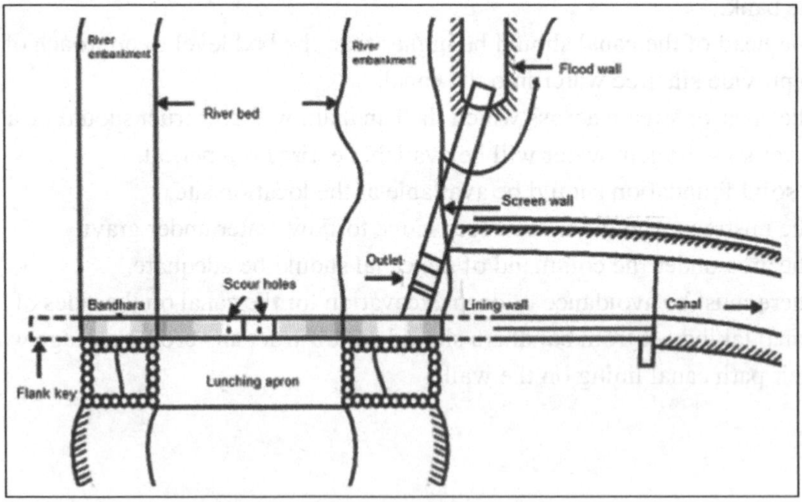

Figure 4.3 Components of Bandhara Irrigation

a. **Bandhara:** There are two types of bandhara

   i. Solid bandhara
   ii. Open bandhara

Solid and open bandhara are the main types of permanent or pucca bandhara. Temporary bandhara is primarily necessary for the development of permanent bandhara, also known as pucca bandhara. Intially a temporary bandhara is constructed on the site, and if it is found suitable for the site in terms of its working objective and performance, after only the permanent bandhara is constructed. Permanent bandhara is usually made of stone or brick masonry and also can be made of concrete. The height of this kind of bandhara varies between 2.5 to 3.5 meters and the top width is usually kept at 3 to 4 meters.

i. Solid Bandhara: To raise the level of water on the upstream side and to reduce the generation of afflux this type bandharas is constructed with a sufficient number of openings. Stone masonry piers are designed with grooves spaced two meters apart, and the spaces between them are blocked with two rows of needles filled with paddles. The piers' grooves are where the needles are situated. These needles are constructed from concrete, stone, or masonry. Solid bandharas range in height from 2.5 to 3.5 meters, with shutters situated atop the peak. Without a shutter, the height ranges from 1.5 to 2.5 meters.

Figure 4.4 Solid Bandhara

ii. Open Bandhara: The objective of this type of bandhara construction is to elevate the water level on the upstream side so the raised water is diverted to the canal on both sides of the bank. It acts as an open weir and consists of several piers with grooves. The grooves are fixed with needles. The meant of provision of needles is to gain the required height of the weir.

Figure 4.5 Open Bandhara

Table 4.1 Difference between Solid and Open Bandhara

Solid Bandhara		Open Bandhara	
i.	In solid-type bandhara, permanent construction of bandhara will be done after the construction of temporary bandhara and there will be no change in structure.	i.	This is also a permanent type and is done after the construction of the temporary bandhara also has allowance to change the needles as per the requirement of height.
ii.	This type of bandhara acts as a solid weir.	ii.	This bandhara acts as an open weir.
iii.	There is no such provision to control flood water in this type of bandhara.	iv.	Flood water can be controlled by removing needles
v.	The height of solid bandhara varies from 2.5m to 3.5m and without any gate 1.5m to 2.5m.	vi.	The height of open bandhara can be easily varied by removing or adding needles as a requirement.

b. **Scour hole:** These holes, which range in diameter from 20 to 50 cm, are spaced evenly across the bandhara's solid wall. They are positioned between 30 and 50 centimeters above the riverbed. These holes are primarily blocked during the off-monsoon season and are used to dispose of silt to the downstream side during the monsoon season when river flows are at their maximum.

c. **The screen wall and outlet of the bandhara**: This wall, which has an exit at an angle of 900 to 1200, is located on the bandhara's upstream side. This wall contains the outlet, which is accessible from the top of the wall via a steel gate. The outlet sill is maintained at a level of 0.3 meters below the full supply of water.

d. **Embankments**: These are installed to prevent people who live outside of Bandhara from drowning during floods caused by backwater flows.

e. **Off-taking canal with lining Wall**: The off-taking canals are provided to carry water from the bandhara site to the commanded area. Based on the discharge carrying capacity they can be classified as main, branch, major, and distributaries.

4.1.4 Temporary Bandhara

Any obstructions, such as stones or tree trunks, are placed beside earth and stone, GI sheet face, etc., to create the temporary. The construction of permanent bandhara mainly depends mostly on temporary bandhara. If the temporary bandhara is found suitable for the site in terms of its working objective and performance, then only it is replaced by a permanent bandhara.

Figure 4.6 Temporary Bandhara

4.1.5 Working with Bandhara

A weir and an off-taking channel both constitute one unit of the bandhara irrigation scheme. A series of Bandharas units may be constructed one after the other. The surplus water of the bandhara is utilized by the subsequent unit of the bandhara. To regulate the amount of water that enters the off-taking channel, a head regulator is built. The commanded area of Bandhara is known as that. A thal is divided into a number of small blocks called pads. One phad contains several units of fields. Each pad has one type of crop grown.

4.1.6 Case Study: Kolhapur Bandhara

a. **Location and working**: This bandhara is located and famous in Kolhapur district. The main purpose of this construction for raise level of water on the upstream side to divert the water to the canals. Known as an open weir, it has several piers with side slots where wooden needles can be inserted. To create a continuous weir, the needles are positioned across the piers at the appropriate height. You can change the height of the weir by taking out or adding extra needles. The needles are removed during a flood to prevent the water level on the upstream side from rising.

Figure 4.7 K.T Weir of Kolhapur District

b. **Construction:** Known as K. T. Weir, it was built in the Kolhapur district. The two rows of needles that are packed with paddles to join them shut these openings. The grooves over the piers are where the needles are positioned. This wooden needle is 2 meters in length, 15 centimeters in height, and 5 centimeters in thickness. These needles are located on the weir during post-monsoon to store water and are removed during the arrival of flood just before the monsoon.

4.2 PERCOLATION TANK

4.2.1 Introduction

To elevate the groundwater table in a command area the percolation tanks are constructed. These are similar earthen dams with masonry structures for spilling excess water to downstream. The construction of percolation tanks helps recharge the groundwater which leads to raising the water table in wells. The raised water level in the well will help in increasing the lift irrigation, reducing losses due to evaporation and hence, reducing the cost of irrigation. Percolation tank is an artificially created storage reservoir having highly permeable land. The tank should be located on a weathered and highly fractured rock to access speedy recharge. It is constructed across the river, stream, or a submerging land area with a pervious nature to allow sufficient infiltration of surface runoff. This is said to be an important structure and efficient method for recharging the groundwater. The downstream of the percolation tank should have enough recharge wells and croplands to benefit from the increased groundwater table. The tank size is governed by the factor of percolation capacity rather than the catchment yield. If the soil does not have enough percolation rates on the site, the impounded water will be lost in terms of evaporation loss, thereby reducing the rate of recharge in the nearby area. Hydrological studies such as rainfall pattern, rate of rainfall, evaporation rates, and number of days of dry period should be taken into consideration for selecting the site location of the percolation tank.

Figure 4.8 (a) Aerial View of a Percolation Tank

Figure 4.8 (b) Percolation Tank

4.2.2 Constructional details of percolation tank

The main component of a percolation tank is an earthen embankment with a cut-off trench. The depth of the cut-off trench varies from 30cm to 90 cm and the bottom width varies from 60cm to 120 cm. This tank is constructed with the available local materials like moorum, stones for chipping, soft rocks, black cotton soil, etc. The embankment or the bund is made of sand covering and a clayey material hearting to retain water. The inner core of the earthen bund is compacted by adding a suitable amount of water. Sandy soil is placed over the inner core as a cover with compaction. The banks are crammed with stones or boulders. A cut-off trench at the core of the hearting in the tank base protects the earthen bund's upstream slope. The bund height does not commonly exceed more than 10m. To control seepage, drainage blanket, toe filter are provided in the downstream side of the embankment.

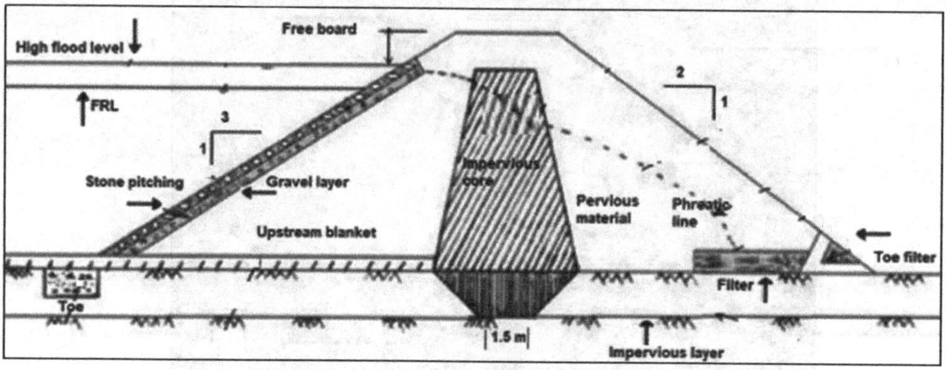

Figure 4.9 Embankment of Percolation tank

4.2.3 Site selection for percolation tank construction.

a. The site for percolation tanks must be containing porous soil so that sufficient recharge is possible.

b. Too high permeability leads to result in the percolated water evading the downstream as regenerated as surface flow, hence it will crush the intent of water conservation

c. The aquifer to be revived should have adequate thickness near about 3m of porous to accommodate recharge.

d. The percolation tank site must have a good catchment for collecting water.

e. The soil of the catchment of the percolation tank should be light sandy to avoid siltation in the bottom of the percolation tank.

f. There must be a study of a long-term pattern of rainfall that will be helpful to fill the percolation tank during monsoon.

g. The area to be recharged should have a sufficient number of wells, hand pumps, etc.

h. The materials and labourers required for percolation tank construction should be accessible close to the site location.

4.3 LIFT IRRIGATION

4.3.1 Introduction

When the irrigated land is at a higher elevation than the source of supply, then the water is lifted from the source by some artificial methods, and the process is called lift irrigation. Because greater elevations make it impossible to redirect gravity flow to irrigable ground and because higher contour canal banks prevent irrigation under gravity, lift irrigation must be installed in these circumstances. Lift irrigation schemes should achieve two main tasks: first to carry water from the source by mechanical means to the water storage reservoir which is situated at a higher elevation point of the command area and second, to distribute the storage water to the field by proper distribution system. Generally, the source of supply is a river source, canal source, and well or tube well source. In most of these types of irrigation systems, the area under command is divided into different blocks according to topographical features. The water required in each block is determined and the pipelines are designed based on the demand and available head the pipelines. The delivery chambers are constructed based on demand requirement and distributed pipelines fitted with valves to control the flow are laid to supply to each block.

4.3.2 Advantages and Disadvantages of lift Irrigation system.

a. Advantages of lift Irrigation system

i. High efficiency due to optimal use of water

ii. Water logging can be avoided by using wells and tubewells as sources of water supply

iii. Conveyance loss due to evaporation loss can be reduced as compared to surface irrigation method

iv. There will be less manpower used in this method.

v. The land acquisition problem can be reduced by lift irrigation method.

b. Disadvantages of lift Irrigation system

1. Maintenance cost of power unit is high which leads to uneconomical
2. Water from a source such as a tube well may be harmful to some crops due to high mineral content.
3. Failure of lifting devices affects the farmers whose depend only source of water supply for irrigation.

Figure 4.10 Lift Irrigation System

4.3.3 Parts of Lift Irrigation

The main components of lift irrigation are given as follows:

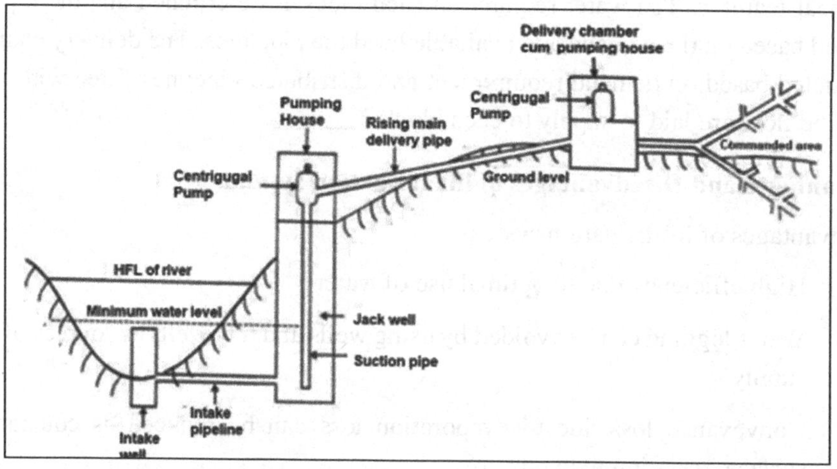

Figure 4.11 Components of Lift irrigation

a. **Intake well:** This is an intake structure used to collect water from the surface as well as a subsurface source of water and divert the water to the inlet chamber of the lift irrigation system.
b. **Inlet chamber:** It protects the jack well from entering debris and silts into it.
c. **Jack well:** Before the water reaches the irrigation field, the water is collected in a structure, called a jack well, and from the jack well the water is lifted through different means to the command area as per the required quantity.
d. **Inlet pipe:** Silt-free water from the inlet chamber is sent to the jack well via an inlet pipe that has the right gradient in it.
e. **Pump House:** The pump house serves as an essential and protected place where pump and the power unit are installed. Since the pump and power unit might get damaged due to water access, pump house is designed in such a way, that it is not affected during flood and extreme climate conditions.

Figure 4.12 Pump House of Lift Irrigation

f. **Rising main:** The rising main is the main transporter through which the water is supplied from the jack well to the delivery chamber or sump well. The diameter of the rising main varies from 0.2 to 5 m depending upon the requirement of water.

g. **Sump well or Delivery chamber**: The delivery chamber or sump well distributes water to the command area through the distribution system of mains or sub mains. Water is pumped from the jack well to the sump well from where it is again distributed to the commanded area under consideration. A delivery chamber or sump well kept at a higher elevation than the commanded area is sometimes housed with a powerhouse.

h. **Water distribution system or Sub mains:** Water from the sump well is distributed to the crop area or commanded area of irrigation through the sub mains. These sub-mains are non-metallic or PVC-type materials. As multiple lines, the diameter of the sub-main varies from 30 mm to 240mm.

i. **Electric Pumps**: Generally, three different types are centrifugal pumps, reciprocating pumps, axial flow pumps, and vertical turbine pumps available for lifting of water. The selection of pumps depends upon

- Total quantity of water to be lifted
- Total head available at the site
- Permissible suction head of the pump
- Speed of the pump
- Cost per unit power
- Monthly demand pattern
- Quality of water
- Maximum discharge required

4.4 SPRINKLER IRRIGATION SYSTEM

4.4.1 Introduction

In the sprinkler irrigation method, the water is applied to the crops with high pressure by using a mechanical pump. This method is called artificial rain in which water is scattered through nozzles placed in the pipes and sprayed on irrigated land. Water is sprayed into the air above the crop using a system of overhead perforated pipes in this technique, which is also known as overhead irrigation. Nozzles are either of fixed type or rotating type with high water pressure.

4.4.2 Necessity of Sprinkler irrigation:

The sprinkler method is suitable for excessively permeable soils especially sandy soil where the depth of soil is shallow and erosive. This method is suitable for crops that require less water and are mostly suitable for undulating irrigation land. Certain crops, such as sugarcane, jute, and rice, require more standing than this watering system can provide.

Figure 4.13 Sprinkler Irrigation System

Figure 4. 15 Sprinkler Irrigation System

It has following advantages over other methods of irrigation.

i. Suitable in all types of soil except clayey soil.

ii. Suitable for undulating land

iii. Reduces soil compaction

iv. Application of fertilizers and chemicals is possible.

v. The cost of labor is reduced.

vi. Bunds are not required. Therefore there a is saving of land area.

vii. Suitable for areas where plant population for irrigation is high.

viii. A portable system helps the system operate easily.

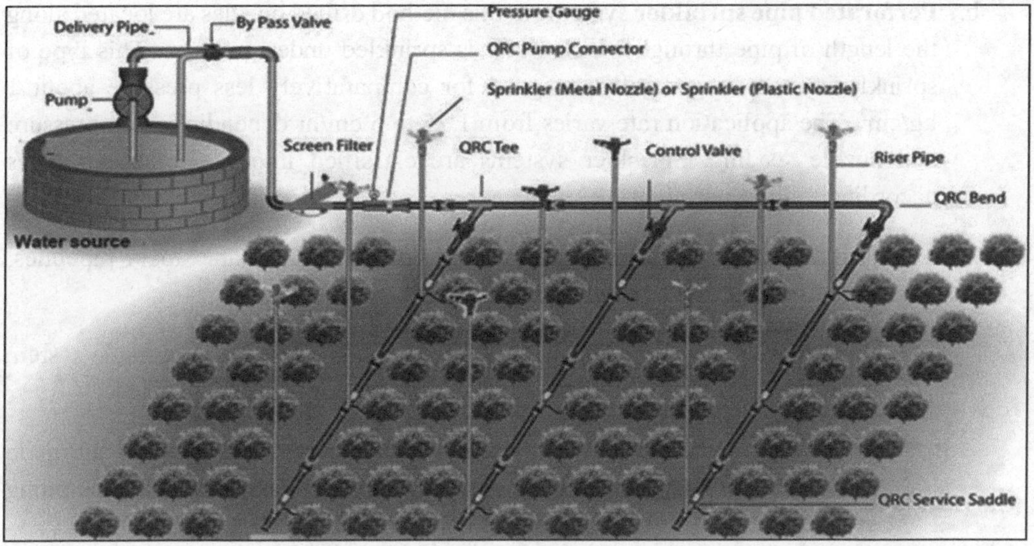

Figure 4.14 Layout of Sprinkler Irrigation

4.4.3 Classification of Sprinkler Systems

The sprinkler systems are divided into two major classes based on the special arrangement for spraying water.

a. **Rotating head type sprinkler system:** Nozzles of small sizes are positioned on riser pipes set at regular spacing along the span of the laterals. The lateral pipes are generally placed on the ground surface. These are mounted on posts, about the height of the crop, and rotated about 900 to the irrigated land. In rotating-type sprinklers, the common device to spin the sprinkler heads is a small strike generated by the force of water striking in opposition to a vane linked to it.

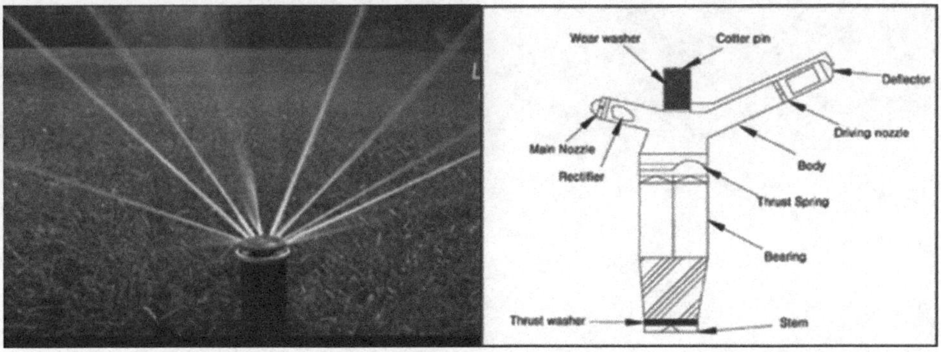

Figure 4.15 Sprinkler head

b. **Perforated pipe sprinkler system:** In this method drilled nozzles are located along the length of pipe through which water is sprinkled under pressure. This type of sprinkler system is generally designed for comparatively less pressure about 1 kg/cm^2. The application rate varies from 1.25 to 5 cm/hr depending upon pressure and nuzzle spacing. Sprinkler systems are classified into the following types according to their portability

   i. Portable system: The portable system consists of portable main pipelines, laterals pipes, and a pumping system.

   ii. Semi-portable system: The semi-portable system is likely to portable system other than the source of water supply and pumping system are fixed.

   iii. Semi-permanent system: This system has permanent main lines and sub-main lines, portable lateral lines, and has fixed source of water source and pumping system.

   iv. Permanent system: A permanent system consists of permanent fixed main lines, sub-main lines, and lateral lines, and a fixed water supply source and pumping system.

4.4.4 Components of sprinkler irrigation system

A sprinkler irrigation unit generally consists of the following components:

a. **Pumping system**: The water is pumped with pressure and sprayed through the nozzles in pipelines to the fields in the form of spray. A high-speed centrifugal pump or turbine pump is used for operating sprinkler irrigation for individual fields. Centrifugal pump is commonly used when the water surface distance from the pump inlet is less than eight meters. For more height turbine pump is used. The driving unit is an electric motor or an internal combustion engine.

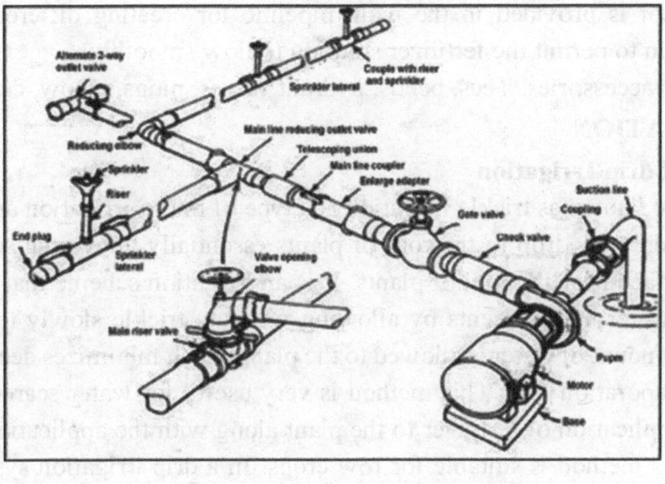

Figure 4.16 Components of Sprinkler System

b. **Tubings or Mains/ Sub-mains with laterals**: The tubings consist of main pipelines, sub mains, and laterals. Water from the source is conveyed to the sub-mains through the main lines. From the sub-mains water is distributed to the laterals which in turn supply water to the sprinklers. Couplers serve as flexible connectors between two pipes, ensuring a leak-proof seal at the joint. They are typically non-corrosive and durable, designed to withstand long-term use.

c. **Sprinkler Head**: The purpose of the sprinkler head is to allocate water homogeneously over the cropland without excess percolation or runoff. Different types of sprinklers are available. They are fixed type or rotating type. The rotating type is applied for a wide range of applications. They are effective for pressure of about 10 to 70 m head of water at the outlet point of the sprinkler. Generally, pressures ranging from 16 to 40 m head are used for practical application. Fixed head types are generally used to irrigate small lawns and gardens.

d. **Fittings with other accessories**: The following are the essential accessories and fittings used in sprinkler irrigation systems.

   i. Water meters are essential tools for measuring the amount of water delivered to a field, facilitating accurate computation of water usage. Flange, couplings, and nipples: These are essential for connection to the pump, delivery pipes, and suction pipes.

   ii. Pressure gauge is required to measure the actual amount of pressure generated at the sprinkler head so as uniform distribution of water on irrigated land.

   iii. Soluble chemical fertilizers are applied to the crops using the sprinkler system. The equipment is moderately low-priced and can be easily available locally. The equipment for fertilizer application consists of an air-tight sealed fertilizer tank with necessary pipes and connections. An essential equipment: venturi injector is provided in the main pipeline for creating differential pressure suction to permit the fertilizer solution to flow smoothly.

iv. Other accessories: Tees, bends, hydrant valves, plugs, elbow, etc.

4.5 DRIP IRRIGATION

4.5.1 Necessity of drip Irrigation

Drip irrigation also known as trickle irrigation is a type of micro-irrigation applying water at a slow rate or drop by drop to the root of plants essentially above the soil surface or below the soil surface near the root of plants. It is an irrigation scheme that is capable of saving irrigation water and nutrients by allowing water to trickle slowly to the roots of plants. A precise amount of water is allowed to the plant which minimizes deep percolation loss as well as evaporation loss. This method is very useful for water scarce zones. This method enables application of fertilizer to the plant along with the application of water to the root zone. This method is suitable for row crops. In a drip irrigation system water is distributed throughout a system of valves, tubing, and emitters. Nutrients mixed with water enter the soil from the exit of the emitters and move towards the root zone of the plants through the force of gravity as well as capillary rise. In this way, the plant's extraction of moisture along with nutrients are replenished without delay, resulting in the water stress on the plant being reduced, enhancing the quality and achieving an optimum yield of crops. It is more efficient than other types of irrigation systems based on its design, installation and operation of the system.

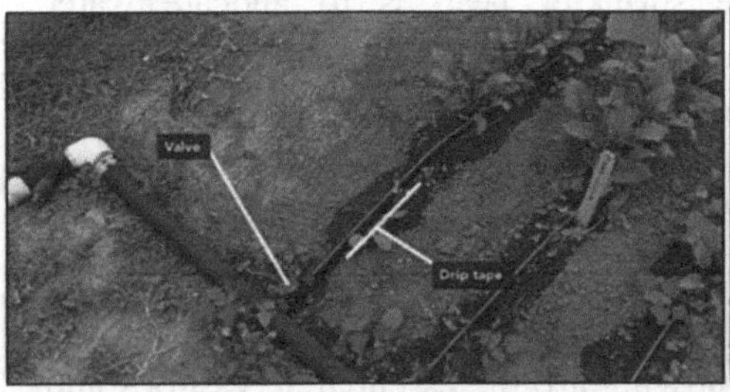

Figure 4.17 View of Drip Irrigation System

4.5.2 Components of drip irrigation:

a. **Pumping Units:** It takes water from the source of supply with enough pressure for delivery into the pipe network.

b. **Control valves:** The drip irrigation system's pressure and discharge are controlled by these control valves.

c. **Filtration system**: There is a system for cleaning the sediment water so that clear water enters the pipeline to prevent blockage in the pipeline. Screen filters and sand-graded filters are the most common types of filters that remove fine material suspended in the water.

d. **Fertilizer tank**: It adds the required dose of fertilizer into the water during irrigation.

e. **Main pipelines, sub mains, and laterals pipes:** They supply water from the pumping station to the fields. They are usually made from PVC and usually buried in the ground to prevent exposure to sunlight. The lateral pipes are usually 13mm to 32 mm in diameter.

f. **Emitters:** They are called drippers essentially required to control the release of water from the lateral lines to the plants. These emitters are generally spaced greater than 1 meter apart for single plants and closely spaced for row crops. The emitters are designed based on producing a precise constant discharge without any variation with pressure changes and reducing the chances of blockage.

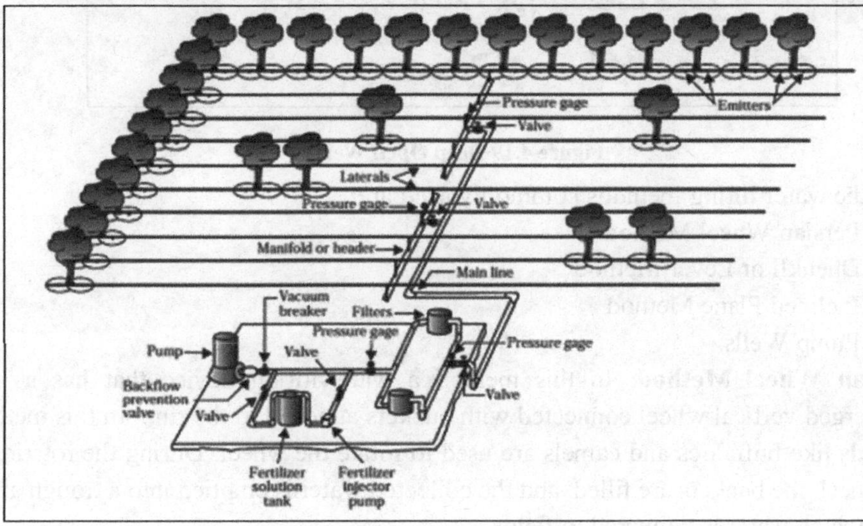

Figure 4.18 Layout of Drip Irrigation

4.6 WELL IRRIGATION

A well is a vertical hole excavated in the earth used to extract water from below for human use. It is a widely used irrigation method in nations like India. Currently, almost 50 lakh tube wells are in use throughout India. In Uttar Pradesh, the first tube well was constructed in 1930. Well, irrigation is generally accomplished in those areas where adequate groundwater is obtainable. In India such areas as the deltaic of Godavari, Mahanadi, Cauvery Rivers, Krishna River, parts of Narmada, and in Ganga Plain there is sufficient groundwater is available. The well may be classified into

4.6.1 Open well

Generally, a shallow open well is about 3-5 meters depth and a deep well depth can vary up to 15 meters. A shallow open well rests over on a porous or pervious stratum having a high-water table. On the other hand, a deep open well rests over an impervious layer and draws water from the underlying beneath the impervious layer that is called the "mota layer" where the previous layer exists. The advantage of the deep open well is that the underlying impervious layer provides enough structural strength.

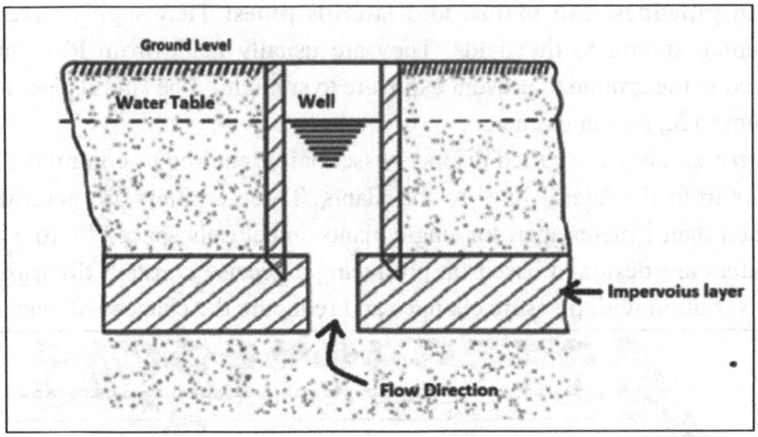

Figure 4.19 Deep Open Well

Some of the water lifting methods commonly used are:

a. Persian Wheel Method
b. Dhenkli or Lever Method
c. Inclined Plane Method
d. Pump Wells.

a. **Persian Wheel Method**: In this method a water-lifting device that has a half-submerged vertical wheel connected with buckets attached to the rim. In this method, animals like buffaloes and camels are used to rotate the wheel. During the rotation of the wheel, the buckets are filled, and the collected water is emptied into a trough above from which water is delivered to fields.

Figure 4.20 Persian Wheel Method

b. **Dhenki or Lever Method**: In this technique, a lever rod oscillates atop a vertical support pole. Top of Form A suitable counterweight is fixed on one side of the lever and a bucket is hovering from the other end into the well. It is widely practiced in Bihar and Andhra Pradesh.

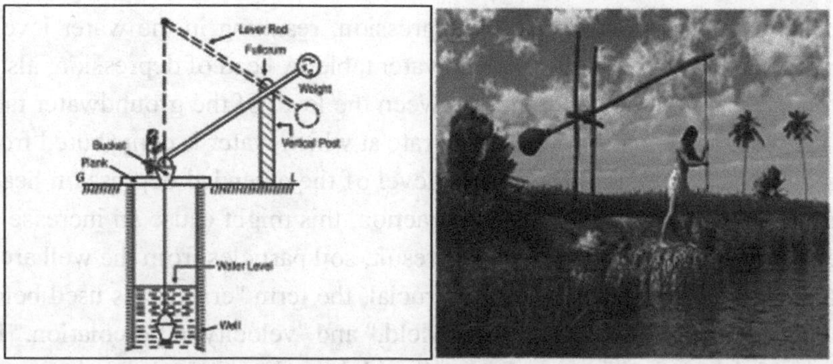

Figure 4.21 Dhenki or Lever Method

c. **Inclined Plane Method:** In this method, a pulley is fixed to the well on two verticals. A large leather bag called a mote is tied on one end of the rope. The other end is used to lift the water-filled leather bag. In this case, a pair of bullocks is used as a lifting force to lift water from the well. This method is used when the level of water in the well is quite deep and about 1.5 hectares of land can be irrigated by this method.

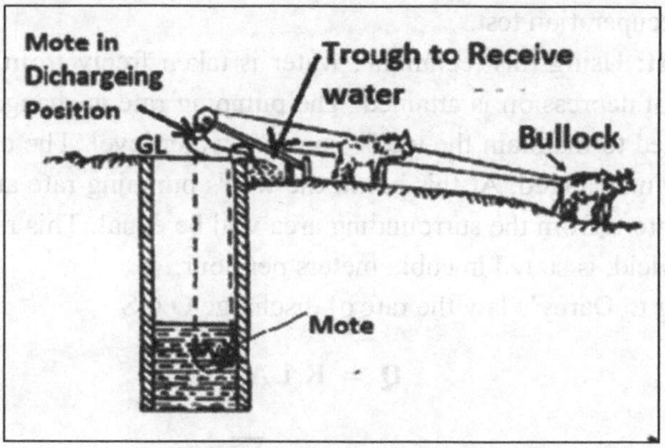

Figure 4.22 Inclined Plane Method

d. **Pumps wells:** In this method, power-driven pumps are used to lift water from wells. Several types of pumps are used for lifting water. Pumps may be divided into

   i. Constant displacement: They deliver the same volume of water against any head within which they can operate.
   ii. Variable displacement pumps: They deliver water in volume varying inversely with the head.

4.6.1.1 Yield of open Wells

Water tries to stay at its initial level when conditions are favorable. It is evident that, in normal circumstances with no withdrawal, the water level in a well roughly corresponds to the level of the water table. When water is extracted from a well, it leads to the formation of a phenomenon known as a cone of depression, resulting in the water level declining more rapidly than the surrounding groundwater table. A head of depression, also known as a cone of depression, is the difference between the level of the groundwater table and the water in the well. In the natural world, the rate at which water is contributed from the well increases with the depression head. If the level of the extended depression head is higher as a result of the well's constant water extraction, this might cause an increase in velocity and the dislodgment of soil particles. As a result, soil particles from the well are carried by the percolating water. Since this stage is crucial, the term "critical" is used before several terms, including "depression head," "well yield," and "velocity of percolation." It is crucial that the critical depression for a certain well withdrawal not be exceeded, since this might lead to unstable circumstances for the well construction.

The rate at which water percolates into the well below the critical depression head or safe maximum working head or from the surrounding previous layer of soil is generally referred to as the "yield of well." In cubic meters per hour, it is expressed. One can ascertain the open well's production or particular yield by

a. Pumping test
b. Recuperation test.

a. **Pumping Test:** Using this technique, water is taken freely from the well up until a critical head of depression is attained. The pumping rate is changed when the crucial stage is reached to maintain the well's constant water level. The depression head will therefore stay unchanged. At this point, the well's pumping rate and the rate at which water seeps into it from the surrounding area will be equal. This rate, which is known as the well's yield, is stated in cubic meters per hour.

According to Darcy's law the rate of discharge Q α S

$$\mathbf{Q = K.i.A} \tag{4.1}$$

Where K is the hydraulic conductivity of soil, i is hydraulic gradient $= \frac{S}{L}$ and S is the drawdown or depression head of the well. L =length of the aquifer, A= cross-sectional area of the well. So the equation (4.1) can be written as $\mathbf{Q = K.\frac{S}{L}.A}$

putting $\frac{K}{L} = C'$ the equation can be written as

$$\mathbf{Q = C'.S.A}$$

$$\frac{Q}{A} = V = C'S \tag{4.2}$$

From eq^n (4.2) it is observed the velocity increases with an increase in depression head 's'. The value of depression head 's' for which velocity becomes critical is called critical depression head. So, to make the pump in suitable working condition to avoid scouring the depression head usually kept $\frac{1}{3}$ th of the critical depression head which is known as the working head. Hence the maximum safe yield from the well depends working depression head of the well

b. **Recuperation Test:** By pumping to any level below the groundwater table, the well's water level is extracted using this approach. Next, the pump is turned off, and the amount of time it takes for the percolating water to fill the well back up to the desired level is tracked. By multiplying the cross-sectional area of the well by the height at which the water level rises following the cessation of pumping, the total volume of water recharged back into the well is calculated. The amount of water that increases over time is then divided to determine the well's output. Typically, this test is conducted during a dry spell to allow for the worst-case scenario.

While the recuperation test is relatively simple to do but does not produce the maximum safe yield, the pumping test is the most reliable, but it is also the most difficult to complete properly. The cause is that throughout the inspection time, the secure maximum operating head is not maintained when the water level in the well rises.

4.6.1.2 Derivation of specific yield from the open well from recuperating test

The rate of discharge per unit time under a unit hydraulic head is known as a well's specific yield. The particular yield is dependent upon:

a. Water-table depth
b. Permeability of the geological formation
c. Quantity of water storage in the well

Rate of withdrawal of water from the well

In this method, the water is first withdrawn from the well with a sufficient amount of drawdown.

Subsequently, when the pumping ceases, the water level in the well begins to rise shortly thereafter. The time taken to raise the water level to its normal level or some other level is observed. The discharge was then calculated using Figure 4.23 below.

From the Figure 4.23 below

CD represents the normal ground water table in the well before pumping

X — X represents the level of water in the well after pumping stopped.

A – B represents the level of water in the well at any time T after the stoppage of pumping.

S_1 = Drawdown in the well after pumping stopped.

S_2= Drawdown in well at any time T

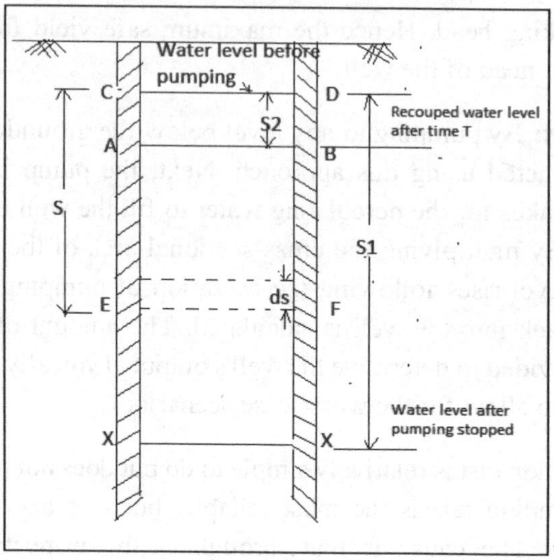

Figure 4.23 Recuperation test

Let at any time 't', EF is the position of the water table after allowing recharge of well. 'S' is the corresponding depression head. Let '*ds*' be the increase in water level at any time *dt*, Consequently, the amount of water replenished at interval time *dt* will be

$$dV = A.ds \qquad (4.3)$$

where A is the crossectional area of the open well. If Q is the rate of recharge of water within time' then the volume of water dV can be written as

$$dV = Q.dt \qquad (4.4)$$

Again we know $Q \alpha S$ or $Q = CS$ where C is a constant depending upon the porosity of the soil.

So putting $Q = CS$ in equation (4.4)

$$dV = C.S.dt \qquad (4.5)$$

Now equating eq^n (4.3) and (4.5) we will get

$-A.ds = C.S.dt$ (-ve sign indicates a decrease in drawdown with time)

$$\frac{Cdt}{A} = -\frac{ds}{S}$$

Now integrating both sides the above equation will be

$$\int_0^T \frac{Cdt}{A} = -\int_{S1}^{S2} \frac{ds}{S}$$

Or $\frac{C}{A}\int_0^T dt = -\int_{S1}^{S2} \frac{ds}{S}$ or $\frac{C}{A} T = -2.3 log_{10} \frac{S_2}{S_1}$

So,

$$\frac{C}{A} = \frac{2.3}{T} log_{10}\frac{S_1}{S_2} \tag{4.6}$$

$\frac{C}{A}$ is the **specific capacity** or **specific yield** of the shallow or open well which is discharge per unit area under the unit depression head.

The discharge can be determined from eq^n $Q = CS = \frac{C}{A}.A.S$

Or,

$$Q = \frac{2.3}{T} log_{10}\frac{S_1}{S_2}.A.S \tag{4.7}$$

$\frac{C}{A}$ value is given in the following table proposed by Marriot

Table 4.2 Marriot table for the value of C/A (Specific Yield)

Types of soil	Value of C/A
Clay	0.25
Fine sand	0.50
Coarse sand	1.0

Example 1. In a recuperation test, the level of water in an open well was declined by pumping to 2.8 m and recuperated back of amount 1.8 m water in 65 minutes. (a) Estimate the yield of the well of diameter 2.5m with a drawdown of 3.2m and (b) For the yield of 15 liters per second with a depression head of 2.8 m determine the diameter of the well.

Solution:

We know that specific yield $\frac{C}{A} = \frac{2.3}{T} log_{10}\frac{S_1}{S_2}$

From the above question the value $S_1 = 2.8$m

The final drawdown $S_2 = 2.8 - 1.8 = 1$ml

The recuperation time T = 65 minutes = 1.083 hr

So Specific yield = $\frac{C}{A} = \frac{2.3}{1.083} log_{10}\frac{2.8}{1} = 0.949\ m^3/hr/m^2$

Now for question (a) As we know the yield $\boldsymbol{Q = \frac{2.3}{T} log_{10} \frac{S_1}{S_2} . A.S,}$

Now putting specific yield $\frac{C}{A}$ = **0.949 m³/hr/m²** equation will be $\boldsymbol{Q = 0.949 . A.S}$

As it is given diameter of well d = 2.5m so Area $\boldsymbol{A = \frac{\Pi d^2}{4} = \frac{\Pi.2.5^2}{4} = 4.9m^2}$ and S= 3.2m in equation $\boldsymbol{Q = 0.949 . A.S = 0.949 \times 4.9 \times 3.2 = 14.88\ m^3/hr}$ **Ans.**

4.6.2 Tube Wells

A tube well is a type of well in which a long stainless-steel pipe of diameter 100mm to 200mm is bored into the underground aquifer. The lower end of the pipe is fitted with a strainer for letting silt-free water into the pipe and at the top, a pump is provided to lift water for irrigation. The irrigation accomplished using a tube well is called tube well irrigation. A tube well can be considered as shallow up to depth varies from 20m to 70m and it is considered as deep if the depth varies from 70m to 300m.

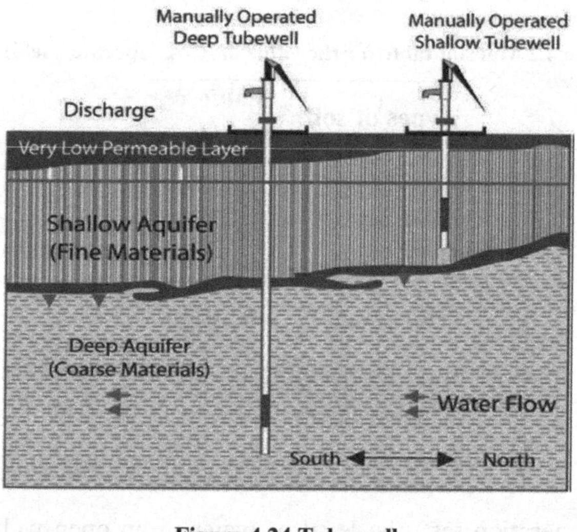

Figure 4.24 Tube well

Classification of Tube Wells

a. Strainer Tube Well: This type of tube well is the most common type of tube well used in India. It consists of strainer pipes screen pipes and blind pipes. Strainer-type tube wells are not suitable for sandy soil stratum as the strainer screen is likely to be choked easily. The boring hole is dug into the ground using a casing pipe whose diameter is about 5 to 10cm larger than the diameter of the main tube well. The main pipe consisting of blind and strainer pipes is then inserted into the boring hole in such a way that the length of the blind pipe covers the impervious layer and strainer pipes run through the previous water-bearing aquifers. The bottom of the well is plugged with cement concrete as shown in the figure.

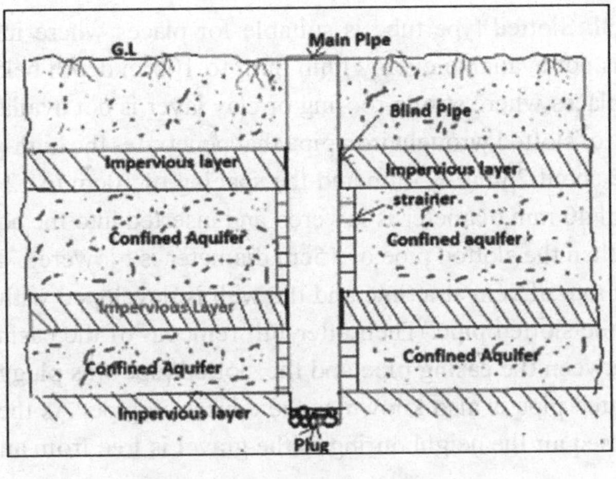

Figure 4.25 Strainer Type Tube well

b. Cavity Tube Well: Cavity tube wells do not require any strainer and blinder alternately unlike strainer-type tube wells. It draws water from the water-bearing stratum at the bottom of the well in which a cavity is developed. The water flows flowing a spherical direction and is normal to the cavity formed at the bottom. The pumping is done with a sand pump by puncturing the impervious layer until a cavity is formed at the bottom of the pipe. As the initial stage of pumping fine sand particles are coming out along with water through the sand pipe. As the surface area of the cavity formed increases with pumping, the radial velocity decreases which results in stopped entry of the sand particles into the pipe. The cavity tube well is economical compared to the strainer type as it requires only a plain well pipe which is lowered into a water-bearing stratum. The cavity needs to be developed at the bottom tube well using a centrifugal pump rather than another turbine or any compressor pump. The cavity tube well is used for domestic water supplies where less water is required.

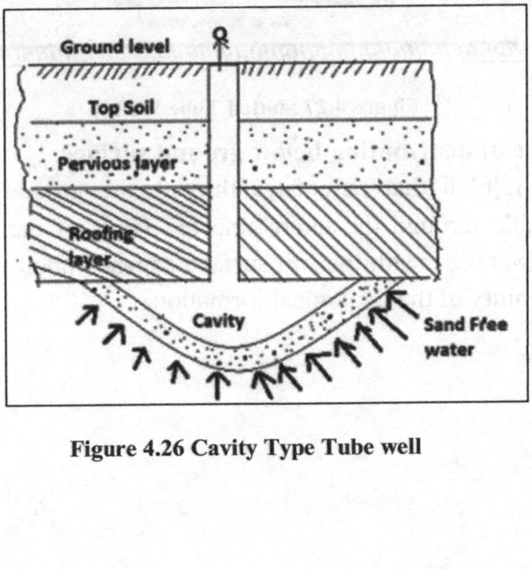

Figure 4.26 Cavity Type Tube well

c. Slotted Tube Well: Slotted type tube is suitable for places where insufficient water-bearing stratum is not available even within 80m to 100 m depth below ground level. It is suitable for places where strong roofing or clay layer is not available. This type of tube well consists of slotted wrought iron pipe that penetrates the high-pervious aquifer. The slot sizes are about 25mm x 3mm and the spacing of 10cm to 12 cm c/c distance. The casing pipe of 40 mm diameter is lowered and inserted into the aquifer for a depth of about 5m and then the slotted pipe of 15cm diameter is t lowered. Then casing pipe is withdrawn at a rate of 5cm at a time and the well is developed with the compressed air pumped into the slotted pipe. Then after full removal of the casing pipe from the well the space between the casing pipe and the slotted pipe was plugged with suitable material. The slotted pipe is also known as the education pipe. As the well developed by using compressed air the neighbouring to the gravel is free from any fine particles.

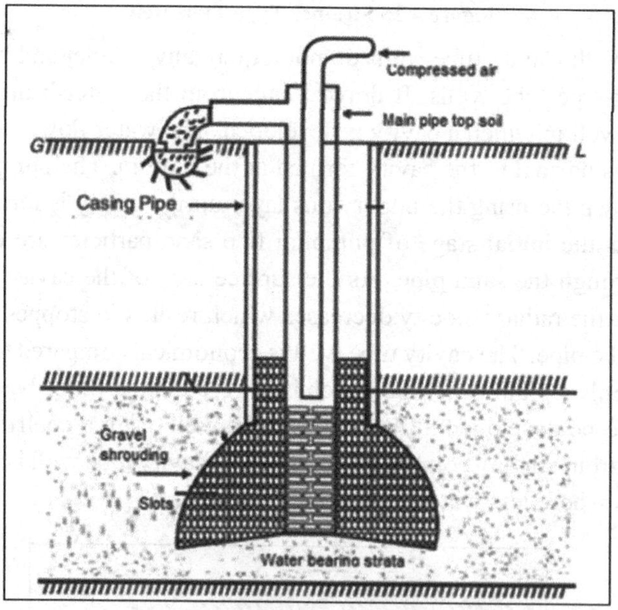

Figure 4.27 Slotted Tube Well

4.7 Soil Moisture zone of distribution below ground surface

The precipitation or rainfall that percolates through the ground surface reaches the underground water table through the interconnected voids of the underlying soil. The availability of groundwater beneath the soil surface depends upon the type of geological formation and permeability of the geological formation.

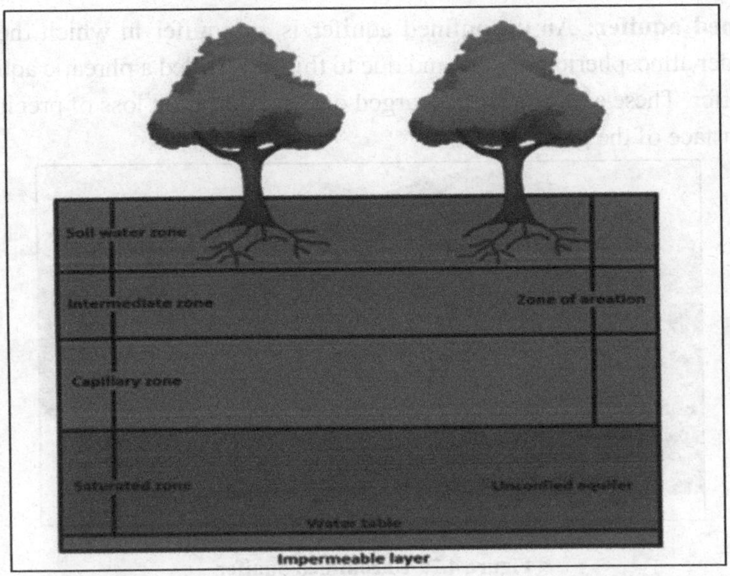

Figure 4.28 Soil Water Distribution

4.7.1 Zone of Aeration

The zone between the groundwater table and the soil surface is called the zone of aeration. The soil's gaps are either filled with water or heavily saturated in this area. It is again classified into three sub-zones

a. Soil water zone: It extends up to the depth of root
b. Intermediate zone: It is intermediate zone between capillary and soil moisture zone.
c. Capillary zone: It is the zone in which the soil is partially saturated by the rise of capillary fringe from the groundwater table.

4.7.2 Saturated zone

This area sits between the impermeable layer and the water table. Every soil gap in this area is filled with water. It is water water-bearing zone of geological formation. So based on the water-bearing capacity geological formations can be classified into aquifers, aquifers, aquitards, and aquiclude.

4.7.3 Aquifer

An aquifer is a type of geological structure that not only holds water but also transfers or produces an adequate amount of it. These aquifers are highly permeable geological formations in nature and hence they are considered an important source of groundwater storage. Unconsolidated sand and gravel bed deposits are examples of aquifers.
Aquifers are again classified into two types based according to the position of groundwater. They are

a. Unconfined aquifer
b. Confined Aquifer

a. **Unconfined aquifer:** An unconfined aquifer is an aquifer in which the water table exists under atmospheric pressure and due to this, it is called a phreatic aquifer or water table aquifer. These aquifers are recharged due to infiltration loss of precipitation from the top surface of the ground.

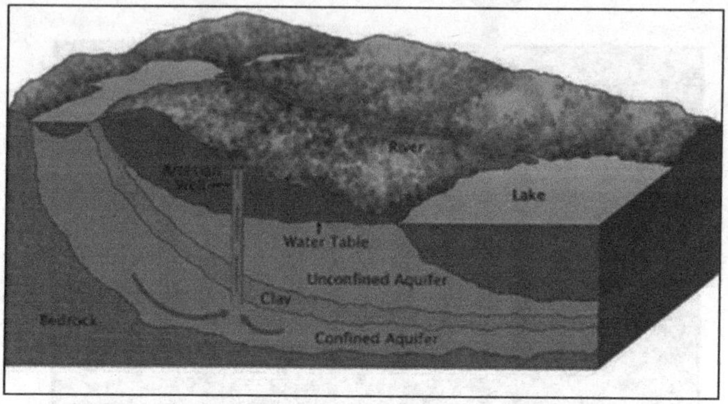

Figure 4.29 Unconfined aquifer

b. **Confined Aquifer:** A confined aquifer is an aquifer that is confined in between two impervious beds such as aquiclude, aquifuge, etc. The water will be under high pressure comparatively higher than atmospheric pressure due to which it is well known as an artesian aquifer. The thickness of this artesian aquifer is constant throughout. The recharge of this confined aquifer occurs through the place which exposed to the ground surface.

4.7.4 Aquifuge

An aquifuge is an impervious geological formation that neither can store water nor able to yield water through it. An example of an aquifuge is compact rock.

4.7.5 Aquiclude

An aquiclude is a geological formation that is highly porous and stores large amounts of water but it is unable to yield water through it. An example of aquiclude is clay soil.

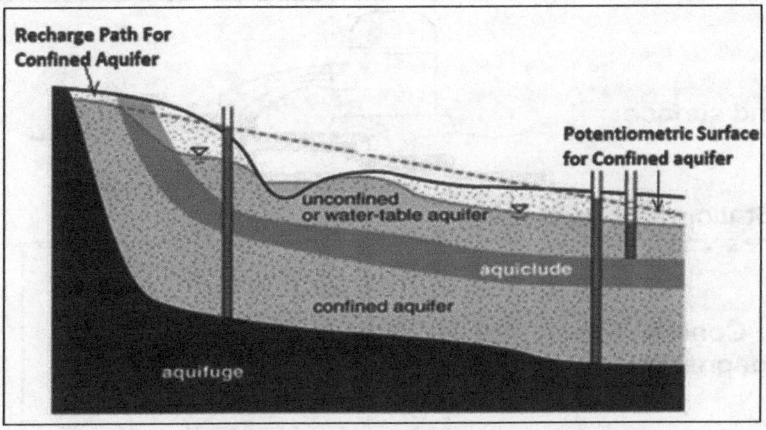

Figure 4.30 Confined aquifer

4.7.6 Aquitard

An aquitard is a saturated geological formation. It stores enough water in it but is unable to yield water in sufficient quantity due partly permeable nature. Sandy clay soil is an example of an aquitard in which clay particles block the voids within the sand to make the formation partly permeable.

Terms used in tube well Irrigation

a. Static water level. The initial level of water inside the well before pumping starts is called static water level.

b. Pumping water level: The level of water in the tubwell during pumping is called the pumping water level.

c. Drawdown: The difference between the static and pumping water levels at a specific moment in time is known as drawdown.

d. Radius of influence: The radius of effect is the horizontal distance measured from the well's center to the point where the decline curve intersects the original, static water table before pumping.

e. Cone of depression: Cone of depression refers to the conical depression in water level caused by ongoing water loss relative to the initial water table.

f. Depression head: The term "depression head" refers to the variation between the water table elevation and the water level within the well.

g. Yield of Tube well: The volume of water that can be pumped per unit of time is known as the yield of the tube well.

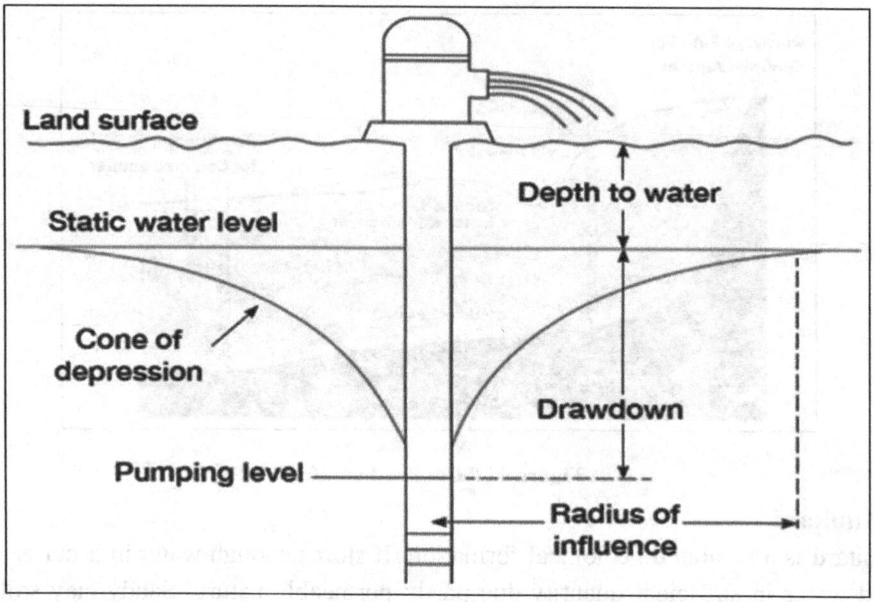

Figure 4.31 Definition Sketch showing drawdown and Radius of Influence

Yield of Tube wells by Theim's Formula

a. **For Unconfined aquifers:**

Let's drill a tube well into an open aquifer and pump water in a method that creates a sufficient decline. A cone-shaped depression is created as the water level surrounding the well falls as the water level inside the well drops due to pumping.

This cone's sloped side is referred to as the drawdown curve, and its base is called the circle of radius of effect (R).

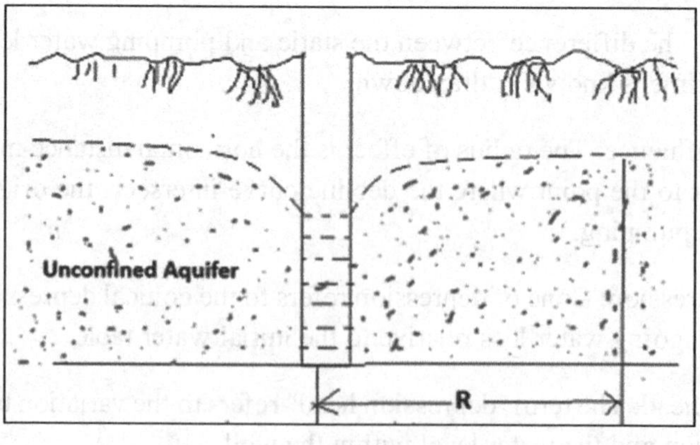

Figure 4.32 Unconfined Aquifer

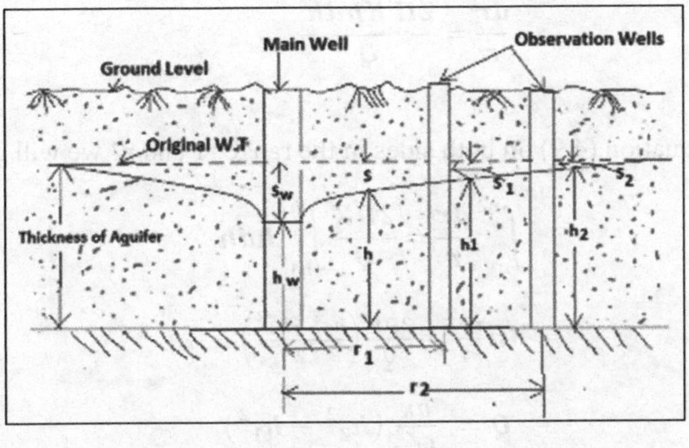

Figure 4.33 Unconfined Aquifer for Thiem's equation derivation

Let two wells be driven at a distance of r1 and r2 from the center of the main well. Let'd' be the depth of water below the initial static water table before pumping. Let the water be pumped from the main well at a high rate to get a significant amount of drawdown. The pumping is then adjusted so there an equilibrium condition is reached in the well i.e. rate of pumping will be equal to the rate of recharge within the main well. Suppose S1 and S2 are the drawdowns in the two observation wells when the equilibrium condition is reached in the well.

According to Darcy's law the rate of discharge

$$Q = KIA \tag{4.8}$$

Where K= hydraulic conductivity of aquifer

Hydraulic gradient of flow= $I = \frac{dh}{dr}$

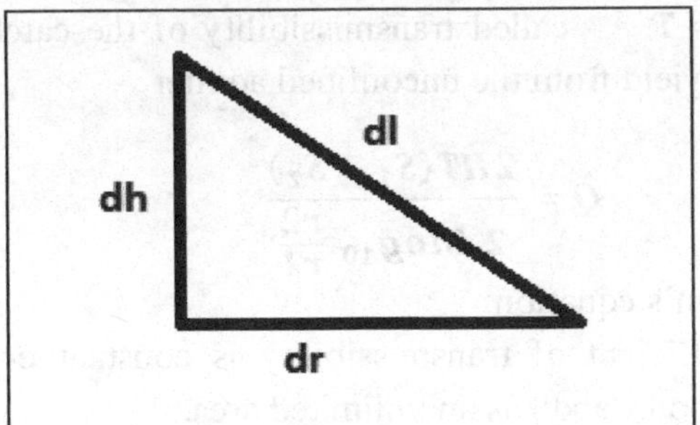

Figure 4.34 Small elements of the drawdown curve

Area of flow per though aquifer at a radial distance r and can be calculated as $A = 2\Pi rh$

Now putting the values I and A in equation (4.8) we will get

$$\frac{dr}{r} = \frac{2\Pi\ Khdh}{Q} \tag{4.9}$$

Now integrating equation (4.9) on both sides in the range r1 and r2 we will get

$$\int_{r1}^{r2} \frac{dr}{r} = \frac{2\Pi K}{Q} \int_{h1}^{h2} hdh$$

$$=> ln\frac{r2}{r1} = \frac{2\Pi K}{Q}\left(\frac{{h_2}^2 - {h_1}^2}{2}\right)$$

$$=> Q = \frac{\Pi K}{ln\frac{r2}{r1}}\left({h_2}^2 - {h_1}^2\right)$$

$$=> Q = \frac{\Pi K\left({h_2}^2 - {h_1}^2\right)}{2.3log_{10}\frac{r2}{r1}} \tag{4.10}$$

Again we know that ${h_2}^2 - {h_1}^2 = (h_2 + h_1)(h_2 - h_1)$

We can observe from the above figure: $(h_2 - h_1) = (S_1 - S_2)$

Also, for a small drawdown compared to the thickness of the saturated aquifer, the value $(h_2 + h_1)$ can be nearly equal to twice the depth of the saturated depth of the aquifer. So we can write$(h_2 + h_1) \cong d + d$. So $(h_2 + h_1) = 2d$

Now putting $(h_2 - h_1) = (S_1 - S_2)$ and $(h_2 + h_1) = 2d$ in equation 4.10 we will get

$$Q = \frac{\Pi K2d(S_1 - S_2)}{2.3log_{10}\frac{r2}{r1}} = \frac{2\Pi Kd(S_1 - S_2)}{2.3log_{10}\frac{r2}{r1}} \tag{4.11}$$

Again $Kd = T$ called transmissibility of the catchment, now the final equation for discharge or yield from the unconfined aquifer

$$Q = \frac{2\Pi T(S_1 - S_2)}{2.3log_{10}\frac{r2}{r1}} \tag{4.12}$$

The assumptions for Theim's equation:

1. The aquifer's coefficient of transmissibility is constant everywhere since it is isotropic, homogenous, and has an unlimited area.
2. Pumping should continue at a constant pace until the steady flow rate or equilibrium stage is attained.
3. To ensure that it receives water from the whole depth or thickness of the aquifer, the well is drilled into the aquifer.
4. The inclination of the water's surface is minimal, allowing Darcy's permeability equation's hydraulic gradient to be calculated using the tangent as a sine function.

5. Flow inside the well is considered as laminar flow lines and they are considered as radial horizontal flow

b. For Confined Aquifer or Artesian well:

For the confined aquifer the above assumptions remain the same but the flow is radial and horizontal, so there is no assumption for it.

The discharge according to Darcy's law

$$Q = KIA = K\frac{dh}{dr}A \tag{4.13}$$

Where, K= Hydraulic Conductivity

$\frac{dh}{dr}$ = Hydraulic Gradient

A radial Flow area = $2\Pi rH$, H = Height of the confined aquifer as shown below in Figure 4..

Now Put A in the above equation (4.13) so

$$Q = K\frac{dh}{dr}2\Pi rH$$

$$\frac{dr}{r} = \frac{2\Pi KH}{Q}dh \tag{4.14}$$

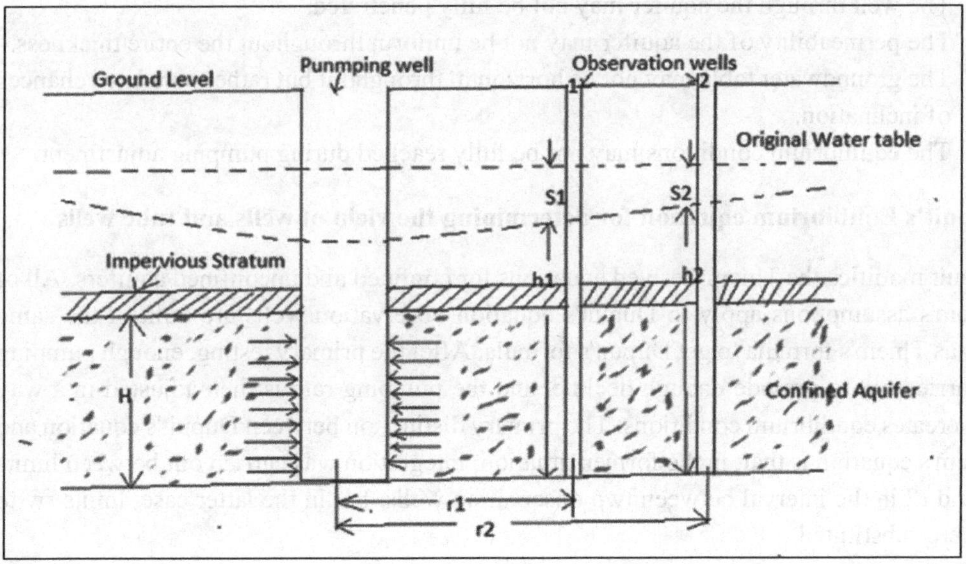

Figure 4.35 Confined Aquifer for Thiem's equation derivation

Now integrating equation (14) on both sides we will get

$$\int_{r1}^{r2}\frac{dr}{r} = \frac{2\Pi KH}{Q}\int_{h1}^{h2}dh$$

$$=> ln\frac{r2}{r1} = \frac{2\Pi KH}{Q}(h_2 - h_1)$$

$$=> Q = \frac{2\Pi KH}{ln\frac{r2}{r1}}((h_2 - h_1))$$

$$=>Q = \frac{2\Pi KH}{2.3log_{10}\frac{r2}{r1}}((h_2 - h_1)) \quad (4.15)$$

Again, from the figure we know that $(h_2 - h_1) = (S_1 - S_2)$ and $KH = T$, so putting this in equation (4.15) we will get discharge from aquifer

$$Q = \frac{2\Pi T(S_1 - S_2)}{2.3log_{10}\frac{r2}{r1}} \quad (4.16)$$

Where T= Transmissibility of the aquifer and S_1 and S_2 are drawdowns in observation wells 1 and 2 respectively.

Limitations of Thiem's Equation

Various assumptions were made by Thiem in derivation yield equations, but in actual cases none of the conditions were satisfied. So the limitations are

a. The soil is not fully homogeneous.
b. The well through the aquifer may not be fully penetrated.
c. The permeability of the aquifer may not be uniform throughout the entire thickness.
d. The groundwater table may not be horizontal throughout but rather may have chances of inclination.
e. The equilibrium conditions may not be fully reached during pumping adjustment.

Dupuit's Equilibrium equation for determining the yield of wells and tube wells

Dupuit modifies the Thiem-derived equations for confined and unconfined aquifers. All of Thiem's assumptions apply to Dupuit's equation observation wells are built in the same way as Thiem's formula to get Dupuit's formula. After the primary testing, enough pumping is carried out to provide enough decline, and the pumping rate is then adjusted in a way that creates equilibrium conditions. The primary distinction between Dupuit's equation and Thiem's equation is that, in the former situation, integration was carried out between limits r1 and r2 in the interval between two observation wells, but in the latter case, limits rw to R were substituted.

The radius of Influence (R): The radius of effect is the length of time between the main well's center and the zero-decline point.

Dupuit's Equilibrium Equation for Unconfined Aquifer

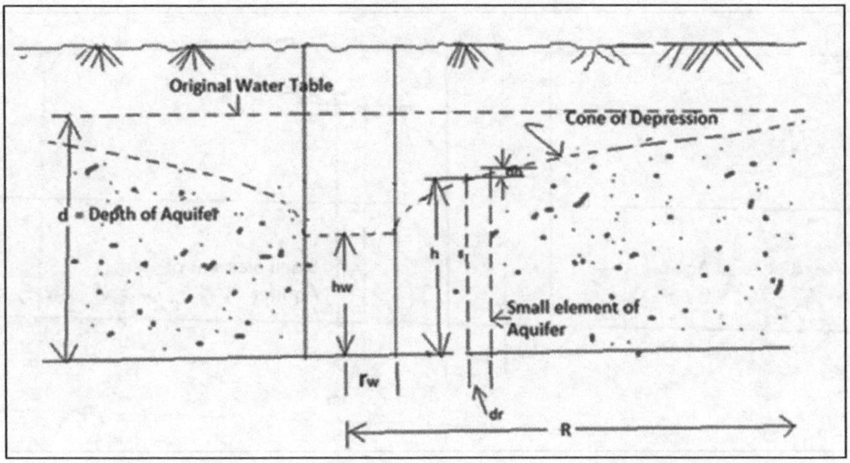

Figure 4.36 Unconfined Aquifer for Dupuit's equation derivation

As per Darcy's law $Q = KIA$

So, the above equation can be written as $Q = K.\frac{dh}{dr}2\Pi rh$ or $\frac{dr}{r} = \frac{2\Pi K}{Q}h.dh$

Now integrating both sides within limits r_w to R we will get from the above equation

$$\int_{r_w}^{R}\frac{dr}{r} = \frac{2\Pi K}{Q}\int_{h_w}^{d} h.dh$$

$$\text{Or}\quad log_e\frac{R}{r_w} = \frac{\Pi K}{Q}\left[d^2 - {h_w}^2\right]$$

$$\text{Or}\quad 2.3\, log_{10}\frac{R}{r_w} = \frac{\Pi K}{Q}\left[d^2 - {h_w}^2\right]$$

$$Q = \frac{\Pi K\left(d^2 - {h_w}^2\right)}{2.3\, log_{10}\frac{R}{r_w}} \tag{4.17}$$

So the above equation no (4.17) is required discharge for the unconfined aquifer. Since the value *R* cannot be accessible easily, the value R can be obtained by relating it to discharge Q from the well. So *R* is directly related to discharge *Q*. *R α Q* or *R= CQ*. C is the constant of proportionality. Now putting the value of R in equation (17) we will get

$$Q = \frac{\Pi K\left(d^2 - {h_w}^2\right)}{2.3\, log_{10}\frac{CQ}{r_w}} \tag{4.18}$$

and Q value is found by the method of Hit and Trial.

Dupuit's Equilibrium Equation for confined aquifer

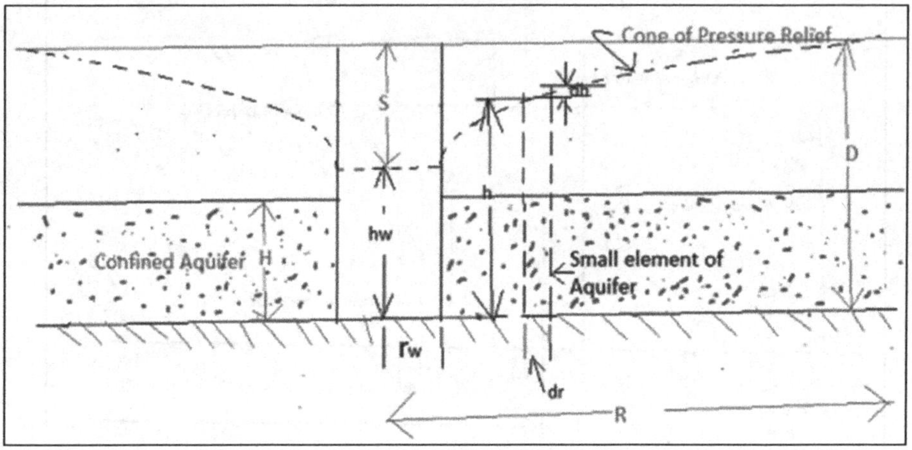

Figure 4.37 Sketch of Confined Aquifer for derivation of Dupuit's equation

We know that $Q = KIA$

So

$$Q = K.\frac{dh}{dr}2\Pi rH$$

$$=> \frac{dr}{r} = \frac{2\Pi KH}{Q}.dh$$

Integrating both sides in between limits r_w to R the above equation will be

$$\int_{r_w}^{R}\frac{dr}{r} = \frac{2\Pi KH}{Q}\int_{h_w}^{D}.dh$$

$$log_e\frac{R}{r_w} = \frac{2\Pi KH}{Q}[D - h_w] \quad (4.19)$$

The above equation (19) can be written as $2.3\ log_{10}\frac{R}{r_w} = \frac{2\Pi KH}{Q}[D - h_w]$

Or

$$Q = \frac{2\Pi KH(D - h_w)}{2.3\ log_{10}\frac{R}{r_w}} \quad (4.20)$$

In the above equation R = Radius of influence; r_w is the radius of the well; K= coefficient of permeability; H is the total height of the confined aquifer; D is the original piezometric surface level; h_w is the height of water level in the well after pumping.

Putting as $D - h_w = S$, where S is the drawdown of the aquifer the final equation for yield from well be

$$Q = \frac{2\Pi KHS}{2.3\, log_{10}\frac{R}{r_w}} \tag{4.21}$$

4.7.7 Well loss

Water pumping out of a restricted aquifer through an artesian well causes drawdown, which is induced by equation (4.21) as well as water flowing through the well's screen and vertically axially moving within the well up to the pump's intake.

In the above figure xx' or yy' is the vertical drawdown known as well loss S_w. This loss occurs due to the flow of water through the screen. The magnitude of this loss S_w is taken as $C_2 Q^2$ where C_2 is a coefficient determined by pumping test data. So the total drawdown will be by adding drawdown due to aquifer loss and drawdown due to well loss.

So, the drawdown S due to aquifer loss found from equation (4.21) $Q = \frac{2\Pi KHS}{2.3\, log_{10}\frac{R}{r_w}}$

so $S =$, Putting C_1 as $\frac{2.3\, log_{10}\frac{R}{r_w}}{2\Pi KH}$ S can be written as $S = C_1Q$. Where C_1 is the coefficient determined from various pumping test data.

So the total drawdown will be equal to

$$S + S_w = C_1Q + C_2 Q^2 \tag{4.22}$$

In the above eq^n (4.22) C_1Q = *Aquifer loss and* $C_2 Q^2$ = *well loss*. The amount of well loss has a great influence on pumping efficiency. More loss indicates more clogging and has a hard coating on good screens requiring immediate recovery to increase the pumping efficiency.

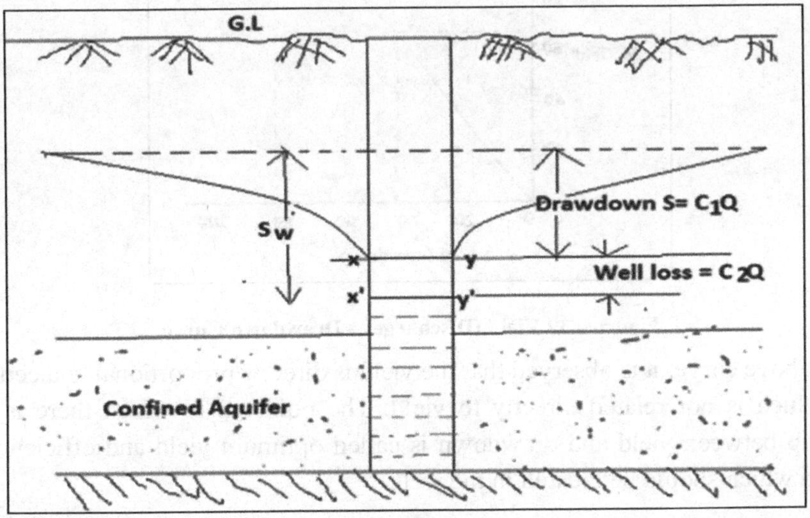

Figure 4.38 Well loss

Specific Capacity of Well

"The rate of yield per unit drawdown from the well is defined as the specific capacity of the well".

So, $\textit{well drawdown} = \frac{Q}{C_1Q+C_2Q^2}$

So Specific Capacity.

$$S.C = \frac{1}{C_1 + C_2Q} \qquad (4.23)$$

From the above eq^n(4.23) it is observed that the specific capacity of the well depends on the discharge of the well. It increases with a decrease in discharge and decreases with an increase in discharge of the well.

4.7.8 Efficiency of the well

As discussed earlier, the discharge of the well is approximately proportional to drawdown(S) i.e. S= C_1Q, neglecting well loss. Also "the discharge per unit drawdown is called the specific capacity of well" which varies with different well designs. To find out the best discharge drawdown condition for a well, it is necessary to plot a graph between the discharge versus drawdown curve of the well which is operated under varying drawdown conditions.

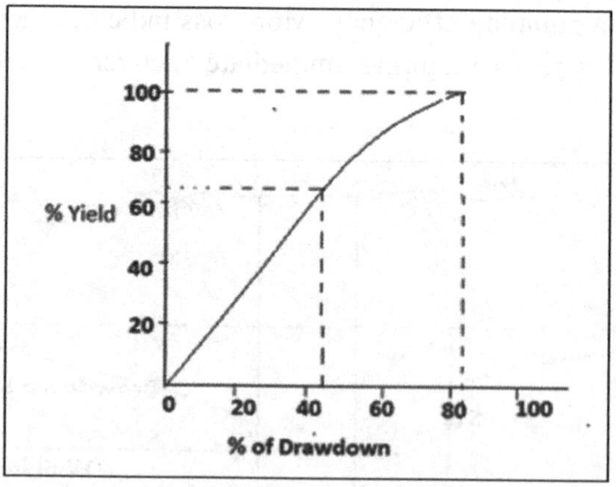

Figure 4.39 Yield (Discharge) – Drawdown Curve

From the above curve, it is observed that the yield is directly proportional to a certain limit beyond which is not related directly to yield. The point up to which there is a direct relationship between yield and drawdown is called optimum yield and efficient limit of drawdown which should be created in the well.

Example 2. A pumping test was prepared in an average sand and gravel medium to a depth of 20m where a bed of clay was encountered. The groundwater level was at the surface.

Observation wells were situated at distances of 3.5m and 8m from the pumping well. At a discharge of 4.5 liters/sec.from the pumping well a steady state was attained in about 24hrs. The drawdown at 3.5m was 1.75m and 7.5 m was 0.4m. Calculate the coefficient of permeability of soil.

Solution:

Given, Q = 4.5 litres/sec; d =20m; r_1= 3.5m; r_2 = 8m; S_1 =1.75m and S_2 =0.4m

So the height of water in observation well 1 will be h_1 = 20 -1.75 =18.75 m and the height of water in observation well 2 will be h_2 = 20 -0.4 =19.6 m.

By using equation (10) $Q = \frac{\Pi K\,(h_2^2 - h_1^2)}{2.3\log_{10}\frac{r2}{r1}}$ we will get

$$\frac{4.5}{1000} m^3/sec = \frac{\Pi K}{2.3}\left[\frac{19.6^2 - 18.75^2}{\log_{10}\frac{8}{3.5}}\right] = \frac{\Pi K}{2.3}\left[\frac{384.16 - 351.56}{\log_{10}\frac{8}{3.5}}\right]$$

or K = $\frac{4.5X2.3}{1000} X\log_{10}\frac{8}{3.5} X\, 32.6X\frac{1}{\Pi}$ =0.0385cm/sec Ans.

Example 3. A 40 cm diameter well penetrates 30m below the static water table. After pumping for 24 hours at an amount of 6200 *litre*/m, the water level in an observation well which is 95m away is decreased by 0.55m, and in another well which is 32m away the drawdown is 1.15m. (a) Calculate transmissibility of aquifer (b) Also determine its value of drawdown in main pumping well.

Solution:

(a) As the well penetrates 30m below the water table the aquifer is considered a confined aquifer. According to Thiem's discharge equation $Q = \frac{\Pi K\,(h_2^2 - h_1^2)}{2.3\log_{10}\frac{r2}{r1}}$

Here h_2 = D- S_2 where D depth of water table, S_2 drawdown at a radial distance r_2,

So h_2 = 30-0.55 =29.55m and h_1 = D- S_1= 30-1.15 =28.85m where S_1 is drawdown at a radial distance r_1.

Given r_2 = 95m, r_1 =32m Q = 6200litres/min = 0.103m³/s

Now in eqⁿ $Q = \frac{\Pi K\,(h_2^2 - h_1^2)}{2.3\log_{10}\frac{r2}{r1}}$ = 0.103= $\frac{\Pi K\,(29.55^2 - 28.85^2)}{2.3\log_{10}\frac{95}{32}}$ or K = $\frac{0.103X2.3\log_{10}\frac{95}{32}}{\Pi\,(29.55^2 - 28.85^2)}$

=0.872 x 10^{-3}m/s.

Therefore, transmissibility T = KD = 0.872×10^{-3}×30 = 0.026 m²/s **Ans.**

(b) The drawdown in the main well as per equation for discharge $Q = \frac{\Pi K\,(h_2^2 - h_1^2)}{2.3\log_{10}\frac{r2}{r1}}$

In the above eqⁿ putting h_1 as h_2 and h_1 as h_w, whereas h_w is the height of water in the main well and r_1 in place of r_2 and r_w in place of r_1, where the r_w is the radius of the main well, the equation can be rewritten as $Q = \frac{\Pi K\,(h_1^2 - h_w^2)}{2.3\log_{10}\frac{r1}{rw}}$

Or $0.103 = \frac{\Pi K\,(28.85^2 - h_w^2)}{2.3\log_{10}\frac{32}{0.20}}$

Or $28.85^2 - h_w^2 = \frac{0.103}{\Pi X0.872X10^{-3}} 2.3\log_{10}\frac{32}{0.20}$ = 190.7

Or $h_w^2 = 641.62$ or $h_w = 25.33$

So, the drawdown will be $S = D - h_w = 30 - 25.33 = 4.67$ m

4.7.9 Advantages and Disadvantages of well irrigation

Advantages:

a. It is easy to operate in case irrigation is done by wells and tube wells.
b. The maintenance cost, as well as construction cost, is affordable in the case of wells and tube wells irrigation systems. So, it is more feasible for the farmers compared to other methods.
c. Wells and tube wells can constructed near the croplands according to requirements.

Disadvantages:

a. Where huge quantities of water are required wells and tube wells cannot be used to draw water.
b. Wells and tube wells become ineffective if the groundwater level decreases significantly.
c. Excessive withdrawal of groundwater through wells and tube wells may source of fluoride and arsenic pollution of water.

UNIT SUMMARY

- Minor and micro-irrigation pro jects play a significant role in expanding global irrigation efforts, utilizing groundwater or surface water for irrigation purposes. These projects are classified as Minor Irrigation Schemes when they cover a Culturable Command Area of up to 2000 hectares.
- This chapter elaborates on Bandhara irrigation, percolation tanks, lift irrigation, drip and sprinkler irrigation, and well irrigation schemes.

EXERCISE

MULTIPLE CHOICE QUESTIONS

1. The storage reservoir created on the upstream side of a small natural stream by constructing of low earthen embankment or bund is known as ____________.
   a) A lake
   b) A reservoir
   c) A tank
   d) A pond
2. The top level of a percolation tank bund is placed at ____________
   a) M.W.L
   b) Full supply level
   c) F.T.L

d) Either M.W.L or F.T.L

3. The planning made in a percolation tank to spill surplus water is called__________
   a) Tank sluice
   b) Tank weir
   c) Tank bund
   d) Tank spillway
4. The most common earthen section for percolation tank __________
   a) Zoned embankment type
   b) Diaphragm type
   c) Homogeneous embankment type
   d) Both diaphragm and zoned type
5. Which of the following irrigation methods is also known as trickle irrigation?
   a) Check Flooding
   b) Drip Irrigation Method
   c) Furrow Irrigation Method
   d) Sprinkler Irrigation Method
6. Which of the following irrigation methods is experienced on a small scale in India?
   a) Artificial sub-irrigation
   b) Natural sub-irrigation
   c) Flood Irrigation
   d) Lift Irrigation
7. Which of the following irrigation methods is helpful for sandy soils and shallow land where leveling of land is not possible?
   a) Sub-surface irrigation
   b) Drip irrigation
   c) Sprinkler Irrigation
   d) Surface Irrigation
8. The irrigation method in which water is slowly applied to the root zone of the plant to reduce the losses due to percolation and evaporation is known as_______
   a) Surface irrigation
   b) Sprinkler irrigation
   c) Drip Irrigation
   d) Lift Irrigation
9. The performance of a well is calculated by its _______.
   a) Specific yield
   b) permeability coefficient
   c) Specific capacity
   d) Storage coefficient
10. The safe depression head in open wells is usually taken to be y times the critical depression head when y is ______.

a) 1/6
b) 1/2
c) 1/3
d) 3/4

11. The open well's diameter varies from
a) 0.5 to 1 m.
b) 15 to 19 m
c) 2 to 7 m.
d) 8 to 14 m.

12. The well draws which is known as deep well draws water from the ____ aquifer
a) Unconfined
b) Perched
c) Confined.
d) None of the above

Answers

1	2	3	4	5	6	7	8	9	10	11	12
c	c	d	c	b	a	c	c	c	c	c	c

SHORT ANSWER TYPE QUESTIONS

1. Explain different types of Bandhara Irrigation system with its function
2. Differentiate between sprinkler and drip irrigation methods.
3. Briefly explain about drip irrigation method.
4. Explain different types of well irrigation
5. Derive the expression for discharge in an artesian well assuming penetrated through homogeneous soil having equilibrium flow condition.
6. Explain the Dupuit flow equation along with assumptions. Derived the expression for confined aquifer according to Dupuit.
7. Explain well loss and well efficiency and their importance.

LONG ANSWER TYPE QUESTIONS

1. In a confined aquifer, a drawdown of about 1.8m at a radial distance 6 meters from the center of the well after 2 hours of pumping. Determine the pumping time required for the same drawdown for a radial distance of 15 meters from the center of the well. Use Thiem's equation.
2. A well of 40 cm diameter will be penetrating 20m below the static water table. The drawdown in the observation wells is 0.6m for 80m away and 1m for 20m away from the main pumping well respectively. The pumping rate in the main well is 4000 liters per minute for 24 hours. What is the transmissibility of the aquifer?
3. Water is pumped at a rate of 1250 liters per minute from an 80cm diameter pumping well. The drawdowns were found 5m at a distance of 5m and 1.6 m at a distance of 16 m in two observation wells respectively. The depth of the well is 80m below the

groundwater table. (a) Find the hydraulic conductivity of the aquifer. (b) What it's the drawdown in pumping well if all observation points were following Dupuit's curve? (c) What is the maximum discharge that can be pumped from the well? (d) Calculate the Specific capacity of the well.

PRACTICAL

Based on the knowledge gained from this unit, perform the following experiments.

Experiment 1: Create a presentation focusing on the technical aspects of a selected micro or minor irrigation system.

Experiment 2: Construct a scale model of an irrigation structure using appropriate materials.

Experiment 3: Compile a maintenance report for a major or minor irrigation project located near your area, drawing upon observations and findings from a site visit.

Experiment 4: Draft a summary that captures the technical specifics of a water resources project located in or near your area, detailing its structure, function, and operational status.

KNOW MORE

Activity 1: Make different groups of students visit nearby sites where a Bandhara Irrigation scheme exists. Interact with the Engineers and the farmers. Compare your knowledge with the real field implementation. Write the gaps.

Activity 2: Let the groups collect the details of the Percolation tank in a nearby area. Classify the soil type of the tank and the catchment area from where the water enters the tank.

Activity 3: Let one group of students visit a Lift Irrigation Scheme and collect data on the command area, crop types grown, yield, and farmer's level of satisfaction and prepare a report.

Activity 4: Let one group of students visit a Drip or Sprinkler Irrigation Scheme and collect data on the irrigated area, crop types grown, yield, and farmer's level of satisfaction and prepare a report.

Activity 5: Let another group of students visit a Well Irrigation Scheme and collect data on the yield of the well, command area, crop types grown, yield, and farmer's level of satisfaction and prepare a report.

Interesting Facts

1. The practice of irrigation is deeply rooted in history, having been a fundamental aspect of Indian civilization since ancient times, along with canal building.
2. Ancient Indian scriptures, the Vedas, are filled with mentions of water management structures like wells, tanks, canals, and dams, with the Samritis also documenting early examples of irrigation systems.
3. India's historical leaders prioritized irrigation infrastructure, establishing early systems based on scientific principles. A prime illustration of ancient engineering prowess is the ambitious creation of a large anicut on the Cauvery River in the second century A.D.

4. In the 19th century, the British began to focus on the development of irrigation, erecting notable dams such as the Periyar and Mettur; similarly, dams like Nizamsagar and Krishnarajasagar were developed by local princes within their domains.
5. The British solidified their approach to irrigation in 1854 by founding the Public Works Department and creating a dedicated fund for irrigation projects.
6. Irrigation efforts were divided into Minor and Major works. Minor works primarily aimed at preserving existing agricultural land and its revenue rather than generating new income and were funded through general state revenues. Over time, minor irrigation increasingly encompassed private projects, particularly renovations, playing a significant role in the Grow More Food Campaign.
7. The introduction of public tube wells as part of minor irrigation initiatives occurred with the establishment of the agriculture department in 1845. Conversely, major irrigation projects were funded through public borrowing, with each project needing to meet specific productivity benchmarks.
8. Subsequent reports by the Famine Commission (1880) and the First Irrigation Commission (1928) emphasized the importance of supporting private irrigation efforts (such as wells and tanks) to mitigate the effects of recurring famines.
9. Over the past century and a half, India has experienced eight major famines, with the most recent occurring in Bengal in 1943. Such famines in tropical and subtropical regions like India are often precipitated by droughts.

In India, the stewardship of the Minor Irrigation (MI) sector primarily rests with the state governments and Union Territories. They are charged with the responsibilities of developing, planning, investigating, and executing MI projects. Despite this state-level autonomy, the central government significantly influences through policy formulation, design guidance, and sector development, involving multiple ministries such as the Ministry of Water Resources, River Development and Ganga Rejuvenation, Ministry of Agriculture & Farmer's Welfare, Ministry of Rural Development, and Ministry of Tribal Affairs. Correspondingly, at the state level, the management of this sector is overseen by respective departments and ministries related to Water Resources, Agriculture, Rural Development, and Tribal Welfare.

Funding for MI initiatives is sourced through various state channels, including the Department of Irrigation/Minor Irrigation and Water Resources Development, in addition to local bodies and Public Works Departments. Financial incentives, often in the form of subsidies, support a broad spectrum of MI activities, ranging from the construction of tube wells and wells to the procurement of water distribution systems and micro-irrigation technologies like drip and sprinkler systems.

The Mahatma Gandhi National Rural Employment Guarantee Act (MGNREGA) significantly contributes to water conservation and management efforts, employing rural projects aimed at water conservation, drought proofing, irrigation canal construction, renovation of traditional water bodies, and flood control measures. These projects not only bolster water resource management for agriculture but also generate employment, addressing economic and environmental challenges simultaneously.

The Indian government's dedication to water conservation culminated in the launch of the Pradhan Mantri Krishi Sinchayee Yojana (PMKSY), with objectives to extend irrigation coverage and enhance water efficiency across farmlands. PMKSY offers end-to-end solutions from water source creation to its field-level application, promoting state-led planning and execution based on tailored irrigation strategies. This scheme also targets the socio-economic upliftment of Particularly Vulnerable Tribal Groups (PVTGs) by incorporating irrigation supports tailored to their needs and respecting their cultural heritage.

The Rationalisation of Minor Irrigation Statistics (RMIS) scheme, a component of PMKSY, endeavors to build a comprehensive MI database, facilitating informed planning and policymaking. Through its regular censuses, RMIS provides insights into irrigation potential, water distribution practices, and energization sources within the MI sector. Each state or UT appoints a Nodal Department for RMIS implementation, ensuring the collection and coordination of minor irrigation statistics, thus enhancing water management and agricultural productivity across India. This systematic approach underscores the government's commitment to advancing water conservation and agricultural prosperity.

Case Study

A case study of a minor irrigation plan of a part of Bargarh District of Odisha is presented below by reproducing the details presented in the District Irrigation Plan. (Ref.: https://pmksy.gov.in/mis/Uploads/2016/20160602021535100-1.pdf)

"DISTRICT IRRIGATION PLAN OF part of BARGARH (ODISHA) Under PRADHAN MANTRI KRISHI SINCHAYEE YOJANA (PMKSY)"

Introduction

In India, the 'Pradhan Mantri Krishi Sinchayee Yojana' (PMKSY) has been initiated under the slogan 'Har Khet Ko Pani' to provide water to every farm. It emphasizes the importance of exploring all possible measures, including river interlinking where viable, to utilize water resources efficiently and avoid the adverse effects of floods and droughts. The overarching goal is to ensure every farm in the district has access to protective irrigation facilities to enhance crop yield per unit of water, leading to rural prosperity. The initiative's main objectives include consolidating farm-level irrigation investments, enhancing both the availability and accessibility of water for farming, expanding the reach of dependable irrigation services ('Har Khet Ko Pani'), optimizing water efficiency within farms to reduce wastage and increase effectiveness, advocating for precise irrigation and other water-saving methodologies ('Per Drop More Crop'), replenishing underground water sources, adopting sustainable methods for conserving water, promoting comprehensive development in rainfed regions through the watershed management technique, attracting private investment into the irrigation sector, and others. All these efforts are directed towards increasing agricultural productivity and elevating the earnings of farmers.

The Minor Irrigation Division in Bargarh manages an area of 19,464.66 hectares through check dams and other minor irrigation structures, having built 600 check dams across the district. Additionally, the Lift Irrigation Division enhances irrigation with community lift projects, shallow tube wells, and powered bore well systems. Currently, there are 625 operational lift irrigation projects covering 12,736 hectares, and 4,800 powered bore wells irrigating 28,898 hectares of agricultural land.

Rationale/ Justification Statement

The development of irrigation potential as a percentage of the net area sown exhibits significant variation across regions, ranging from 26% in Bijepur block to 104% in Attabira & Bheden block, as shown in the table below. This uneven distribution of irrigation facilities has led to considerable disparity and dissatisfaction among farmers, especially in less irrigated blocks. There is a pressing need for the construction of government-supported irrigation projects, tailored to the specific needs of the terrain and groundwater characteristics, in numerous villages. Implementing such schemes would not only expand the irrigated land but also support the national initiative of ensuring water for every field (Har Khet Ko Pani). Bargarh district's soil and climatic conditions are conducive to a diverse range of crops. The positive effects of irrigation have been observed within the district, where farmers, out of necessity, have been practicing rainfed agriculture due to a lack of irrigation infrastructure. The importance of irrigation and its potential benefits are well recognized. The district hosts several potential sites for minor irrigation projects. The Padampur Minor Irrigation Division, within the district, has completed numerous such projects and plans to initiate more, incorporating both gravity and lift irrigation methods. A significant portion of the agricultural land remains outside the scope of the Command Area Development and Water Management (CADWM) program, offering an immediate opportunity to enhance irrigation coverage through the construction of field channels. Additionally, there is a considerable demand for bore wells, with about 8000 farmers expressing interest in lift irrigation solutions. Where electricity is available or can be promptly connected, bore wells can provide reliable irrigation across various locations in the Bargarh district. Under the rebranded PMKSY (previously IWMP), projects from batch 1 to batch 6 have received commitments for financial support from the Government of India, contingent on budget allocations. The construction of check dams, farm ponds, and other infrastructure for protective and, where possible, guaranteed irrigation could significantly enhance water availability. These measures will not only serve as irrigation sources but also contribute to groundwater recharge.

Status of Command Area

Currently, the Bargarh district boasts a net irrigable area of 181,896 hectares. The major irrigation infrastructure is overseen by the Canal Division of Bargarh and the Sambalpur Irrigation Division, primarily utilizing canal-based methods. The Canal Division extends its services to six blocks within the Bargarh district, while the Sambalpur division covers three. Additionally, the Nuapada Irrigation Division supports two blocks with medium canal-based irrigation. The Minor Irrigation (MI) Division manages a 19,464.66-hectare area through check dams and other minor systems, having constructed 600 check dams across the district. Specifics about the check dam's coverage are explored in the section discussing existing irrigation types. The Lift Irrigation Division offers irrigation via community run-of-the-river projects, shallow tube wells, and powered bore wells. Currently, there are 625 operational Run-of-the-River projects covering 12,736 hectares, and 4,800 powered bore wells irrigating 28,898 hectares. Watershed management further contributes to irrigation, covering 8,283.30 hectares of farmable land.

For a practical understanding of the minor irrigation initiatives planned, an excerpt from the Bargarh District Irrigation Plan for 2016 in Odisha is provided:

i. Document Title: District Irrigation Plan of Bargarh, Odisha for the Year 2016
ii. Cluster Name: Bandeswaria Nalla, within the Padampur Block
iii. Cluster's Total Area: 21,973 hectares
iv. Gram Panchayats Included: 6
v. Number of Minor Irrigation Schemes: 6
vi. Area Under All Minor Irrigation Schemes: 2,631 hectares
vii. Length of Lined Channels: 483.406 kilometers
viii. Length of Unlined Channels: 175.784 kilometers
ix. Construction Cost for Channels under Command Area Development: INR 94,483,900
x. Demonstration Costs under Command Area Development: INR 3,295,950
xi. Training Costs: INR 3,515,680

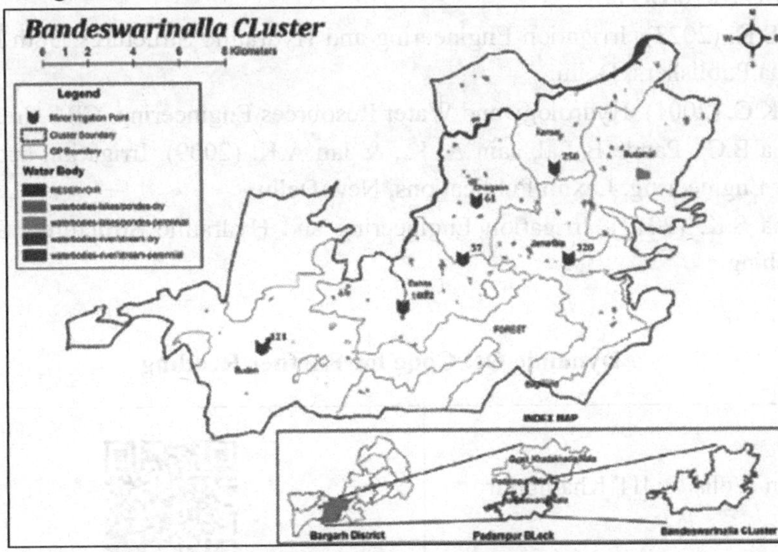

Figure 4.40 Bandeswari Nalla Cluster

(**Source:** *https://pmksy.gov.in/mis/Uploads/2016/20160602021535100-1.pdf*)

REFERENCES & SUGGESTED READING

- Asawa G.L. (2005). Irrigation and Water Resource Engineering. New Age Publishers.
- Basak N.N. (1999). Irrigation Engineering. McGraw Hill Education.
- Brouwer C., & Heibloem M. (1986). Irrigation Water Management: Irrigation Water Needs. Training manual no. 3. FAO.
- Dahigaonkar J.G. (2006). Text Book of Irrigation Engineering. Asian Book Pvt. Ltd., New Delhi.
- FAO. (1984). Crop Water Requirements. By: J. Doorenbos & W.O. Pruitt. FAO Irrigation and Drainage Paper 24, Rome, Italy.
- FAO. (1986). Yield Response to Water. By: J. Doorenbos & A.H. Kassam. FAO Irrigation and Drainage Paper 33, Rome, Italy.
- FAO. (1992). CROPWAT: A Computer Program for Irrigation Planning and Management. Developed by: Martin Smith. FAO Irrigation and Drainage Paper 46, Rome, Italy.
- FAO. (1993). CLIMWAT for CROPWAT: A Climatic Database for Irrigation Planning and Management. Developed by: Martin Smith. FAO Irrigation and Drainage Paper 49, Rome, Italy.
- FAO. (1998a). Crop Evapotranspiration: Guidelines for Computing Crop Water Requirements. By: Richard Allen, Luis Pereira, Dirk Raes & Martin Smith. FAO Irrigation and Drainage Paper 56, Rome, Italy.
- FAO. (1998b). Guidelines for Investigation, Design, Construction and Management of Irrigation Schemes. Prepared by: FAO TCP/BOT/4451 and FAO UTF/BOT/010/BOT.
- Garg S.K. (2023). Irrigation Engineering and Hydraulic Structures, 38th Edition. Khanna Publishers, Delhi.
- Patra K.C. (2001). Hydrology and Water Resources Engineering. CRC Press.
- Punmia B.C., Pande B Lal, Jain A. K., & Jan A.K. (2009). Irrigation and Water Power Engineering. Laxmi Publications, New Delhi.
- Sharma S.K. (2017). Irrigation Engineering and Hydraulic Structures. S.Chand Publishing.

Dynamic QR Code for Further Reading

Irrigation Wells by IIT Kharagpur	

Drip Irrigation Design by IIT Kharagpur	
Aquifer Properties by IIT Kharagpur	

5 DIVERSION HEADWORKS & CANALS

परिचयः ॥ Introduction

Diversion headworks and canals are critical components of water management systems, designed to control and direct water flow for various purposes such as irrigation, flood control, and water supply. These structures play an essential role in the efficient and sustainable use of water resources, particularly in agricultural regions where water distribution is vital for crop production.

"यथा धारा निझरिभ्यः समुद्रं गच्छन्ति, तथा जीवनं जलमेव साधयति ।।"

"Just as streams from the mountains flow to the ocean, so does life thrive through water."

UNIT SPECIFICS

The following aspects will be discussed elaborately in this unit.

- Diversion head works
- Weirs
- Barrages
- Canals
- Canal lining
- Cross Drainage works
- Canal regulators

This chapter will introduce the practical uses of the subjects covered to enhance curiosity, creativity, and problem-solving abilities. It features a vast array of multiple-choice and both short and long-answer questions, organized into two levels according to Bloom's taxonomy's lower and higher orders. Additionally, learners are provided with numerical assignments, along with a compilation of references and recommended readings for further practice.

To enrich the learning experience with more in-depth information on selected topics, QR codes are strategically placed throughout the text. These codes lead to additional supportive material upon scanning.

Following the practical exercises, the chapter introduces a "Know More" segment, carefully crafted to offer extra information that is of great value to readers. This segment focuses on the foundational activities, intriguing facts, analogies, and the historical progression of the subject, emphasizing key observations and discoveries. It outlines the timeline of the subject's evolution to present times and discusses its application in everyday life and various industries. Case studies are included to give the reader a real-life experience. The purpose is to stimulate curiosity and inquisitiveness about the topics discussed in the unit, enriching the reader's understanding.

RATIONALE

This introductory course on is designed to build students' knowledge and skills in the field. By the end of the course, students will have a solid foundation on “Diversion Headworks and Canals”, which they will be able to apply specifically in civil engineering context. They will possess the capability to employ techniques for selection of sites, layout, planning and execution of Weirs, Diversion headworks, Barrages, Canals, CD Works and Canal Regulators.

PRE-REQUISITES

Science: Fundamentals of Intermediate Science

Mathematics: Fundamentals of Intermediate Mathematics

UNIT OUTCOMES

At the end of the course, the student will be able to:

U5-O1: Differentiate various types of weirs and construct K.T. weir.
U5-O2: Select site, give layout and construct Diversion Headworks
U5-O3: Execute the construction of Barrages
U5-O4: Plan and Execute the construction of canals, their linings and canal regulators.
U5-O5: Decide to choose and construct a given type of cross-drainage structure

ALIGNMENT WITH COURSE OBJECTIVE

UNIT OUTCOMES	EXPECTED ALIGNMENT WITH COURSE OUTCOMES (1: Low Correlation; 2: Moderate Correlation; 3: High Correlation)				
	CO:1	CO:2	CO:3	CO:4	CO:5
UO-1	-	-	3	-	2
UO-2	-	-	3	-	2
UO-3	-	-	3	-	2
UO-4	-	-	3	-	2
UO-5	-	-	3	-	2

5.1 DIVERSION HEAD WORKS

5.1.1 General

Headworks are hydraulic structures that provide water to the off-taking canal. Headworks may be further subdivided into storage and diversion headworks.

a. Storage headworks - Structure built across a river to store water is known as storage headworks. Hydroelectric energy production, floods control and fishery are some of the multidisciplinary functions that exist in these headworks. Dam is constructed across a river valley to form storage in the reservoir for storage headworks.
b. Diversion headworks - When a structure is put in place to improve the water level or divert it through canals with shallow heads, that's known as diversion headwork. Weirs and barrages are constructed across a perennial river to raise water level and then diverted the water to canal system.

5.1.2 Functions of diversion headworks

a. It raises the water level at the canal's head on the upstream side.
b. It controls water supply into the canals.
c. It regulates the influx of silt into canals.
d. It controls the water level fluctuations during different seasons.
e. It creates small ponds on its up-stream and provide pondage throughout the season.

5.1.3 Components of diversion headworks

a. Weir or barrages
b. Divide wall
c. Under sluices or scouring sluices
d. Fish ladder
e. Canal head regulator

f. Silt excluder/ silt ejector
g. River training works

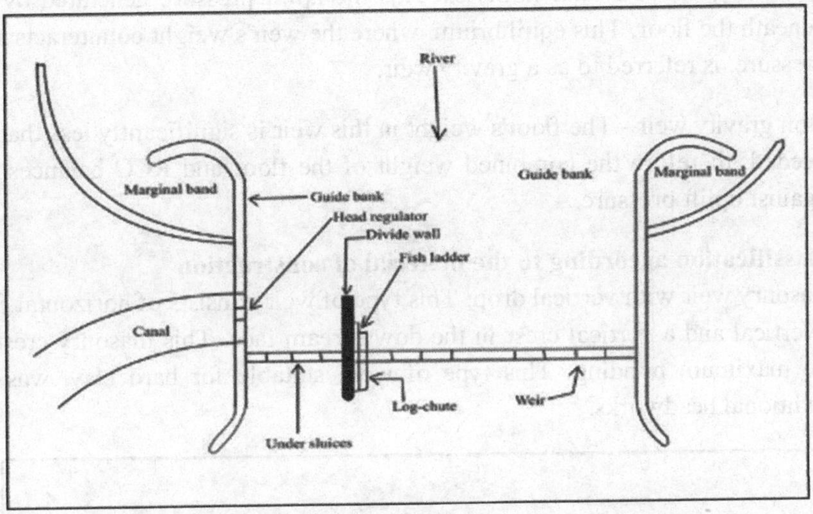

Figure 5.1 Layout of Diversion Headworks with its components

5.2 WEIRS AND BARRAGES

5.2.1 Weirs

A weir is a small dam built across a river to control the upstream water level. Weirs have been used for ages to control the flow of water in streams, rivers, and other water bodies. Unlike large dams which create reservoirs, the goal of building a weir across a river isn't to create storage, but only to gain some control over the water level.

Normally the water of the river cannot be diverted to the canal because of low head. Therefore, to raise the water level and for ponding effect, a structure is constructed across the river. A weir is a barrier where a substantial or complete ponding of water is accomplished through a raised crest, and a smaller or no part of it is achieved by shutters. It leads to a rise in the water level on the side of the canal head facing upstream.

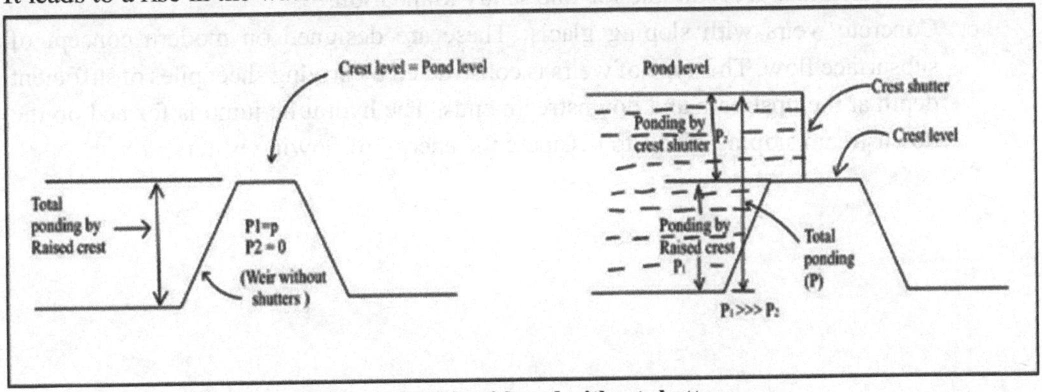

Figure 5.2 Weir with and without shutter

5.2.1.1 Classification of weir with respect to floor

a. Gravity weir - In a gravity weir, the combined weight of the weir structure (including the body and floor) exceeds the uplift pressure generated by seepage beneath the floor. This equilibrium, where the weir's weight counteracts the uplift pressure, is referred to as a gravity weir.

b. Non gravity weir - The floor's weight in this weir is significantly less than what is needed, therefore the combined weight of the floor and RCC balances stability against uplift pressure.

5.2.1.2 Classification according to the material of construction

a. Masonry weir with vertical drop: This type of weir consists of horizontal floor and a vertical and a vertical crest in the downstream face. This masonry crest creates the maximum ponding. This type of weir, suitable for hard clay, was used in traditional headworks.

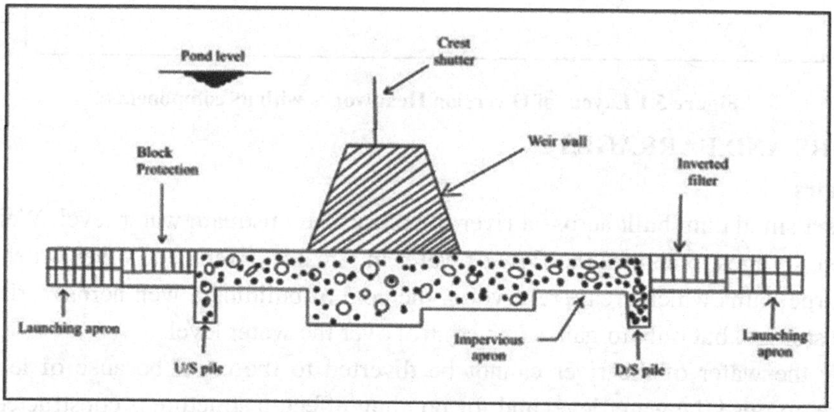

Figure 5.3 Components of a Vertical drop weir

b. Rock fill weirs: This type of weir is suitable for area where huge quantities of stone are available and is suitable for fine sandy foundation.

c. Concrete weirs with sloping glacis: These are designed on modern concept of subsurface flow. This type of weirs is constructed by driving sheet piles of sufficient depth at the upstream and downstream ends. The hydraulic jump is formed on the downstream sloping glacis to dissipate the energy of flowing water.

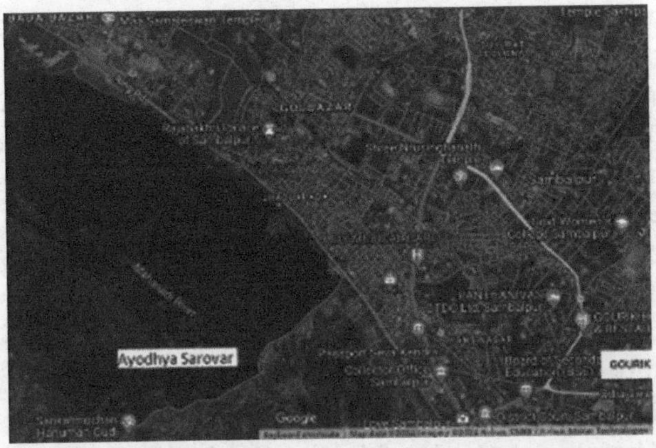

Figure 5.4 View of Ayodhya Sarovar created behind a Weir, Sambalpur, Odisha (Source: ***Google map*****)**

Figure 5.5 Ayodhya Sarovar behind the Weir, Sambalpur, Odisha

In the following, we will present few special types of weirs which may fall under any one of the weirs classified in previous paragraphs. Out of these, the Kolhapur Type Weir (K. T Weir) is discussed in detail since this type of weir is cheap from view point of construction and easy to construct with local manpower.

The Kolhapur type (K.T) weirs

The Kolhapur-Type (K.T.) weir, often referred to as a bridge-cum-bandhara, derives its name from its place of origin, the Kolhapur District. Designed to serve a dual function, it not only captures or stores water following the monsoon season, thereby ensuring a steady base flow, but also functions as a bridge. This innovative structure facilitates vehicle and pedestrian movement across it while also addressing the water supply needs of adjacent communities. The construction of a K.T. weir requires specific environmental conditions, such as the presence of nonporous rock or soil and impervious riverbanks, to effectively hold water. Once water is collected, it is strategically released or utilized to meet the local demands, especially during the dry period from March to May, providing crucial support to the surrounding areas.

Design Philosophy

The channel is segmented into multiple narrow sections, each spanning between 2 to 3 meters, allowing for water accumulation up to a height of 3.5 meters. This storage capacity is adjusted based on the river's flow during dry seasons, catering to diverse needs. To mitigate the risk of damage from sudden water surges, overflow weirs may be installed along one or both banks. Additionally, protective measures are implemented both upstream and downstream to ensure the structure's integrity. Water retention is facilitated using gate panels measuring 2 meters by 0.5 meters, with each panel's weight ranging between 50 and 100 kilograms, depending on its dimensions.

Design Loads

In the engineering of barrage structures, the design accounts for various forces to ensure stability and durability. These include:

i. Dead Load: The inherent weight of the structure itself.
ii. Static Weight of Water: The pressure exerted by the water against the structure when the gates are closed.
iii. Moving Water Pressure at Highest Flood Level (HFL): The force exerted by water in motion when the structure is gateless during peak flood conditions.
iv. Earth Pressures: The lateral pressures from the surrounding soil that affect the structure.
v. Buoyancy: This occurs at the highest flood level when there are no gates, affecting the structure's stability.
vi. Earthquake Forces: The seismic forces considered when the water reaches 50% of its total depth, impacting the structure's integrity under seismic activity.

Gates

Historically, barriers such as weirs and gates were crafted from wooden planks. These planks were slotted into grooves, with soil or mud packed into the spaces between them to halt water flow during dry periods following the rainy season. Nowadays, advancements in materials technology have introduced lighter and stronger alternatives capable of withstanding modest water pressures. These modern gates are typically installed towards the end of the monsoon season and removed well before the next monsoon begins to prevent any potential damage to the primary structure. The timing for gate installation is determined through careful analysis of rainfall patterns.

Kolhapur-type weirs, or K.T. Weirs, are specific structures designed to control and store water, predominantly seen across rivers. Named after their prevalent construction in the Kolhapur district, these weirs feature a series of piers equipped with grooves for the placement of wooden needles or contemporary materials. These needles span across the piers to a specified height, creating a uniform barrier. The height of the weir can be easily adjusted by adding or removing needles, allowing for flexible water management based on seasonal needs.

Selection of Site for K.T Weir

For the optimal placement of a Kolhapur-Type (K.T.) Weir, certain site conditions are imperative:

i. The presence of quality rock material at the site is crucial as it ensures straightforward foundation construction, providing a stable base for the weir.

ii. The stream or nalla bed where the weir is to be constructed should be relatively flat or have a gentle slope. This characteristic is vital for maximizing water storage capacity while minimizing the height of the bandhara, facilitating efficient water management within the structure's design constraints.

Procedure of Construction

i. A suitable location for construction is chosen.

ii. This structure resembles a barrage-type construction.

iii. Adequate openings must be maintained in the nalla portion to prevent afflux during monsoon discharge.

iv. Masonry piers, featuring regular grooves, are equipped with standard 2-meter openings. These openings are sealed using needles placed in two rows, filled with paddle material in between.

v. The needles are inserted into the grooves of the piers.

vi. The wooden needles, measuring 15 cm in height, 5 cm in thickness, and 2 m in length, are inserted into the openings towards the end of the monsoon season to retain post-monsoon water.

vii. Limiting the number of openings is necessary due to the significant challenges involved in placing the wooden needles towards the end of the monsoon season and removing them just before the onset of monsoon.

viii. The height and top width of the bandhara are determined.

ix. In some cases, the height and top width of the bandhara are determined considering other functions of the structure, such as bridge-cum-bandhara:

   a. The width is 2 m if the structure is intended for use as a footbridge.

   b. The width is 4 m if the structure is intended for use as a road bridge.

Replacement of Needles

The wooden needles utilized in KT weirs generally require replacement approximately every five years, resulting in significant recurring expenses. To address this issue, there's a consideration to substitute wooden needles with mild steel needles, contingent upon the cost-effectiveness of the materials and local circumstances. This modification has the potential to provide a more long-lasting and economically feasible solution.

KT Weirs have become increasingly favoured, especially in areas with sugar factories, owing to their efficiency and usefulness. The standardization of KT weir gates underscores their broad acceptance and the refinement of their design to facilitate efficient water management and meet irrigation requirements.

Figure 5.6 Standard K.T Weir Gates

Various developments over the old type of gates have been done. The advanced version of such gates are as follows, which will help in easy operation of the gates.

Figure 5.7 Steel Gate, Fibre Reinforced & Fibre Concrete (from left)

Figure 5.8 Godbole Gates in closed and open condition

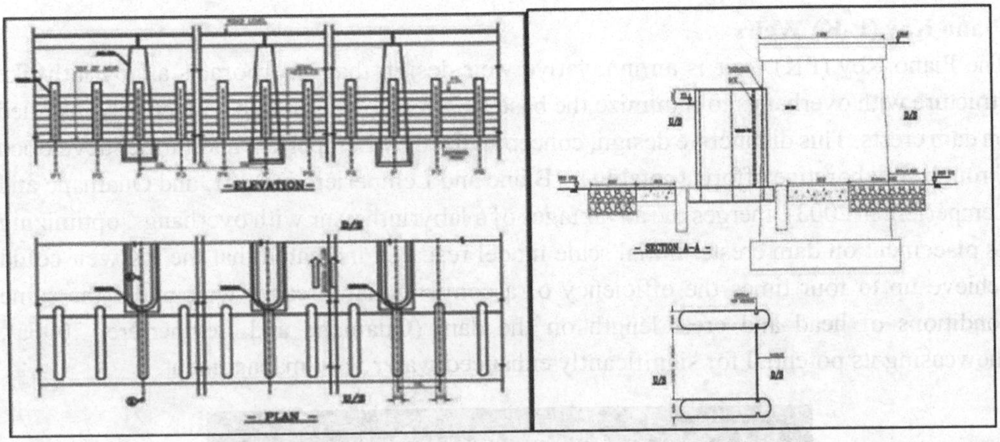

Figure 5.9 Typical Arrangement of Bandhara/Barrage Structure (Ingle, 2016)

Advantages

The primary benefit of KT weirs includes the efficient use of water for irrigation and supply purposes. Unlike check dams, they don't require regular site clearance and eliminate the need for energy dissipation setups. KT weirs play a crucial role in controlling and storing water flow.

Labyrinth Weirs

A labyrinth weir is engineered to manage substantial water flows at low hydraulic heads, achieving this by extending the effective length of the weir crest beyond the width of the channel. While it may not reach the efficiency levels of other weir types with equivalent effective lengths, the significant augmentation in the length of the weir effectively compensates for this discrepancy. This design allows for greater water discharge capacity within constrained spaces, making it a valuable solution for flood control and water management in various settings.

Figure 5.10 Labyrinth weir (after Crookston and Tullis, 2013)

Piano Key (P-K) Weirs

The Piano Key (PK) weir is an innovative weir design that incorporates a labyrinth-like structure with overhangs to minimize the base length, allowing it to be effectively installed on dam crests. This distinctive design, conceptualized by Lempérière and further developed through collaborative efforts (notably by Blanc and Lempérière in 2001, and Ouamane and Lempérière in 2003), merges the advantages of a labyrinth weir with overhangs, optimizing its placement on dam crests. Initial scale model research indicated that the PK weir could achieve up to four times the efficiency of a conventional Creager weir under the same conditions of head and crest length on the dam (Ouamane and Lempérière, 2006a), showcasing its potential for significantly enhanced water flow management.

Figure 5.11 View of Piano-Key Weir

5.2.1.3 Component parts of a weir

Body wall of weir, Upstream Apron, Downstream apron, upstream curtain wall, downstream curtain wall, Crest and shutters are the major components of weirs, which are common to barrages also.

5.2.2 Barrages

Barriers known as Barrages are those in which raised crests perform little or no ponding and major portion of ponding is done by the gates.

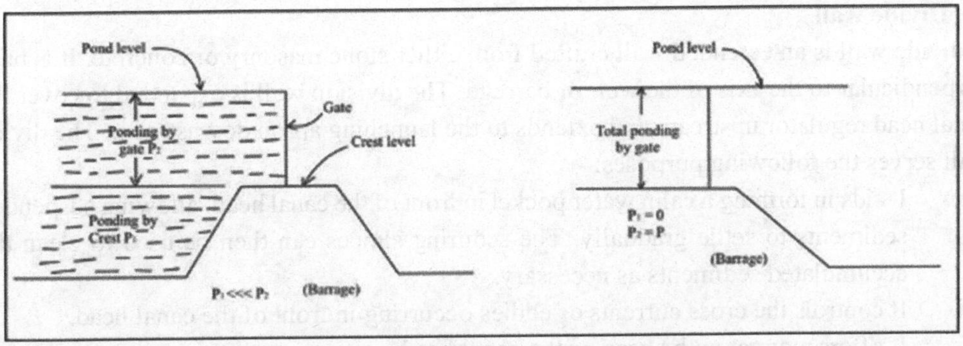

Figure 5.12 Conceptual view of a Barrage

Advantages of barrages

a. Better control on the river floods
b. both inflow and outflow are regulated by mcans of gates
c. better control over the silt entry into the canal.

To have a feel, the photograph of a portion of a barrage, near Cuttack city, Odisha is presented below:

Figure 5.13 Portion of Jobra Barrage, Cuttack, Odisha

5.2.2.1 Components of Barrage

The components of a barrage are:

a. Divide wall
b. Under Sluices or scouring sluices
c. Fish Ladder
d. Canal Head Regulator
e. Silt Excluder

The detailed discussion on the components is discussed in the following paragraphs.

a. Divide wall

A divide wall is an extended wall crafted from either stone masonry or concrete. It is built perpendicular to the axis of the weir or barrage. The division wall is expanded to cover the canal head regulator upstream and extends to the launching apron downstream. The divide wall serves the following purposes: -

i. It aids in forming a calm water pocket in front of the canal head, allowing suspended sediments to settle gradually. The scouring sluices can then be used to clean the accumulated sediments as necessary.
ii. It controls the cross currents or eddies occurring in front of the canal head.
iii. It offers a direct path ahead of the canal head.
iv. It stabilizes the division wall and prevents the overturning impact of water pressure imposed by the weir or barrage.

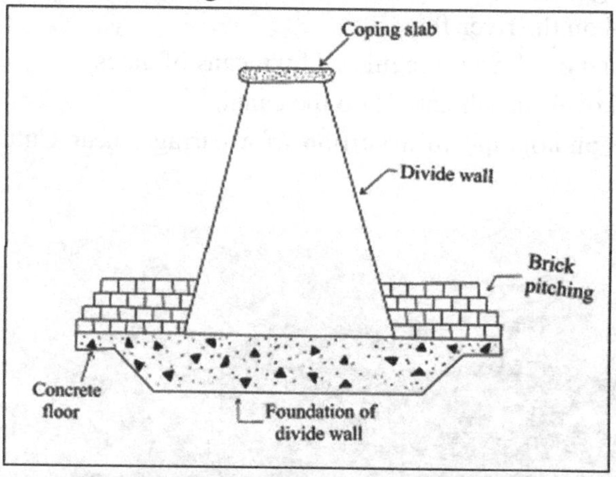

Figure 5.14 Divide wall showing various parts

b. Under Sluices or Scouring Sluices

The scouring sluices are openings provided at the base of a weir or barrage. They are equipped with suitable gates that are normally kept closed, but during floods, the gates are opened.

Under sluices perform the following functions:

i. Silt entry into the off taking canals are controlled by providing under sluices.
ii. When under sluices remain closed silt gets accumulated at the upstream sides of under sluices approaching to the gate which can easily be scoured to the downstream side by opening under sluices in selective interval.

Under sluices are designed as per the intensity of discharge per metre length. The crest of the under-sluice section of the weir is maintained at a level lower than the crest of the normal position of the weir. A deep channel forms that makes it easier for discharge to flow towards the under-sluice pocket because of the low level of the pocket's crest. As a result, this eases the procedure of channelling water into the canal through the canal head regulator.

c. Fish ladder

A fish ladder is a construction meant to facilitate fish migration across river obstacles. Depending on the season, fish move from one place to another; during the winter, they migrate upstream to downstream, and during the monsoon, they migrate downstream to upstream. Fish migration can be hampered by structures like barrages and weirs. Fish ladders are built to allow fish to pass through the river more easily. Swimming against a stream of water is the only way to access the climbing pools that make up these ladders. The zigzag shape of the fish ladder's design keeps the water flow rate at 3 m/sec. This guarantees that fish can move at a speed of roughly 3 to 3.5 m/sec with ease.

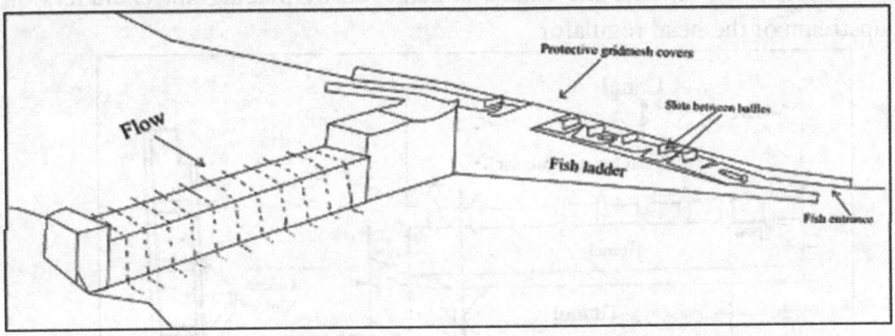

Figure 5.15 Layout of a Fish ladder

d. Canal head regulator

A canal head regulator is a construction situated at the beginning of the off-taking canal to manage the water flow. It comprises several piers that divide the canal's total width into sections called bays. Each pier is equipped with gates, which are appropriately placed and operated by mechanical devices. Water from the under-sluice pocket is directed into the regulator bays to release a full supply of water into the canal. The canal head regulator serves functions, including:

i. It manages the regulation of water flow into the canal.
ii. It regulates the influx of silt into the off-taking or main canal.

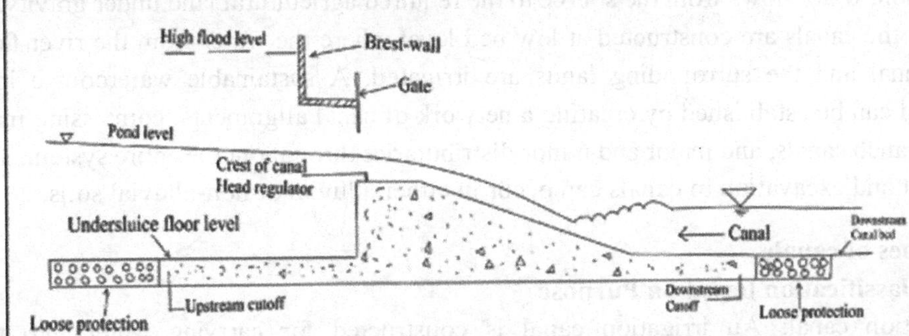

Figure 5.16 Canal head regulator

e. Silt excluder

When the divide wall is constructed to create a calm water pocket in front of the canal head, the lower layer of water holds dense silts, while the upper layer contains finer silt particles. The presence of heavy silts leads to sedimentation in the pocket. Therefore, to remove the suspended heavy silts, a silt excluder is installed. It comprises a sequence of tunnels extending from the side of the head regulator to the divide wall. These tunnels are capped with an RCC (Reinforced Concrete Cement) slab, and their elevation is maintained below the silt level of the head regulator. The water-borne suspended heavy silts enter the tunnels of the silt excluder and exit through the scouring sluices. Therefore, the removal of silt from the water before it reaches the canals is achieved by placing silt excluders on the riverbed upstream of the head regulator.

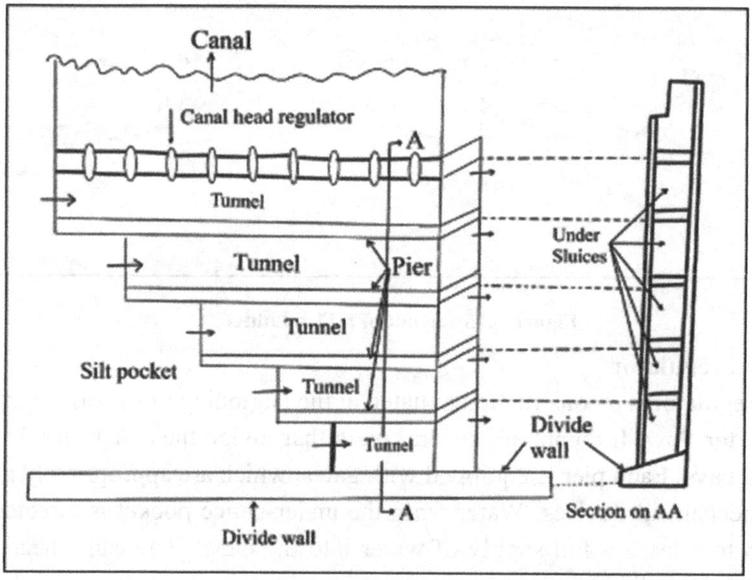

Figure 5.17 Silt excluder

5.3 CANALS

In irrigation, water flows from the source to the required agricultural land under gravity. In irrigation the canals are constructed at low bed level where the water from the river flow to the canal and the surrounding lands are irrigated. A sustainable watercourse in a watershed can be established by creating a network of canal alignments, comprising main canals, branch canals, and major and minor distributaries throughout the entire system. The alignment and excavation of canals can occur in either alluvial or non-alluvial soils.

5.3.1 Types of canals

5.3.1.1 Classification based on Purpose

a. Irrigation canal: An irrigation canal is constructed for carrying water into the agricultural land for irrigation.

b. Navigation canal: A navigation canal is built to facilitate inland navigation, allowing small ships and steamers to traverse these waterways.
c. Power canal or Power Channel: It is constructed to convey water specifically for the purpose of hydropower generation.
d. Feeder canal: This type of canal, constructed specifically to deliver water to another canal, is known as a feeder canal. Positioned outside the service area of the main canal system, its primary role is to augment the water supply to the canal network, ensuring sufficient water flow and distribution for irrigation or other purposes within the command area.
e. Water supply canal: It is designed to supply water for drinking purposes and industrial use.
f. Multi-purpose canal: These canal systems serve multiple purposes, including irrigation, water supply, hydropower, and navigation.

5.3.1.2 Classification based on nature of supply

a. Inundation canal- These canals use excess water of rivers at the time of floods and remain operational during rainy season and used for the purpose of irrigation.
b. Permanent canals- A canal featuring a uniform channel design, equipped with masonry structures for controlling and distributing water, and backed by a reliable source of water supply, is typically referred to as a regulated canal. This type of canal is designed to ensure consistent water delivery for irrigation, navigation, or other purposes, thanks to its engineered channel and built-in mechanisms for water flow management.

5.3.1.3 Classification based on Position in the Canal Network and Discharge

a. Main Canals: These are the primary channels that transport water from a reservoir, initiating from a Head Regulator. Main canals are capable of conveying discharges exceeding 10 cubic meters per second and are often referred to as arterial canals. In a drainage context, the main canal is pivotal, gathering water from subsidiary drainage canals to direct it towards a water intake point. Originating directly from a river, these canals derive their flow from the upstream side of weirs, headworks, or dams, serving to distribute water for agricultural purposes through gravity flow. However, they are not typically used for direct irrigation but instead feed into secondary channels.
b. Branch Canals: Positioned along either side of the main canal, branch canals function to distribute water to both major and minor distributaries, with flow rates ranging between 5 to 10 cubic meters per second (cumecs). Serving as feeder channels, they do not engage in direct irrigation but rather facilitate water flow to direct outlets.
c. Distributary Canals: Specifically designed for direct irrigation purposes, these canals are divided into major and minor distributaries and manage the delivery of water directly to agricultural lands through distributary outlets.
    i. Major Distributary: These canals, drawing water from main or branch canals with a head discharge between 0.25 and 5 cubic meters per second, primarily

function to distribute water further to minor distributaries. Often stemming from branch canals and occasionally from main canals, their discharge is typically less than that of branch canals. Referred to as 'major' when they feed into 'minor distributaries', they are crucial for irrigation, directing water flow to the fields.

ii. Minor Distributary: Characterized by carrying discharges of less than 0.25 cubic meters per second, these canals sometimes receive water from branch canals and are instrumental in supplying water directly to the fields through outlets, facilitating precise irrigation practices.

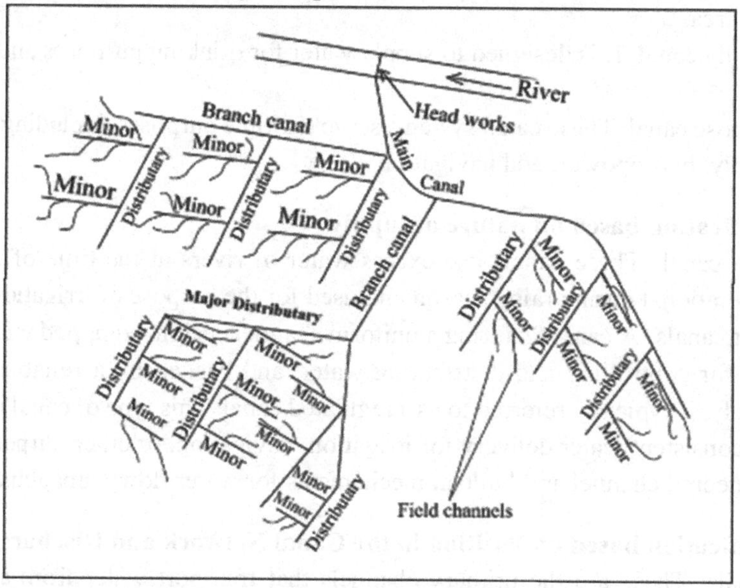

Figure 5.18 Classification of canals based on discharge

(Ref.: IS:5968-1987 Indian Standard GUIDE FOR PLANNING AND LAYOUT OF CANAL SYSTEM FOR IRRIGATION.)

5.3.1.4 Classification based on alignment

a. Ridge canal or watershed canal– The dividing ridge line separating the catchment areas of two streams is referred to as the watershed. The main watershed, positioned between two major streams, serves as the boundary that divides the drainage areas of the two streams on either side. Ridge canals are appropriate for flat and uniformly sloped plain areas. Canal that follows the course of a natural watershed is referred to as a watershed canal. This alignment ensures gravity irrigation on both sides of the canal.

b. Contour canals – Ridge line canals are not considered cost-effective in hilly areas characterized by substantial changes in elevation. So, contour canals are frequently aligned in hilly and mountainous region. Contour canals adhere to the natural contour lines of the land, with the exception of incorporating the necessary longitudinal slope to enable water flow along the canal. As these canals run along a contour, many cross-drainage works are required to be constructed to allow the overland flow flowing along the natural slope of the ground.

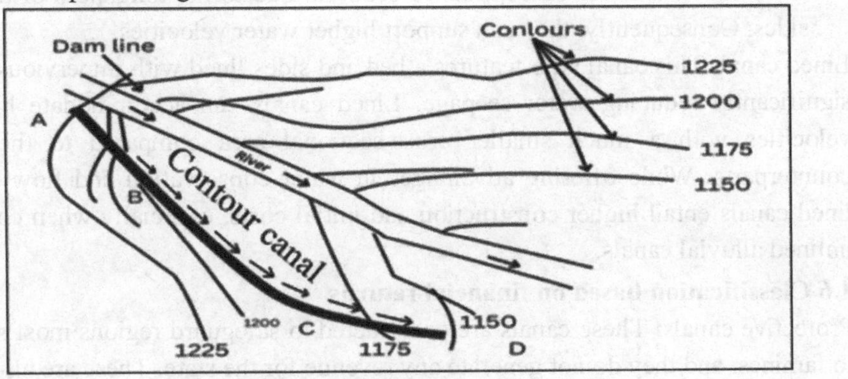

Figure 5.19 Contour canal

c. Side slope canals – These are aligned at the right angles to the contours. These canals align with the natural drainage flow and avoid intercepting drainage canals, thereby reducing the need for cross-drainage structures. These are also known are inclined or sloping canals as the canal bed is inclined or sloped instead of being completely level. The purpose of side slopes in canals is to prevent erosion, maintain structural integrity, and provide proper drainage.

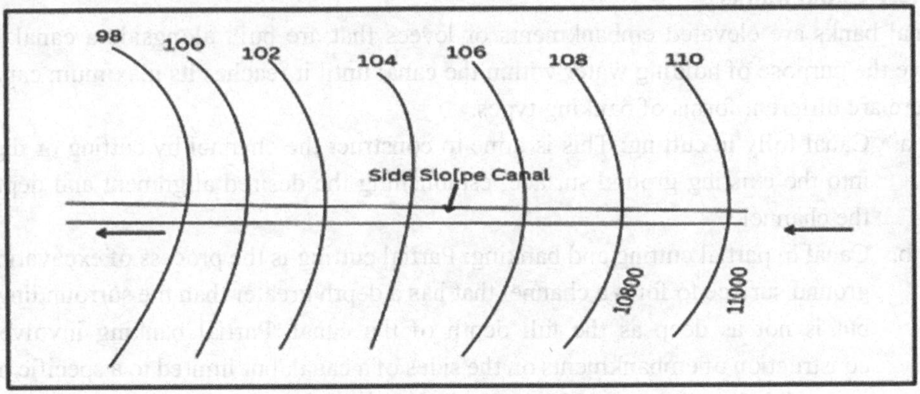

Figure 5.20 Slide slope canal

5.3.1.5 Based on Type of Boundary Surface of the Canal

a. Unlined canal: This type of canal maintains the natural material of its construction site without any added lining. Unlined canals are categorized into two types:

   i. Alluvial canals: Constructed in areas with alluvial soil, typically found in river deltas, these canals navigate through loosely held silty soils prone to erosion and deposition. Designed to minimize both scouring and silting, they operate at lower velocities, requiring larger cross-sectional areas for water flow. Among unlined canals, their construction costs are the most economical.

ii. Non-alluvial canals: Built through areas with hard or disintegrated rocky substrates, these canals are less susceptible to scouring due to the toughness of the bed and sides. Consequently, they can support higher water velocities.

b. Lined canal: This canal type features a bed and sides lined with impervious materials, significantly reducing water seepage. Lined canals can accommodate higher flow velocities with a much smaller cross-sectional area compared to their unlined counterparts. While offering advantages in water conservation and flow efficiency, lined canals entail higher construction and initial costs, especially when compared to unlined alluvial canals.

5.3.1.6 Classification based on financial returns

a. Protective canals: These canals are constructed to safeguard regions most susceptible to famines, and they do not generate any revenue for the state. These are also designed and constructed to mitigate the risks and impacts of flooding in a particular area.

b. Productive canals: When fully developed, these canals generate revenue for the state. These are designed and built to facilitate the distribution of water for agricultural purposes. The purpose of designing these canals is to effectively distribute water, ensuring adequate coverage and delivery to the agricultural areas they serve.

5.3.2 Cross-section of canal

5.3.2.1 Canal banks

Canal banks are elevated embankments or levees that are built alongside a canal. They serve the purpose of holding water within the canal until it reaches its maximum capacity. There are different forms of banking types.

a. Canal fully in cutting: This is done to construct the channel by cutting or digging into the existing ground surface, establishing the desired alignment and depth for the channel.

b. Canal in partial cutting and banking: Partial cutting is the process of excavating the ground surface to form a channel that has a depth greater than the surrounding land but is not as deep as the full depth of the canal. Partial banking involves the construction of embankments on the sides of a canal, but limited to a specific height or depth below the ground level. Unlike having uniformly raised banks throughout the entire canal length, partial banking includes leaving certain sections of the canal at a reduced height.

c. Canal in banking: A Canal in banking refers to the construction of raised embankments or banks along the entire length of the canal. It involves creating elevated sides that are designed to contain the water within the canal's boundaries, providing stability and preventing overflow. This technique is commonly used in canals with higher flow velocities or areas where there is a need for maximum containment of the water flow. Full banking helps maintain the desired water levels and provides a secure and controlled pathway for the canal's flow.

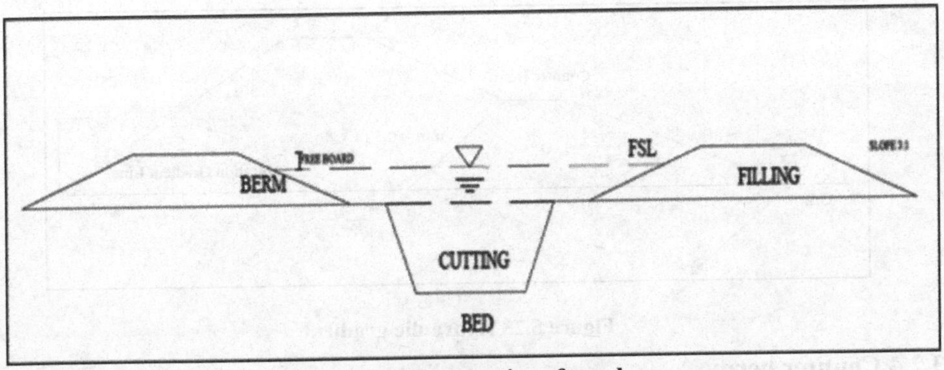

Figure 5.21 Cross section of canal

5.3.2.2 Berm

It represents the vertical distance from the canal bottom to top edge of canal bank. It is provided because:

a) It helps to protect the bank from erosion
b) It helps the canal section in widening
c) It helps the bank to prevent from sliding down towards the canal section.

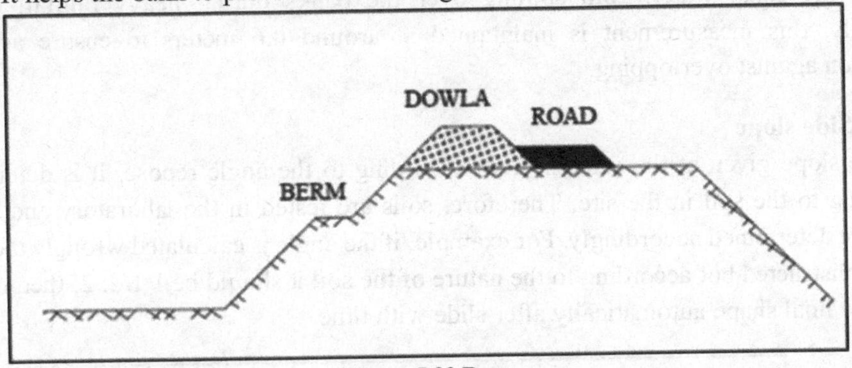

Figure 5.22 Berm

5.3.2.3 Hydraulic gradient

It is also known as saturation gradient. This forms a saturation line below this the soils are saturated and above this the soil is dry. The hydraulic gradient depends on the type of soil.

a. Clayey – 1:4
b. Alluvial – 1:5
c. Sandy soil – 1:6

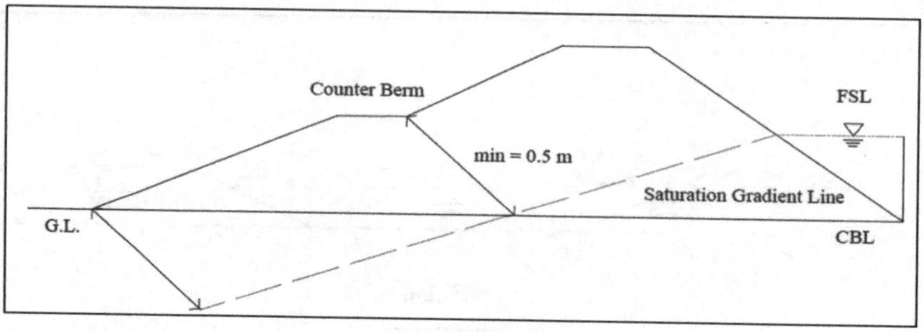

Figure 5.23 Hydraulic gradient

5.3.2.4 Counter berm

Elevated embankments placed on the outside of canal banks in irrigation systems are called counter berms.

5.3.2.5 Free board

This describes the freeboard of a canal, which is the vertical distance between the full supply level of the water and the top edge of the canal bank. The freeboard is essential to prevent the canal water from spilling over the banks during heavy rainfall events. Typically, this measurement is maintained at around 0.6 meters to ensure adequate protection against overtopping.

5.3.2.6 Side slope

It is the slope given at the canal section according to the angle repose. It is determined according to the soil in the site. Therefore, soils are tested in the laboratory and repose angle are determined accordingly. For example, if the angle is calculated wrongly the slope 1:1 is constructed but according to the nature of the soil it should be 1 1/2: 2, then the soil takes the final shape automatically after slide with time.

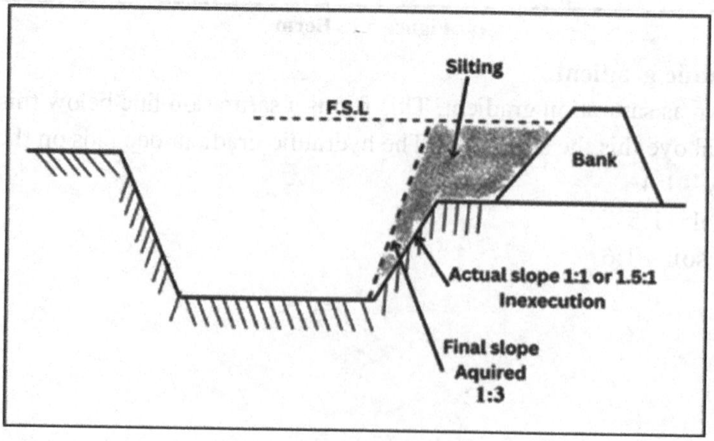

Figure 5.24 Side slope

5.3.2.7 Service Road

This road is constructed for maintenance and inspection on the top of the canal. It also serves the purpose to connect the two village for communication purpose. In the main canal it is provided on both side and in branch canal on one side.

5.3.2.8 Dowla

This refers to a low embankment or a raised bank constructed alongside a canal, adjacent to the service road. Its primary purpose is to ensure the safe passage of vehicles by acting as a protective barrier between the road and the canal. The height and width are generally 0.5m and 0.5m respectively.

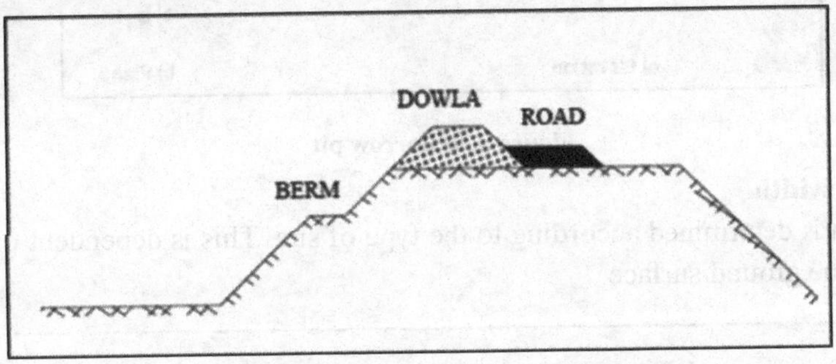

Figure 5.25 Schematic presentation of Dowla and Service road

5.3.2.9 Borrow pit

During the construction of embankments or levees, the excavated earth obtained from the site may not always be adequate to fulfil the required volume. In such cases, additional soil is sourced from designated areas known as borrow pits. These pits are excavated to provide the necessary earth for completing the construction. It may be found inside or outside of the canal. In the canal it acts as pocket where silt gets deposited.

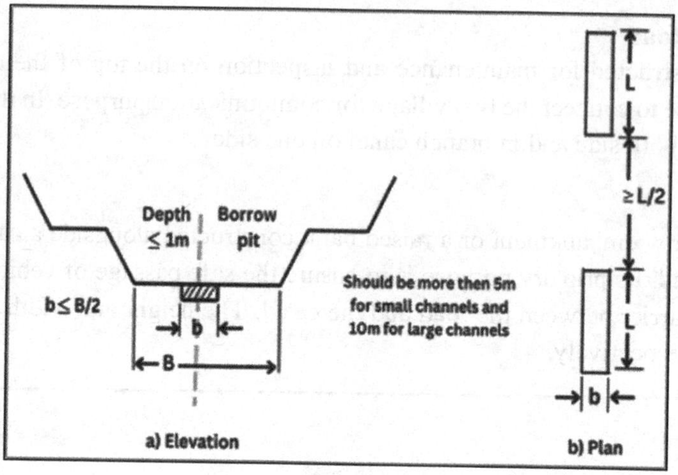

Figure 5.26 Borrow pit

5.3.2.10 Land width

The land width is determined according to the type of site. This is dependent on the canal bed level and the ground surface.

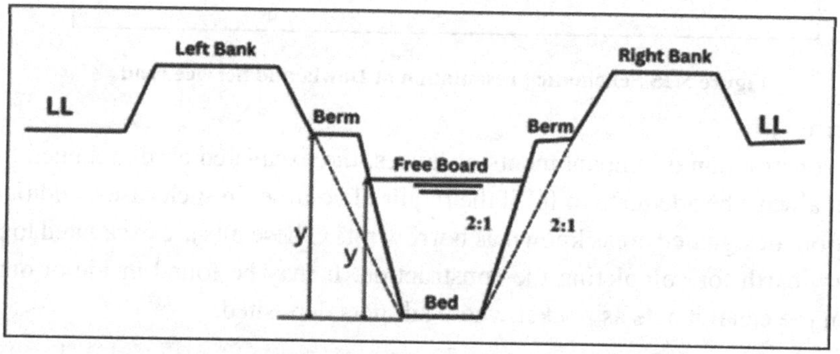

Figure 5.27 Figure to guide the calculation of Land width

The total land width is calculated by adding

a. Top width if the canal
b. Twice the Berm width
c. Bottom width of banks twice
d. One metre margin from the bank heel on both sides.
e. External borrow pit width
f. Margin of 0.5m from the outer edge.

5.3.2.11 Balancing depth

Balancing canal depth comes when the canal is in partially embankment and partially in cutting. It is the depth of the canal which gives equal amount of filling (i.e earth required for formation of Banks) and cutting (i.e earth from digging). For a given cross-section of a canal, it has only one balancing depth. For this depth the canal sectional will be economical. The following worked out example will illustrate the process of calculating and arriving at a balancing depth for a canal.

Example 1. An irrigation canal has a bottom width of 8 meters and a side slope of 1.5 H: 1V in cutting and 2 H: 1 V in filling. The width of the crest of the bank is 2 meters and its height above the ground level is 3 meters. Compute balancing depth of the canal and draw net x-section of the various dimensions and level it.

Solution:

Given,

Bed width (b) = 8 meter

Side Slope (z) = 1.5 in Cutting

Side slope (z1) = 2 in Filling

Width of embankment (w) = 2 meter

Hight of embankment (h1) = 3 meter

Balancing depth (h) =?

Now, we have area of Trapezoidal Section = $b \times h + 2 \times \left(\frac{1}{2} \times h \times z \times h\right)$

Therefore, Area of cutting = $8h + 2\left(\frac{1}{2} \times h \times 1.5h\right) = 8h + 1.5h2$

Area of filling = $2\left[2 \times 3 + \left\{\frac{1}{2} \times (3 \times 2) \times 3\right\} \times 2\right]$ = 48m2

For balancing depth; we have

Area of cutting = Area of filling

Or, $8h + 1.5h2 = 48$

Or, $8h + 1.5h2 - 48 = 0$

Solving; we get,

H = 3.58m

Hence, the balancing depth of canal is 3.58 m

5.3.3 Design of most economical canal section

The design of open channels involves a variety of terminologies that describe the geometric and hydraulic characteristics essential for effective water conveyance. Here's a breakdown of these key terms:

a. **Area of Cross Section (a):** This refers to the area within the channel that is in contact with water. For channels with a rectangular cross section, the area can be calculated by multiplying the width of the channel (b) by the depth of water (y), resulting in the formula **(a) = b. y**.

b. **ii) Wetted Perimeter (p):** The wetted perimeter is the total length of the channel sides and bottom that are in direct contact with water. For a rectangular channel, it is determined by adding the width of the channel to twice the depth of water, leading to **(p) = b + 2y.**

c. **iii) Hydraulic Radius (R):** This is a measure of the efficiency of the channel cross section in conveying water, calculated as the ratio of the area of the wetted cross section to the wetted perimeter. For a rectangular channel, the hydraulic radius is given by

d. $(R) = \frac{a}{p} = \frac{by}{b+2y}$

e. **iv) Hydraulic Slope (S):** The hydraulic slope represents the gradient of the channel, defined by the ratio of the vertical drop along a longitudinal section of the channel (h) to the length of that section (l).

f. $(S) = \frac{h}{l}$

g. **v) Freeboard:** Freeboard is a safety margin, representing the height difference between the maximum anticipated water level in the channel and the top edge of the channel banks. This margin helps prevent the water from overflowing and causing damage to the channel embankments. Freeboard is typically set to a minimum of 15-25% of the normal depth of flow to ensure adequate protection.

h. *Understanding these terminologies is crucial* for the design and construction of efficient, safe, and functional open channels for water conveyance, whether for irrigation, drainage, or flood control purposes.

5.3.3.1 Discharge Capacity of Channel

To estimate the capacity of a channel, which is crucial for determining how much water it can transport within a given timeframe, the following equation is utilized:

$$Q = \frac{(16667)(DDIR)(A)}{(HPD)(Ei)}$$

Where,

Q represents the channel capacity, measured in liters per minute (L/min).

DDIR stands for the design daily irrigation requirement, which is the amount of water needed per day, measured in millimeters per day (mm/day).

A is the area that the canal or ditch serves, measured in hectares (ha).

HPD denotes the hours per day that water is delivered through the channel.

E_i is the irrigation efficiency, which includes the conveyance efficiency of the canal or ditch, expressed as a percentage.

This formula helps in planning and managing irrigation systems by calculating the optimal flow rates to meet the irrigation requirements of a given area efficiently.

Additionally, it's important to maintain the velocity of water flow within the channel at a level that prevents erosion and sediment deposition. As per Schwab et al., 1993, a flow velocity exceeding 0.6 meters per second (m/s) is generally considered non-silting, meaning it won't lead to the accumulation of sediments that could block the channel. However, the maximum velocity that avoids causing erosion depends on the type of soil or the materials lining the channel. For both lined canals and unlined ditches, standard maximum allowable velocities are available, but it's advisable to refer to local data for more precise guidance, as soil and lining material erodibility can vary significantly across different locations.

5.3.3.2 Economical Section of a Channel

A channel design is considered cost-effective when it achieves the lowest possible construction cost. This cost is primarily influenced by the excavation depth and the expense involved in lining the channel. Achieving the lowest construction cost while allowing for the highest flow rate for a specific cross-sectional size is key. According to fluid dynamics, particularly the continuity equation and uniform flow principles, the flow speed is at its peak when the hydraulic radius is largest, given a constant slope and surface roughness. This maximum hydraulic radius occurs when the wetted perimeter is at its smallest for the specified area. Therefore, minimizing the wetted perimeter for the required flow rate is essential for reducing construction expenses. This principle guides the determination of the dimensions for cost-effective channel shapes. Such an optimal design, known as the most economical or hydraulically efficient section, allows for the maximum flow rate through a channel of a specific cross-sectional area, bed slope, and roughness coefficient.

The conditions for the most economical section of channel

i. A rectangular channel achieves its most cost-effective design when the flow depth is half the width of the bottom, or the hydraulic radius equals half the flow depth.

ii. For a trapezoidal channel section to be considered the most cost-efficient, the condition is that half of the top width should match the length of one of the channel's sloping sides, or the hydraulic radius should be half the depth of the water flow.

iii. A triangular channel section reaches its optimal cost-effectiveness when each sloping side forms a 45-degree angle with the vertical, essentially making it half of a square positioned diagonally with equal sloping sides.

The formula for discharge from a channel can be represented as:

$$Q = AV = AC\sqrt{RS_0} = AC\sqrt{\frac{A}{P}S_0} = K * \frac{1}{\sqrt{P}}$$

Q represents the discharge in cubic meters per second (m³/s),
A is the cross-sectional area of the channel in square meters (m²),
C stands for Chezy's constant,
R is the hydraulic radius in meters (m),
P denotes the wetted perimeter in meters (m),
S_0 is the bed slope (expressed as a fraction or m/m),
K is a constant specific to the given cross-sectional area,
Bed slope, defined as $A^{3/2}\ C\ S_o^{1/2}$.

According to this equation, the discharge Q reaches its maximum value when the wetted perimeter P is at its minimum. This relationship highlights the importance of optimizing the channel's shape and size to achieve the least possible wetted perimeter for maximizing discharge efficiency.

i. **Channel Shape:** Among the different geometries for open channels, the semi-circular shape stands out as the most hydraulically efficient cross-sectional design. However, constructing a semi-circular channel, especially if it is an earthen and unlined one, presents significant challenges. As a result, the trapezoidal section is the more frequently adopted cross-sectional shape for practical applications.

ii. **Channel Dimensions:** Channel dimensions can be determined using the uniform flow equation expressed as $\boldsymbol{Q = A\,V}$

Where,

V represents the flow velocity in meters per second (m/s),

A stand for the cross-sectional area of the canal perpendicular to the direction of flow, measured in square meters (m^2),

Q is the channel's capacity, quantified in cubic meters per second (m^3/s).

To calculate the velocity, one can employ either Manning's formula or the Chezy formula:

Manning's Equation = $V = \frac{1}{n} R^{2/3} S^{1/2}$

Chezy's equation = $V = C R^{1/2} S^{1/2}$

Where,

n denotes Manning's roughness coefficient,

C represents Chezy's roughness coefficient,

R is the hydraulic radius in meters (m), defined as the area of flow divided by the wetted perimeter,

S is the bed slope, represented as a fraction (m/m).

5.3.4 CANAL LINING

5.3.4.1 General

Importance of canal lining:

a. Seepage control: It plays a vital role in conserving water, enhancing irrigation efficiency, preserving the structural integrity of the canal, preventing waterlogging and soil salinization, protecting the environment, and reducing costs. Most of losses which occurs in unlined canals are because of seepage loss. The seepage loss affects the storage capacity of a reservoir.

b. Prevents water logging: Canal lining helps in the prevention of waterlogging in agricultural fields by reducing the transfer of water from the canal to the surrounding soil. It helps maintain the water table at an optimal level, ensuring it does not reach a point where it causes waterlogging in the fields. Proper water distribution ensures that each field receives the necessary amount of water without causing waterlogging in any particular area.

c. Canal capacity increases: In unlined canal the flow velocity is fixed because of silting and scouring. Therefore, lining helps in the increase of velocity resulting in the discharge in minimum cross section area.

d. Command area increases: Since the discharge increases due to lining and all other losses are reduced therefore the command area increases.

5.3.4.2 Types of lining:

a. Cement concrete lining: Cement concrete lining involves applying a layer of cement-based material to the inner surfaces of canals. It offers long-lasting protection against water loss, enhances water conveyance efficiency, and contributes to the durability and sustainability of the canal system. When the canal is in the full banking type, this type of canal is used.

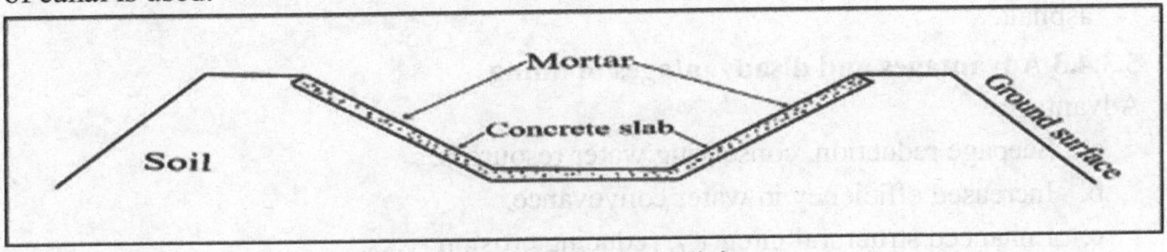

Figure 5.28 Cement concrete lining

b. Precast concrete lining: In order to construct a smooth, waterproof lining inside canals, precast concrete lining uses prefabricated concrete panels or segments. The seamless fit of these precast panels creates a continuous barrier that runs the length of the canal's interior. Numerous advantages come with this technology, including improved quality control, quicker production, and greater durability.
c. Cement mortar lining: Applying a protective layer of cement mortar to the inside surfaces of pipes or conduits is known as cement mortar lining. This is done by first mixing a cement, sand, and water combination and then applying it to the inside surfaces of the pipes or conduits via centrifugal casting, spraying, or troweling.
d. Brick lining: Brick lining is the process of placing bricks to a canal's inner surface to create a protective layer. Bricks are bonded with mortar in a prearranged arrangement, typically in staggered order.

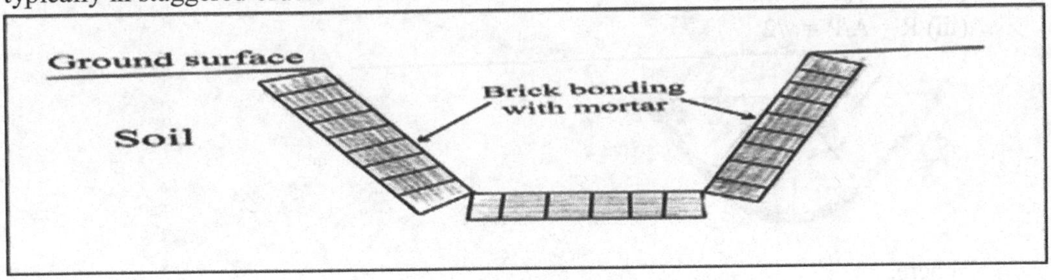

Figure 5.29 Brick lining

e. Boulders lining: Boulder lining is a method of lining canals and waterways inside with large rocks or boulders to provide stability, resistance to outside forces, and a protective layer.
f. Shotcrete lining: A mixture of concrete, water, and additives is sprayed onto surfaces, like canal walls or tunnels, in the process of shotcrete lining, often referred to as sprayed concrete lining. Strong adhesion and consolidation are ensured by this method,

producing a smooth and long-lasting finish that improves structural integrity and stops erosion.

g. Asphalt lining: The process of lining canals or channels with asphalt involves coating the inside surfaces with a layer of bitumen or asphalt. This procedure produces a flexible and waterproof lining that manages seepage, stops erosion, and promotes easy water flow. Smaller drainage channels and irrigation canals are frequently lined with asphalt.

5.3.4.3 Advantages and disadvantages of lining

Advantages

a. Seepage reduction, conserving water resources.
b. Increased efficiency in water conveyance.
c. Enhanced structural integrity, reducing erosion risks.
d. Protection of water quality from contamination.

Disadvantages

a. High initial cost of implementation.
b. Limited flexibility for future modifications.
c. Potential environmental impacts.
e) Regular maintenance requirements.

Design of Lined Canals

a. Triangular Section

Used when $Q \leq 150$ cumecs

(i) $A = \gamma^2(\theta + \cot\theta)$

(ii) $P = 2\gamma(\theta + \cot\theta)$

(iii) $R = A/P = \gamma/2$

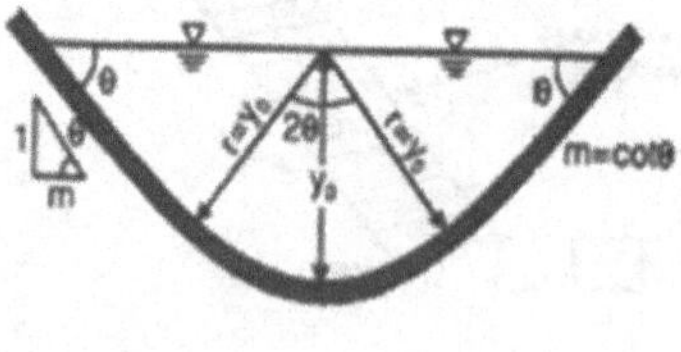

Where,

A = Area (m^2)

γ = Central depth = Radius of circle

θ = Angle

R = Hydraulic mean depth.

b. Trapezoidal Section

$A = By + \gamma^2(\theta + \cot\theta)$

$P = B + 2\gamma(\theta + \cot\theta)$

$R = A/P$

b. **Trapezoidal Section**

$A = By + \gamma^2(\theta + \cot\theta)$

$P = B + 2\gamma(\theta + \cot\theta)$

$R = A/P$

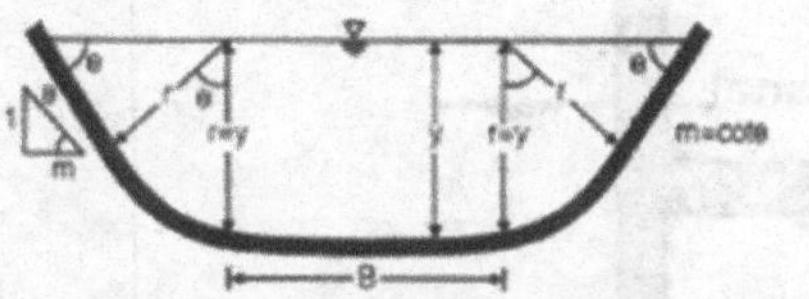

5.4 CROSS DRAINAGE WORK

5.4.1 General

In order to prevent flooding, cross drainage work entails building infrastructure that allow water to flow smoothly over highways, railway lines and canals. These constructions like culverts, aqueducts, and bridges, for example it allow water to move under or over the infrastructure, guaranteeing efficient drainage and preserving its operation.

5.4.2 Types of cross drainage work

a. Aqueduct: Aqueducts are elevated water transportation systems that cross railway tracks, highways and waterways. They are made comprised of pipelines or supported channels that allow water to flow across the barrier continuously.

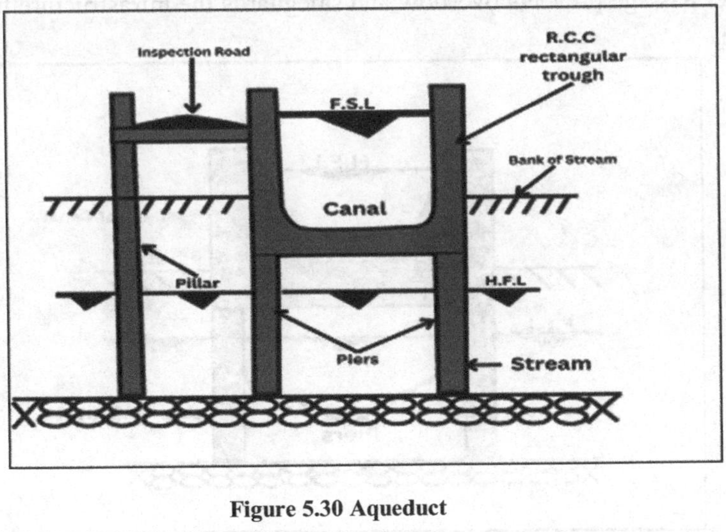

Figure 5.30 Aqueduct

b. Siphon aqueduct – Pumps are not necessary when using a syphon aqueduct, which uses an inverted U-shaped curving tube to convey water over barriers with a steady gravity-driven flow. It works well in the region where the canal bed is below the drainage system's peak flood level.

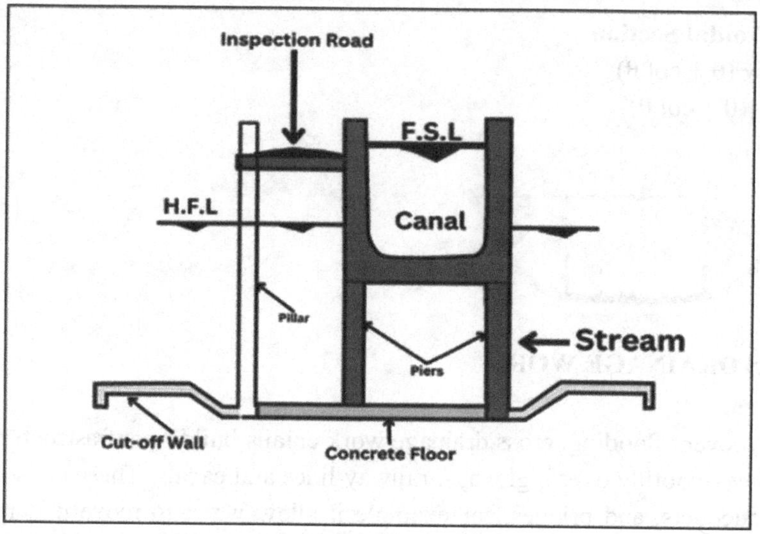

Figure 5.31 Siphon aqueduct

c. Super passage: It is the structure where drainage is over the canal. A super passage in cross drainage work is an additional channel or passage constructed alongside the main structure, such as a culvert or bridge. It is specifically designed to manage flood or excess water flow during heavy rainfall or flood events. By offering extra capacity, the super passage prevents overflow and safeguards the infrastructure from potential damage.

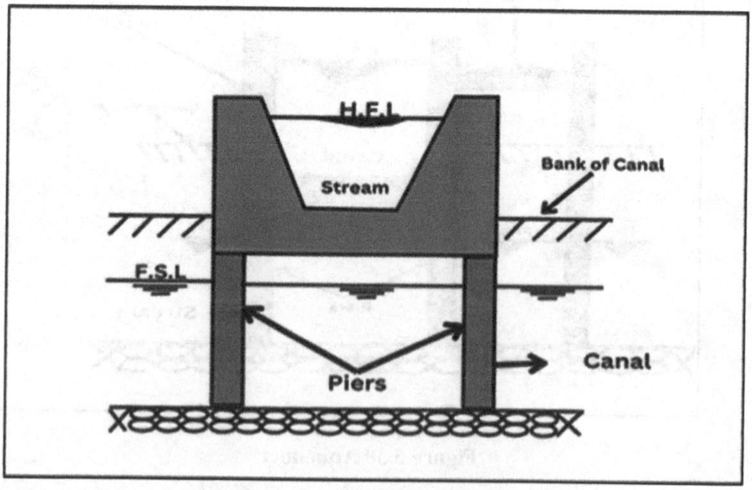

Figure 5.32 Super passage

d. Siphon super passage: A siphon super passage ensures uninterrupted water flow when the main siphon reaches its capacity. It diverts excess water away from the primary siphon, preventing flooding and maintaining efficient drainage. It serves as a vital backup, safeguarding the functionality of the cross-drainage system.

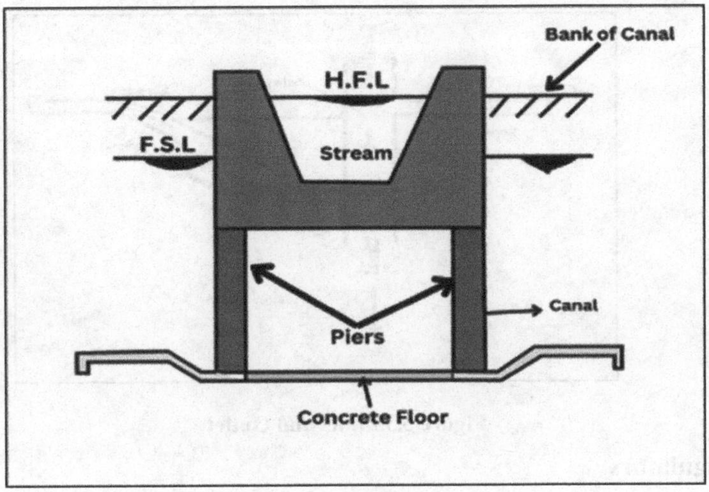

Figure 5.33 Siphon super passage

e. Level crossing: A level crossing in cross drainage work ensures uninterrupted transportation routes while allowing unobstructed water flow beneath or alongside the crossing. It eliminates the requirement for bridges or culverts by maintaining a consistent level between the intersecting channels.

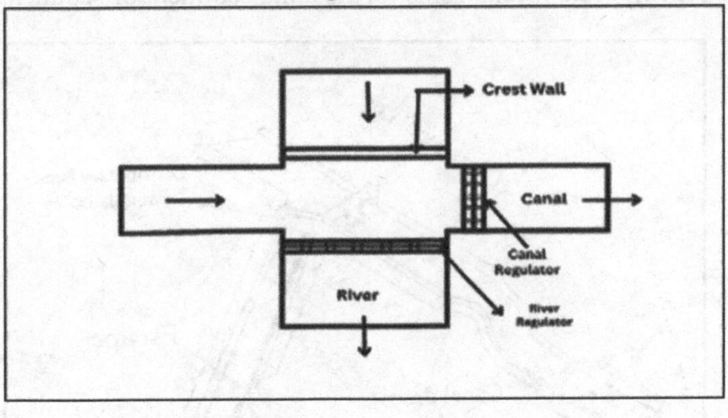

Figure 5.34 Level crossing

f. Inlets and outlets: Inlets collect and direct water into the structure, while outlets regulate the flow and release of water downstream. Proper design and placement of inlets and outlets are crucial for efficient water flow.

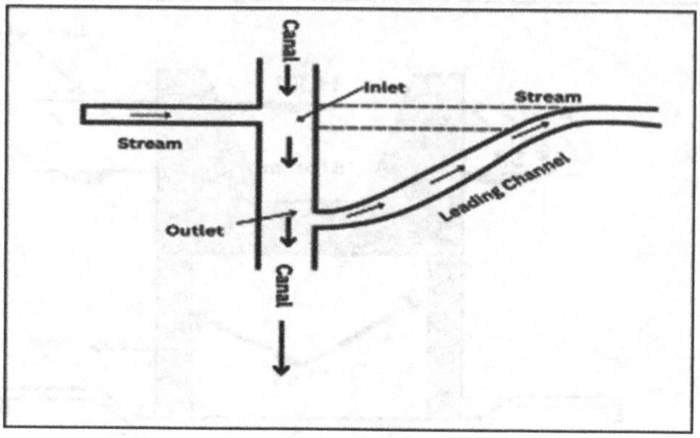

Figure 5.35 Inlet and Outlet

5.5 Canal regulators

5.5.1 General

Canal regulators are hydraulic structures used in canal systems to regulate and control the movement of water. They are strategically positioned along the canal to oversee water distribution, uphold desired water levels, and optimize the functionality of the canal network. To maintain the hydraulic effectiveness of the canal and prevent obstructions, regulators often incorporate mechanisms for flushing sediment or sedimentation basins.

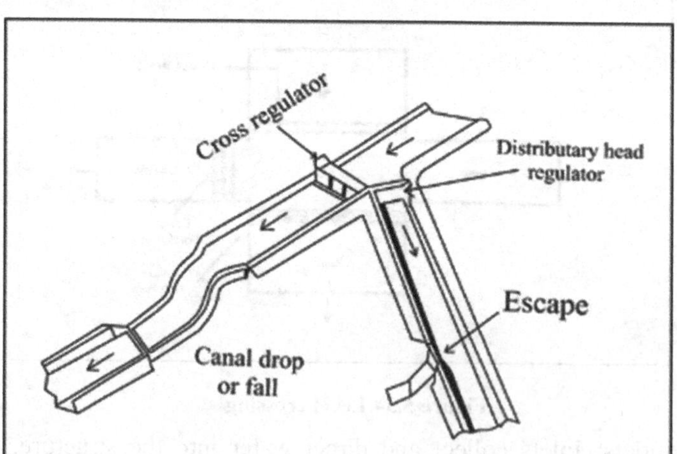

Figure 5.36 Canal Regulator

5.5.2 Cross regulator

The purpose of a cross regulator is to regulate the flow of water between two connected canals. It modifies the water flow by gates, valves, or comparable devices. The water flow between the canals can be controlled or diverted by the cross regulator by adjusting these controls.

Function of cross regulator

a. Water distribution between interconnected canals.
b. Flow control by adjusting gates or valves.
c. Water level maintenance in the canals.
d. Flood control during heavy rainfall.
e. Effective water management in the canal network.

5.6 Canal falls

5.6.1 General

Canal falls are critical structures within canal systems, designed to facilitate the smooth transition of water from higher to lower levels. These structures become necessary when the natural gradient of the terrain is steeper than the canal's designed slope. By incorporating canal falls, the canal maintains its designated slope, ensuring a controlled and steady water flow, while preventing erosion and minimizing turbulence as water moves downstream.

Canal falls adjust the elevation difference through the construction of vertical drops at strategic intervals along the canal bed. These drops effectively lower the water surface in the canal, dissipating the excess energy generated by the descent, thus safeguarding the canal's structural integrity.

The velocity of water in a canal correlate directly with its slope, and there exists a specific velocity threshold that, if exceeded, risks eroding the canal's bed and sides. This threshold is determined by the type of soil the canal traverses. Consequently, there's also a maximum slope for the water surface beyond which the canal could suffer damage. If the terrain's slope surpasses this limit, introducing a fall in the canal becomes imperative to prevent erosion.

While early canal constructions often circumvented steep gradients by aligning with the contours of the landscape to avoid the need for falls, this method introduced several drawbacks. Following the natural contours increases the canal's length, which not only proves to be economically inefficient but also leads to greater water loss through absorption, loss of potential service area (loss of command), and increased risks of silting and scouring. Therefore, despite their complexities, canal falls play a vital role in modern canal design by balancing the need for efficient water conveyance with the structural and operational integrity of the canal system.

5.6.2 Requirement of canal fall

a. Manage slopes and changes in elevation.
b. Dissipate energy and prevent turbulence and erosion.
c. Regulate water flow and maintain a stable water level.
d. Control sediment and prevent blockages.
e. Enhance the aesthetic and recreational value of the canal system.

5.6.3 Types of falls

a. Ogee falls - Ogee Falls are distinguished by a curving crest that reduces turbulence and controls water flow. Water flows easily from a higher to a lower height as it crosses the curving crest. This layout guarantees a constant water level downstream and inhibits erosion.

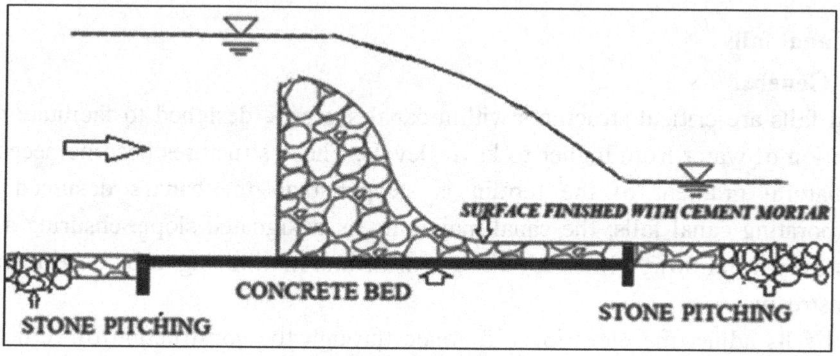

Figure 5.37 Ogee fall

b. Rapid fall – Rapid falls are constructed to create a sudden drop in water level, causing a fast flow downstream. They typically utilize gates or sluices to control water flow, enabling accelerated descent when opened. The main goal is to efficiently transfer water from higher to lower elevations while maintaining a consistent flow rate. Rapid falls find applications in irrigation and water conveyance projects where swift water flow is necessary for meeting downstream water delivery needs.

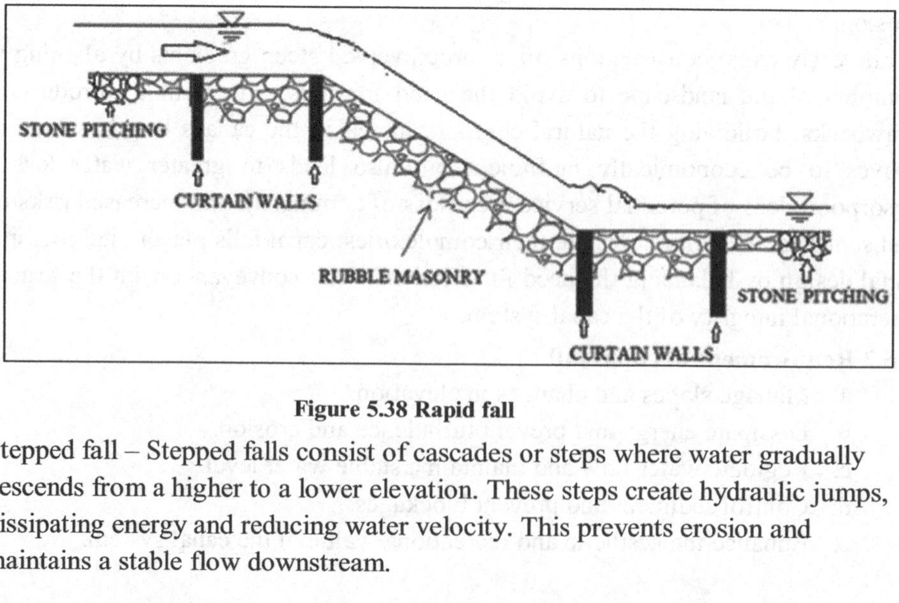

Figure 5.38 Rapid fall

c. Stepped fall – Stepped falls consist of cascades or steps where water gradually descends from a higher to a lower elevation. These steps create hydraulic jumps, dissipating energy and reducing water velocity. This prevents erosion and maintains a stable flow downstream.

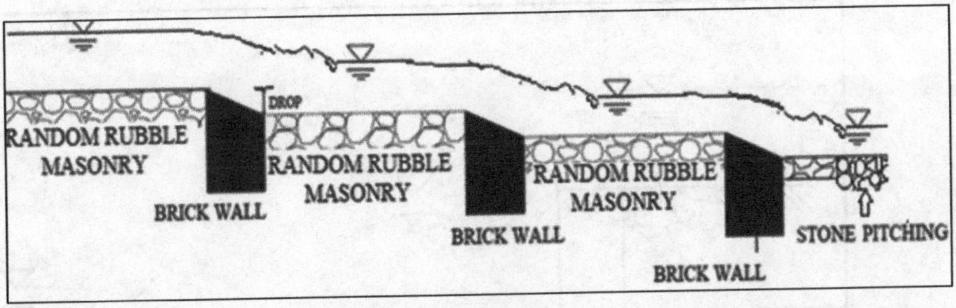

Figure 5.39 Stepped fall

d. Trapezoidal notch fall – The trapezoidal shape of the notch enables effective energy dissipation and flow control. The narrowing width and sloping sides reduce water velocity and turbulence, ensuring a smooth and controlled flow. This design minimizes erosion risk and maintains a stable water level downstream.

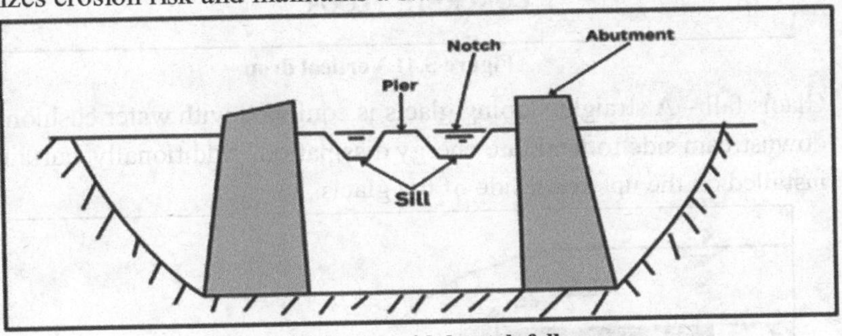

Figure 5.40 Trapezoidal notch fall

e. Vertical drop – Water flows over crest of the wall and falls over the cistern on the downstream side which is provided to act as a water cushion, this helps in the dissipation of the water energy and downstream is provided with cement grouting.

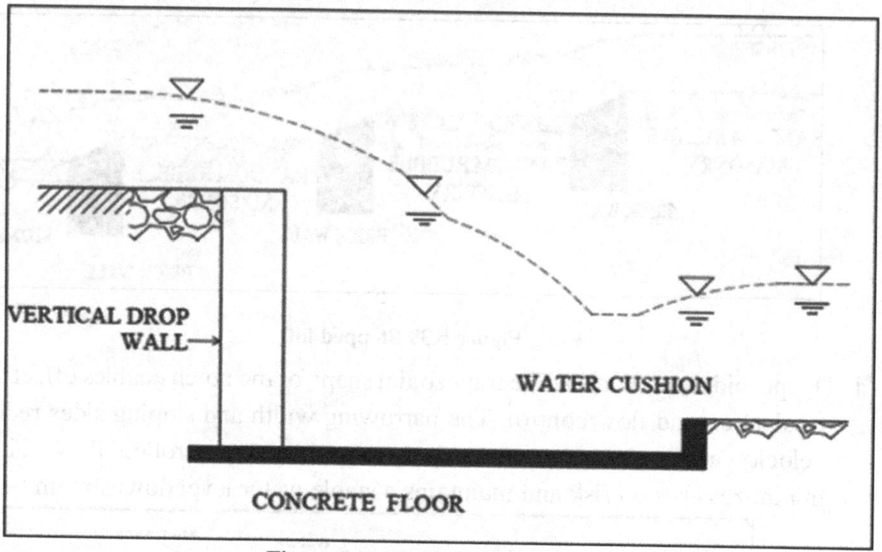

Figure 5.41 Vertical drop

f. Glacis fall – A straight sloping glacis is equipped with water cushions on the downstream side to facilitate energy dissipation. Additionally, curtain walls are installed on the upstream side of the glacis.

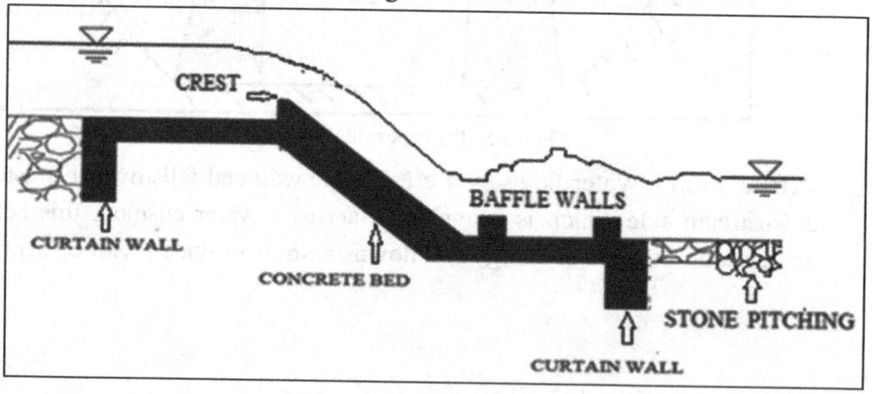

Figure 5.42 Glacis fall

It is modified in to two types are:

i. Montague type fall: Here parabolic shaped glacis is used instead of the straight sloping glacis.

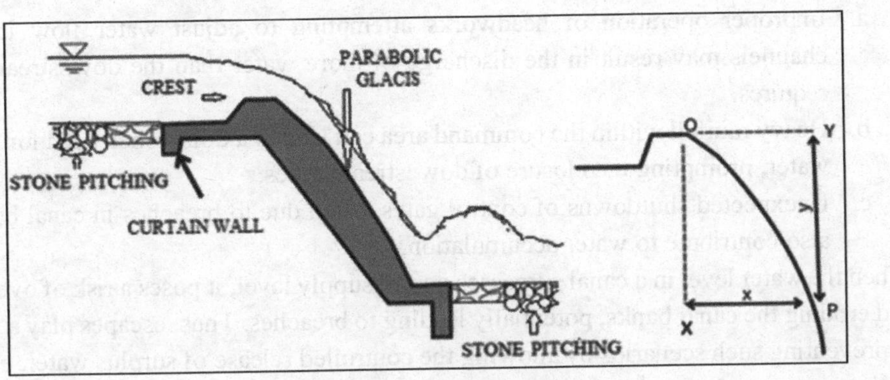

Figure 5.43 Montague fall

ii. Inglis type fall: In this scenario, although the slope remains straight, curtain walls are installed on the downstream floor to dissipate energy. The structure of the fall is comprised of cement concrete, ensuring stability and durability.

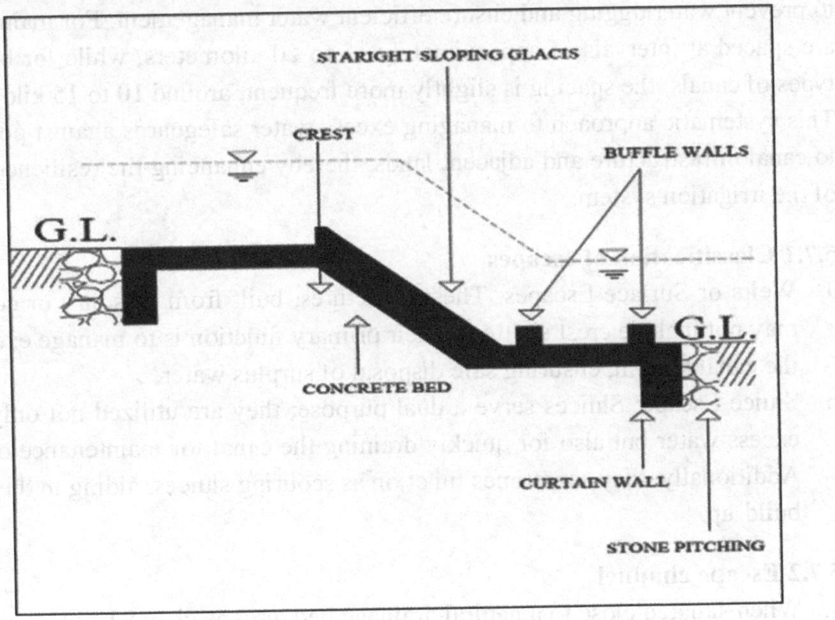

Figure 5.44 Inglis fall

5.7 Escapes

Escapes are critical structures within canal systems, designed to safely release excess water from various segments of the network, such as the main canal, branch canals, distributaries, and minors. Despite the common issue of water scarcity in irrigation systems as they age, there are instances where excessive water accumulates due to several factors:

a. Improper operation of headworks attempting to adjust water flow in lengthy channels may result in the discharge of more water than the downstream system requires.
b. Heavy rainfall within the command area can lead to a diminished need for irrigation water, prompting the closure of downstream gates.
c. Unexpected shutdowns of control gates, often due to breaches in canal banks, can also contribute to water accumulation.

When the water level in a canal surpasses its full supply level, it poses a risk of overflowing and eroding the canal banks, potentially leading to breaches. Thus, escapes play a vital role in preventing such scenarios by allowing the controlled release of surplus water, especially during emergencies. Additionally, these structures facilitate the drainage of canals for maintenance and repair works.

Escapes are strategically installed at the termini of minors and at various points across the canal network to ensure the maintenance of optimal water levels. The selection of sites for escapes typically depends on the proximity to natural drainage paths, such as rivers, drains, or depressions, which can expediently carry away the excess water. Positioning is crucial to prevent waterlogging and ensure efficient water management. For main canals, escapes are spaced at intervals of approximately 15 to 20 kilometers, while for branch and other types of canals, the spacing is slightly more frequent, around 10 to 15 kilometres.

This systematic approach to managing excess water safeguards against potential damages to canal infrastructure and adjacent lands, thereby enhancing the resilience and efficiency of the irrigation system.

5.7.1 Classification of escapes

a. Weirs or Surface Escapes: These structures, built from masonry or concrete, may or may not include crest shutters. Their primary function is to manage excess water from the canal system, ensuring safe disposal of surplus water.
b. Sluice Escape: Sluices serve a dual purpose; they are utilized not only for managing excess water but also for quickly draining the canal for maintenance or repair works. Additionally, they sometimes function as scouring sluices, aiding in the removal of silt build-up.

5.7.2 Escape channel

a. When situated close to a natural drainage bed, escape channels might not be necessary if the water can be discharged directly, with any elevation difference managed through a designed fall. However, if an escape channel needs to be constructed; its bed level and the drop should align with the drainage it leads into.
b. For sluice escapes, ideally, the escape channel's bed should be positioned lower than the canal's bed level to facilitate smooth water flow.

c. The design of the escape channel should prevent silt deposition and erosion, ensuring velocities that do not erode or deposit material. The channel should also have stable side slopes to prevent collapse.
d. Escape channels are typically designed as either concrete-lined chutes or earthen channels. If required, a series of falls may be incorporated to address the difference in height between the canal's full supply level and the water level in the natural drainage system.
e. The escape channel's capacity must be sufficient to handle the maximum expected discharge, ensuring that it can efficiently manage the water flow without overflow or damage.
f. Before utilizing a natural channel for discharge, its capacity to handle both the escape flow and any natural drainage simultaneously should be assessed. If the natural channel's capacity is found lacking, it should be modified or expanded to accommodate the increased flow.
g. This comprehensive approach to managing excess water through escape channels ensures the integrity and functionality of canal systems, highlighting the importance of detailed planning and design in water management infrastructure.

5.8 Outlets

A device which is constructed for delivering water from a government canal to the field channel is termed as outlet. The area which is irrigated by the outlet is called as outlet chak. Some factors which decide the size of the chak are

- Discharge required for the chak
- Intensity of rainfall
- Nature and slope of the area to be irrigated.

5.8.1 Classification of outlets

a. Modular outlet – In this type of outlet the water level in the channel and the discharge are independent. Here the discharge from the outlet is constant under the working limits. It can be either of moving parts or can be without moving parts.
b. Semi modular outlet- Here the outlet discharge is dependent on the channel water level but is independent on the water course water level. This includes the open flume outlet and free fall pipe outlet.
c. Non modular outlet- The discharge in this particular type of outlet is determined by the water level differential between the watercourse and the channel.

Following are the requirements of a good outlet:

- It should be simple- in design, construction and working.
- It should not he easily tampered with by the cultivator: but if tampered, it should be easily detected.
- It should work efficiently with a small working head.
- The outlet should draw its fair share of sediment carried by the parent channel.

- From the point of view of distribution, it should take proportional discharge with varying supply in the parent channel.
- From the point of view of the cultivator, it should give design discharge irrespective of any fluctuation in the parent channel.

UNIT SUMMARY

- This chapter delves into the principles and practices of hydrology and water resources engineering.
- Key topics include the hydrological cycle, precipitation, evapotranspiration, infiltration, groundwater flow, and surface runoff.
- The chapter emphasizes the importance of understanding these processes for effective water resource management. Practical applications are explored through exercises and case studies, with a focus on solving real-world problems.

EXERCISE

MULTIPLE CHOICE QUESTIONS

1. What is the primary function of a diversion headwork?

a) To generate hydroelectric energy
b) To control floods
c) To provide water to off-taking canals
d) To regulate water supply to fishery areas

2. Which structure is specifically built across a river to store water?

a) Weir
b) Barrage
c) Divide wall
d) Dam

3. What is the purpose of a fish ladder in a diversion headwork?

a) To regulate water flow
b) To control silt entry
c) To facilitate fish migration
d) To create small ponds

4. In the classification of weirs based on floor design, which type relies on the combined weight of the structure to counteract uplift pressure?

a) Gravity weir
b) Non-gravity weir
c) Rock fill weir
d) Concrete weir with sloping glacis

5. What is the purpose of a divide wall in a diversion headwork?

a) To create small ponds
b) To control water flow

c) To regulate silt entry
d) To stabilize the division wall
6. Which type of canal is constructed to facilitate inland navigation?
a) Irrigation canal
b) Navigation canal
c) Power canal
d) Feeder canal
7. What is the primary function of a canal head regulator?
a) To control water flow into the canal
b) To regulate silt entry
c) To create small ponds
d) To stabilize the division wall
8. How does a silt excluder function in a diversion headwork?
a) By regulating water flow
b) By preventing silt entry into canals
c) By creating small ponds
d) By stabilizing the division wall
9. What is the primary purpose of canal lining?
a) To increase water flow velocity
b) To control floods
c) To prevent waterlogging
d) To reduce seepage loss
10. What is the function of a level crossing in cross drainage work?
a) To regulate water flow
b) To control sediment
c) To maintain a consistent level between intersecting channels
d) To facilitate fish migration

Answers

1	2	3	4	5	6	7	8	9	10
c	d	c	a	d	b	a	b	d	c

SHORT ANSWER TYPE QUESTIONS

1. a) What is the purpose of a feeder canal

   b) How are perennial canals different from inundation canals?

   c) Define a multi-purpose canal.

2. a) Name three types of canal lining.

   b) What is the importance of canal lining in preventing waterlogging?

   c) When is cement mortar lining used?

3. a) What is the primary function of storage headworks?

b) Give two multidisciplinary functions of storage headworks.

c) How does diversion headwork differ from storage headwork?

4. a) List three components of diversion headworks.

b) What is the function of a fish ladder in a diversion headwork?

c) Why is a divide wall necessary in a diversion headwork?

5. a) What is the distinguishing factor between a gravity weir and a non-gravity weir?

b) In which type of weir is a vertical drop used?

c) What is the purpose of a rock fill weir?

PRACTICAL

Experiment 1: Visit the site and draw a neat labelled sketch of a diversion head work existing in the vicinity of your place.

Experiment 2: Visit the site and draw a neat labelled sketch of the Cross Drainage work existing in the vicinity of your place.

Experiment 3: Design a canal section for carrying a discharge of $25m^3/s$. Draw the section of the canal and estimate the quantity of materials which will be required for lining of this canal. Assume all other data of required.

Experiment 4: Visit the site, have a close look on the canal fall. Take salient photographs. Do you have any suggestion on the site selected for the purpose? Give a detailed note on the canal fall visited.

Experiment 5: Design a canal section for carrying a discharge of 16m3/s. Estimate the quantity of materials which will be required for lining. Choose any other data as per the site conditions.

KNOW MORE

Activity 1: If a fall is to be provided in a navigable canal, what is the difficulty and how to come out of it. Additional structures are permitted to be constructed, if you suggest.

Activity 2: Discuss about the process of removal of **silt by silt** excluders. If silt is not removed, then what will happen?

Activity 3: Discuss about the concept of a non-silting non-scouring canal.

Interesting facts

In 2019, Chennai experienced a severe water shortage during the summer, with the city facing a daily shortfall of at least 200 million liters of water. To address this critical situation, a remarkable initiative was undertaken starting July 12, 2019, where a train equipped with 50 tank wagons, each carrying 50,000 liters of water, transported a total of

2.5 million liters of water from Vellore to Chennai. Approximately 100 inlet pipes were installed near the railway tracks to facilitate the transfer of this vital resource to a treatment plant, addressing the city's urgent need amidst its water crisis.

In a related development aimed at enhancing water conservation and groundwater recharge, the Ministry of Road Transport and Highways (MoRTH) of the Government of India issued a directive on April 18, 2017. It stated that sites of all new and old, abandoned bridge structures are to be utilized for water tapping through the construction of Bandhara/Barrages/Weirs, thereby improving groundwater recharge and boosting the availability of water for drinking and other uses.

Furthermore, the Ministry of Jal Shakti, Government of India, has initiated water conservation efforts across 255 districts nationwide, aiming to secure water accessibility for the population. A strategy for conserving water involves the construction of bandhara/barrage type structures on the downstream side of bridges to facilitate water storage upstream. These structures are designed with piers and gates not exceeding 3.5 meters in height to capture water during the final phase of the monsoon season. The pond level of the Bandhara is meticulously set to maximize storage capacity without necessitating land acquisition or causing submergence issues. The innovative aspect of storing water within the riverbanks is that it obviates the need for additional land acquisition, making this approach highly feasible and attractive for widespread adoption. This strategic measure not only mitigates water scarcity but also supports sustainable water management and conservation practices.

The main purpose of constructing such bandhara/barrage type structure can be defined as:

a. Water Harvesting Structure: The main objective of constructing bandhara/barrage type structures is to capture and store water following the monsoon season, ensuring its availability for extended periods. Successful implementation of these structures necessitates specific site conditions, including the presence of nonporous rock or soil and impervious banks, which are essential for preventing water seepage and ensuring efficient water storage. Stored water is then strategically utilized to meet the demands of local communities, especially during the peak dry season from March to May, when water scarcity is most acute. This approach plays a crucial role in water resource management, significantly alleviating water scarcity in arid regions and supporting the needs of the population during critical times.

b. Artificial Recharge Structure: In locations characterized by pervious soil, sandy soil, or fissured rock, water harvesting structures can be effectively utilized for the purpose of artificial groundwater recharge. This strategy enhances the overall groundwater availability in the surrounding area, offering a valuable resource that can be tapped into by local communities. Numerous bandhara/barrage structures have been established across the country to facilitate this process. Recognizing the benefits of such initiatives, the Government of Maharashtra has proactively embarked on constructing these types of structures, with some standard designs now readily accessible for the development of bandhara/barrage structures, as documented by Ingle in 2016. This approach not only bolsters water security but also supports sustainable water management practices, benefiting society at large.

Bandhara/Barrage Structures

In response to the seasonal rain pattern in India, where precipitation is limited to just 3-4 months followed by extended dry periods, Maharashtra pioneered the strategy of constructing low-height dams along rivers downstream of bridges. This innovative approach, aimed at conserving water post-rainy season, ensures water availability for agricultural and drinking purposes during the dry months. The technique, first employed in Kolhapur, Maharashtra, during the reign of Rajarshi Shahu Maharaj, involves building a special type of weir, known as the KT weir (Kolhapur Type Bandhara), across river beds. This structure is designed with significant gaps between piers to permit water flow, which can be regulated by needle gates to conserve water for future use, particularly when the stream is unable to meet water demands.

The KT weir, a non-overflowing structure with a concrete deck, doubles as a bridge facilitating light to medium traffic. Its gates are typically closed at the monsoon's end, trapping a considerable volume of water that can be drawn upon as needed. Historically, these gates were made of mild steel, reinforced for added strength, but modern advancements have seen the adoption of Fiber Reinforced Plastic (FRP) for needle gates, enhancing operational efficiency.

Despite their crucial role in water management, KT Weirs have suffered from neglect over the past 15 years. These gravity structures, which can be built in various suitable locations or in conjunction with bridge structures, are now experiencing a resurgence, with over 100 bandhara/barrage structures currently under construction or in the planning phase in Maharashtra, indicating a revitalized commitment to improving water availability across the region.

REFERENCES & SUGGESTED READINGS

- Sivaraman V., Devanathan D., & Marak A. K. C. (2022). Water Storage and Supply System in Ancient India. Journal of Pharmaceutical Negative Results, Volume 13, Special Issue 1, pp. 1088-1093. DOI: 10.47750/pnr.2022.13.S01.130.
- Hager W.H., & Castro-Orgaz O. (2017). Ogee Weir Crest Definition: Historical Advance. Proceedings of the 37th IAHR World Congress, August 13–18, 2017, Kuala Lumpur, Malaysia.
- FAO. (1998a). Crop Evapotranspiration: Guidelines for Computing Crop Water Requirements. By: Richard Allen, Luis Pereira, Dirk Raes & Martin Smith. FAO Irrigation and Drainage Paper 56, Rome, Italy.
- FAO. (1998b). Guidelines for Investigation, Design, Construction and Management of Irrigation Schemes. Prepared by: FAO TCP/BOT/4451 and FAO UTF/BOT/010/BOT.
- Garg S.K. (1977). Water Resources and Hydrology. Khanna Publishers, New Delhi.
- Michael A.M. (2008). Irrigation Theory and Practices. Vikash Publishing House Pvt. Ltd., New Delhi.
- Raghunath H.M. (1985). Hydrology: Principle Analysis and Design. Wiley Eastern Limited, New Delhi.
- Raghunath H.M. (2003). Groundwater. New Age International Pvt. Ltd., Publishers, New Delhi.
- Reddy P.J.R. (2016). A Textbook of Hydrology. Laxmi Publications, New Delhi.
- Sharma R.K. (1993). A Text Book of Hydrology and Water Resources. Dhanpat Rai & Sons Publisher, New Delhi.

Dynamic QR Code for Further Reading

For further information on the DESIGN OF WEIRS, BARRAGES AND CANALS, the QR code be scanned	
For further reading refer "GUIDE FOR LOCATION, SELECTION AND HYDRAULIC DESIGN OF CANAL ESCAPES, IS: 6936 : 1992 (Reaffirmed 2012)" by scanning the QR Code.	

CO AND PO ATTAINMENT TABLE

Course outcomes (COs) for this course can be mapped with the programme outcomes (POs) after the completion of the course and a correlation can be made for the attainment of POs to analyse the gap. After proper analysis of the gap in the attainment of POs necessary measures can be taken to overcome the gaps.

Course Outcomes	Attainment of Programme Outcomes (1- Weak Correlation; 2- Medium correlation; 3- Strong Correlation)						
	PO-1	PO-2	PO-3	PO-4	PO-5	PO-6	PO-7
CO-1							
CO-2							
CO-3							
CO-4							
CO-5							

The data filled in the above table can be used for gap analysis.

INDEX

U

V

W

Y

Z